Stanford's Voyaging Companion

Captain R J F Riley

STANFORD MARITIME LONDON

Stanford Maritime Limited
Member Company of the George Philip Group
12-14 Long Acre London WC2E 9LP

Stanford Maritime Limited

First Edition © 1976

Printed in Great Britain by
Lowe & Brydone (Printers) Ltd, Thetford, Norfolk

NOTE
The Publishers, while exercising the greatest
care in compiling this publication, do not hold
themselves responsible for the consequences arising
from any inaccuracies therein.

ISBN 0 540 07264 X

Contents

Preface

The object of this book is to assist yachtsmen who wish to make short sea crossings from our shores to the continent and the islands which surround us. It is hoped that it will be found a worthy successor to Stanford's Sailing Companion, now being published in third edition. The writer of this publication is the co-author of the earlier Companion.

It has been assumed that the reader has already served the first part of his apprenticeship to the sea about the reassuring coasts of Britain. This most important step having been made, the world can well become his oyster. "The distance is nothing", said one to St. Denys before he commenced his two-mile walk with his head in his hands, "it is the first step that counts!" One more headland, one more stretch of sea: is there so much difference between coasting, and dropping a coastline astern to seek new cruising grounds?

Except where necessary, no differentiation has been made between small sea-going craft, whether they be propelled by machinery or by sails. This difference, which looms large in the minds of most yachtsmen, has relatively small place here. Accent throughout has been upon the practical rather than the theoretical approach. The best way to voyage safely and cheaply has been preferred to the idea of voyaging at any cost. After all, the sea is a great leveller which takes no account of man's estate. Certain views of the author may evoke controversy, even disagreement. However, one cannot gainsay his experience the world over in dinghies and yachts, in merchantmen and naval vessels.

Latterly, twenty two short sea crossings outward from England have been discussed. In each of them the factors which no yachtsman can afford to ignore have been included, together with advices upon how the author himself would conduct them. Of course, as with the way to heaven, there are many roads to the same goal. Guidance for crossing the narrow seas is here: necessary preparation: equipment which one should buy or hire – or indeed do without: how one can handle the tides and the vexed problem of yachtsmen versus merchantment at sea; and, of course, general passage advices.

There is, perhaps, an element of illusion about foreign harbours and cruising abroad. If this is so, then it is of the same stuff as the illusion of life itself. Those who own small sea-going craft usually have something of the gypsy in them. More often than not they prefer the unconventional, rather than orthodoxy and the habits of the madding crowd. Above all, most of them have a zest for life. It is a zest which will probably, sooner or later, urge them to cross the narrow seas.

R.J.F.R.

Acknowledgements·

Mr. C. Schofield, M.A.; Mr. W.J. Bailey, B.D.S., L.F.S., R.C.S.(Eng.); Miss Elizabeth Rider, Secretary, The Cruising Association; Drawings and artwork by John Pezare, A.R.C.A., A.S.I.A., N.R.D.

CHAPTER 1

Preparatory Considerations

'Bloody January again!' sing Flanders and Swann, and all but the yachting fraternity. For these fortunate few January brings the Boat Show with its display of craft of all types and sizes, and its dreams of summer voyaging. On fibreglass, teak and polished salesmen, arc lamps shine with an equal impartiality. Every device known to the boat builder is on show except perhaps for one: the means by which a purchaser's pocket book can be stretched. But many a worthwhile enthusiasm can be costly in terms of time or money or, quite commonly, both. Especially is this true for those whose zeal is directed in leisure periods towards the sea.

Bearing this in mind, the man relatively new to the world of small boats accepts as inevitable, albeit with dismay, the expenditure of a few hundred pounds on 'extras' to transform a boat builder's 'Ready to Sail' sea-going craft into one he considers adequate to meet his modest needs for sailing in and around his home port.

As his efficiency in handling the craft improves, and his confidence increases, there frequently grows a desire to be more adventurous. However, the further a yachtsman intends to voyage, the greater amount of preparation he must make and the more equipment he will need. Extra preparation costs time, at the very least; extra equipment inevitably costs money. He whose means are limited may question the need of this extra expenditure and effort. Unfortunately, deciding to do without and making no preparation is short sighted and could result in placing his own and the lives of others in jeopardy; and no sailor can afford to cut his throat according to his cloth. With this realisation, the responsible but impecunious small boat sailor may feel condemned for ever to short passages inshore, never to fulfil his ambition to travel to new and distant havens across the sea.

Is the problem so clear cut? In this and succeeding chapters the writer endeavours to bring the subject into perspective, placing needs as he sees them before the weekend sailor, so he himself may decide the equipment he should purchase, and that he can safely do without; what he might consider hiring and those preparations he may consider doing for himself.

The average man, no matter what his resources, may be loth to take his problems to a yacht chandlery where, because of uncertainty, he may find himself buying goods he does not really need and paying too much for those he does. Yachting is still considered to be a luxury pastime and prices generally tend to reflect this attitude. As a result, any yachtsman who enters a large chandlery is commonly assumed to have the means to afford the pound it costs him to open his mouth and the two it needs to close it again. In no sense is this intended to denigrate yacht chandlers. The majority only desire to be constructive and

helpful. Even so, in Abenazer's cave an inexperienced Aladdin may well become confused, surrounded by so many treasures. Any one of them may tempt his desire. He really needs a Genie of the Lamp to illumine the cave and to help him dispassionately choose what he requires.

The hire of equipment

At this early stage let it be stated that there are many strong arguments against the purchase of expensive equipment, essential when a long, deep water cruise is planned, if it is going to be used only for a very few weeks in a year. The first objection is obviously financial; the second is the knowledge that most equipment deteriorates with age. Pride of possession turns sour in the long winter months. Where appropriate within this publication, reference is made to articles which may be rented.

PART 1 EXTERNAL FACTORS

Progress at sea

Good progress through the water is not just a matter of personal satisfaction to the owner, or the pleasure obtained from showing a clean pair of heels to another craft of similar design. It reduces the adverse effects of tidal streams, shortens sailing time and therefore lessens the possibility of a weather change, it gives greater manoeuvrability and offers more time on foreign shores. Assuming sound sails or engines, and a competent crew to handle them, two factors can effect speed to an extent that none can afford to ignore them. The first is weight; the second, cleanliness of underwater surfaces.

The Weight factor

Let the weight factor be related to similar problems in a car. Motoring performance can be greatly improved by reducing weight. Increased car load can, in part, be overcome by a wider throttle opening, but more fuel is consumed. In this sense the owner of a motor cruiser has something in common with a motorist. Not so the sailing man; he has no reserve of power.

These facts were learned long ago by the racing fraternity and so a racing car has become an engine and wheels built around a single person: a sailing yacht designed for racing is a stripped, stark, hollow racing machine. Of course, between the greatly overladen family cruiser and the racing machine lies common sense. It dictates that one leaves on shore all the superfluous paraphernalia which is so easily accumulated on a boat, and that crew members are firmly discouraged from bringing aboard personal effects which are not strictly essential.

It also implies that if 10 gallons of fresh water and 5 gallons of fuel meet estimated needs plus a good safety factor, then double these quantities can be transposed into about 150 lbs. of additional weight which must be propelled through the water. Theoretical though these comments may appear, the weight factor is real.

The Hull factor

Not unlike the gradual falling off of the performance of a car between periodic services, so does the gradual roughening and fouling of underwater surfaces insidiously effect speed. A relatively short while after docking, an owner might blame wind and sea conditions for slight loss in performance because he is loth to accept the probable reason: one which could cost him time and money to rectify. The motor cruiser owner should not feel that these effects have little substance in his case. To quote extremes, badly fouled hulls have been known to produce propellor slip and cavitational effects, causing further loss of speed, and perfectly functioning engines to give trouble.

Fouling and anti-fouling

Fouling of a hull is inevitable so long as a craft remains afloat. This inexorable process, speedy enough when under way, is hastened when she is at rest, and the average yacht spends considerably more time on moorings than she does under way. These are dolorous realities with which yachtsmen must live.

Salt water, brackish water, fresh water, water so polluted by industrial effluent that no tadpole could live in it; each type in its own particular way will allow marine growth to bedevil underwater surfaces. There are spores which are peculiar to salt water, those which can exist in fresh water alone and others which can thrive in either. In polluted water less natural effects occur. Oil and other pollutants form a slimey coat on wetted surfaces. Thereafter, certain types of marine growth which thrive in turgid, apparently lifeless water will attach themselves to the viscid seal and so fouling progresses.

Certainly, misconceptions are nurtured by many yachtsmen about the properties of anti-fouling compositions, even to the belief that, by applying a single coat, hull protection may be expected for up to two years. Perhaps the paint is blamed if this period is not obtained. Anti-fouling paints contain toxins, lethal to spores, which are released from it over a protracted period – but not two years. At least this is the claim of paint manufacturers and no doubt these properties have been proved in test conditions. Watching week by week the insidious growth of marine organisms on a hull, a yachtsman needs quite a lot of convincing. It might be assumed that two coats of anti-fouling composition can be no more effective than one. Paradoxically, two coats are not just twice as effective: they are three or four times more so. Yet, for the reasons given above, it may well be that this cannot wholly apply in polluted waters.

With reservations about the water in which a yacht is berthed, there is a strong case for applying two coats of anti-fouling paint annually, and in ordinary circumstances for the bottom to be scrubbed off once between times.

Hull treatment before cruising

When pottering locally at weekends it is unusual to concern oneself very much about the state of a hull's wetted surfaces.

Nevertheless it must be accepted that with very little fouling and few barnacles, a half a knot and more can be lopped off the potential speed of the average craft. For this reason, unless a hull has been scrubbed clean within two months of commencing an extended sea passage, it is sensible to do so again before sailing. Whether or not anti-fouling paint is applied at the same time must be a case of individual need. Boatyards will of course undertake this work, yet at a cost which might seem disproportionate to the work involved. For many yachtsmen an alternative is often available.

In sundry ports and havens round our coasts, suitable public and privately owned hards will be found for both single- and bilge-keeled craft. Settling a craft in position is a pleasantly challenging undertaking well within the competence of most. Bilge-keelers present no problems but, an owner invariably having to lie on his back to treat the bottom between the keels, a large sheet of polythene or ground-sheeting is a sensible provision. A single-keeled craft is laid alongside the jetty or the piles and so moored that she will lean against the support at an angle of 5° or 10°. Fenders with a thickness equivalent to two or three car tyres are needed to hold her clear of the support. A stout two-fold purchase tackle is set up between jetty or piles and a position, say, 10' up the mast. Before the craft takes the ground, with thick fenders in position the tackle is tautened to give her the required list. In the absence of a stout tackle, improvisation can be adopted; with double mooring ropes used as strops, the main sheet tackle can be shackled to them and the same object is achieved. Obviously, owners of motor cruisers with minimal keels and near flat bottoms cannot adopt these do-it-yourself methods, but the disadvantages of loss of speed and increased fuel consumption may well be regarded as preferable to a boatyard's docking charges.

Where these methods are possible, considerable satisfaction is obtained from completing the task oneself, and even this is overshadowed by the knowledge that the work could cost £50 to £150 for an average craft at any good boatyard using modern techniques.

Fig. 1.1

Underwater fittings

A craft being high and dry, no owner will fail to minutely examine every square foot of wetted surface for leaks and defects. Apertures such as self-draining outlets and sea closet openings call for special attention, not just to ensure they are clear and to scrape clean their openings but, if necessary, to re-seat underwater fittings. It is the opportunity to re-pack leaking or binding sea cocks. None of these tasks are outside the ability of the average yachtsman who, by nature, is usually a practical man. Echo sounder transducer fittings call for special care. They should be gently cleaned and at no time should more than one coat of paint cover them.

Never using a wire brush except perhaps on a steel hull; weed and slime should be scrubbed carefully away. Ideally, barnacles should be pinched off with pliers but they can generally be removed with a thumbnail or scraper when the hull is dry. Sanding down then becomes necessary because seldom is scrubbing so efficient that a truly clean surface is obtained by that alone.

Rudders somewhat naturally call for special attention and most defects can be detected by the amateur. A good shaking will usually reveal defects in traditional rudders. Defects may be undue wear on gudgeons, pintles and bearing pintle, or slackening fastenings. It is fair comment to say that balanced or suspended rudders either function or they do not. However, any rudder defect even though slight is a reason for cancelling a voyage until proper repair is obtained.

Work aloft

This sub-title is not intended to imply that all yachtsmen should carry out every repair aloft. Neither is the implication that all yachtsmen carry out minor tasks aloft. There are, however, a considerable number who are quite capable of checking the condition of standing rigging from top to bottom, retrieving a lost halliard, changing a failed spreader light bulb, and undertaking sundry other tasks.

Most masts on sailing craft of 24 feet and under can be lowered and so an owner, with a little help from his friends, can in a leisurely manner carry out maintenance and repairs on it. Taller masts requiring similar attention must usually be lifted off by a crane, although subsequent work is not necessarily a boatyard undertaking. But for mid-season checks such as might be carried out by an owner who wishes to ensure that mast and rigging are in good order before commencing a cruise, a considerable number of owners are capable of going aloft, yet few do so. It needs neither steely nerves nor remarkable fitness.

Bosun's chairs are not usually stocked by chandlers but they are so easy to make that it is of no consequence. Although canvas chairs with cheek pockets for tools are used by the racing fraternity for use under way if necessary, for the average owner whose only intention is to quietly carry out checks and minor repairs in port on a still day, there is much to commend the old fashioned wooden type. It gives equal security, is more comfortable and tools can easily be secured to it.

It can be made from $\frac{3}{4}''$ plank, 18″ long by 6″ wide. Holes are drilled through the four corners to take two beckets both of which are short spliced beneath the chair. The length of the beckets should be such that, when peaked over the chair, the apex is at about chin height.

The main or jib halliard is secured to the chair with a double sheet bend. A trusted, practical man is required on deck to hoist and he is assisted by the man in the chair who also hauls lustily on the running part of the halliard. One other person is necessary.

Fig. 1.2

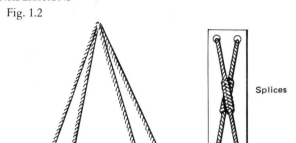

Splices

With a couple of security turns round the halliard winch barrel or a single turn round a cleat he takes in the slack and immediately turns up the halliard on the cleat when necessary. Any other system is risky and unseamanlike. By the same token, one *never* lowers a person from aloft except from two turns or more on a winch barrel or from a single full turn on a cleat.

Fig. 1.3

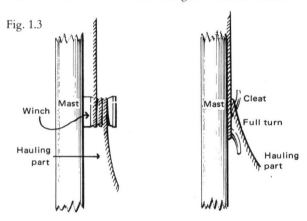

Winch · Mast · Hauling part · Mast · Cleat · Full turn · Hauling part

Standing rigging

Apart from the obvious necessity of checking the condition of rigging wires and ensuring that shackles and rigging screws are free and greased, tension is important. It may generally be said that, in the case of most modern craft, all standing rigging, when plucked, should sing. If tension needs to be restored on certain stays or shrouds, care must be taken that the mast is not bent slightly in the process, or that the usual slight cant aft is not disturbed. A common tightening order is: (a) forestay and backstay; (b) topmast shrouds; (c) lower shrouds and inner forestay. A check to ensure that the mast is vertical in the athwartship plane can be obtained by reference to the masts of other craft in the vicinity. Absence of bend in the mast can be checked by sighting up the mainsail luff groove. Thereafter, all bottle screw locking nuts must be tightened, for obvious reasons.

Running rigging

Despite the fact that a craft is properly maintained, it must be borne in mind that on a long passage all running rigging will be tested for a much longer duration, and perhaps more severely, than usual. Main and jib halliards are items of running gear about which one never harbours doubts. Their reliability must be such that the possibility of failure need never cross a skipper's mind. In most cases it is not necessary to either place a craft under a crane or lower the mast to renew these or any other halliards. If old

3

and new halliards are placed end to end, they may be joined so that halliard changing is just a matter of reeving off through the sheave. With a sailmaker's needle and palm, the ends are sewn together and then whipped, so that smoothness and continuity is produced at the meeting point.

Fig. 1.4

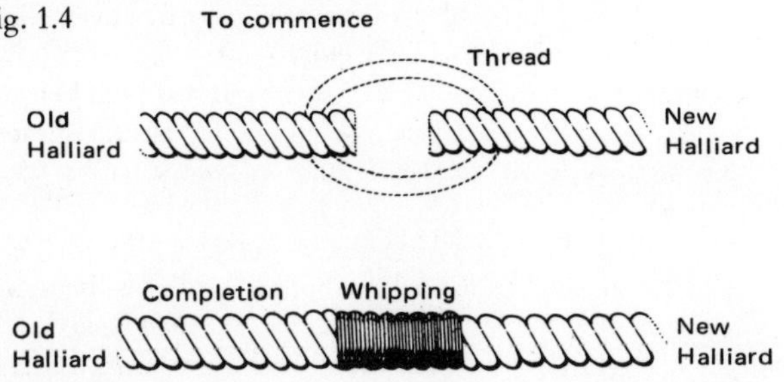

To commence

Thread

Old Halliard

New Halliard

Completion   Whipping

Old Halliard

New Halliard

Guard rails

Guard rails must be bar taut and should be kept so by whatever means are provided. Slack guard rails are potentially dangerous.

Taping of snags

In modern craft split pins are frequently used in rigging screws and guard rails. In sea conditions they can, and will, rip a sail if they are not covered. Trousers are vulnerable too. All rigging screws and abrasive guard rail fitments are best bound with white adhesive tape to guard against this happening. Why white? It looks better than black.

Side dodgers

On sailing craft with after cockpits, side screens have value. Reaching from deck level to upper guardrail and from forward of the cockpit to near the transom, they give helmsmen wind and spray protection. For a price one can have them specially made, with the name of one's craft emblazoned across them yet, with the appropriate amount of suitable material obtainable from any chandlers, these simple oblongs can be produced on a sewing machine. In the absence of a punch and die to secure brass eyelets for lacing, it should be remembered that a sail needle and twine, and the common buttonhole stitch, will achieve the same object.

Spray screens

Spray screens, worn with side dodgers, give even greater protection to the cockpit area. Specially designed for each make of craft, and therefore costly, they might well be regarded as a luxury. They have a negative value too. The higher the screen, the more difficult it is to keep an effective lookout ahead and the perspex windows often fitted give no effective forward vision when wet. It may be said that these screens have value when one has a large and active crew and the passage is relatively short. The lone and tired helmsman whose only desire is to keep horizon, compass and sails in view with the minimum of effort would, it is suggested, prefer to lower the screen and accept the occasional lash of spray from the weather bow.

When the wind comes from any bearing forward of the beam, the condition when they have most value, both spray screens and side dodgers produce two effects, one beneficial and one unwanted. They provide welcome protection at the same time as they produce windage, which is any upward protrusion upon which the wind can act to slightly retard speed and increase leeway.

Weather boards

In sailing yachts with after cockpits the only way of preventing rain or occasional spray from entering a cabin is to keep the weather boards in place. Whilst these boards are essential in heavy weather, in conditions which are merely wet it is rather like using a marquee when an umbrella would have sufficed. With all weather boards in place, daylight in the cabin below is severely restricted, claustrophobia is real, seasickness is brought considerably nearer; and all this because one is blanketted from the open sea, the stability of the horizon and the sanity of the cockpit.

A substitute for weather boards is a sheet, perhaps two, of $\frac{1}{4}''$ rigid transparent perspex which will slot into the weather board keyways. In ordinary sea conditions and when it is raining such sheets will provide cabin protection and will totally overcome the disadvantages to those below of weather boards. They are also rather pleasant to use in port.

Security of working handles

Although additional reefing and mast winch handles are highly desirable equipment, they are often overlooked. Difficulty in obtaining the precise type of spare can be a reason for an owner deciding to manage with the single one he carries. He should consider this: of the sundry items of equipment on a sailing craft fitted with roller reefing gear, there is no article more important when the wind is freshening than his reefing handle. A crew member claws cautiously forward with the handle in his hand or his pocket, thereafter to manipulate it in difficult conditions. At the very time he most needs it, he places it at greatest risk. With the only reefing handle over the side, he is left with the choice of carrying full mainsail or none at all. The choice is unpleasant and one ruminates upon the absolute security of old fashioned reef points which, for other reasons, tend to be returning to favour.

In the manner portrayed in Fig. 5, it is good seamanship to fit a grommet capable of being slipped over the wrist, and to use the grommet whenever the reefing handle is needed. Less importance can be attached to mast winch handles but, their replacement price being considerable, there is good reason for fitting them with grommets as well.

Fig. 1.5

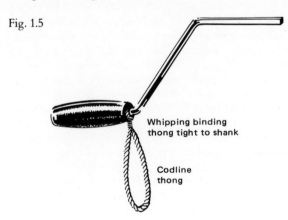

Whipping binding thong tight to shank

Codline thong

Some may argue that the shape of many types of handle and their highly polished finishes preclude one's ability to fit them in this manner. The writer must disagree. Yes, the grommet will work up a handle from time to time but sliding it back again is no problem and it in no way detracts from the value of this virtually costless security device.

Tiller locking device

With tiller lashed, many sailing craft will sail themselves. This quality is inherent more in long craft than short; in craft with long, traditional keels rather than fin keels; in single keeled craft rather than bilge keelers. In short, a 20 foot bilge keeled craft may be difficult to encourage to sail itself for more than a minute or two: the period generally tends to increase as the virtues listed above are met. A tiller left unattended for a half an hour or so is not unknown. Even the minimum time quoted is of value to the lone helmsman whose crew may be below and perhaps asleep.

A common means of achieving tiller lock is to use cords akin to tent guys which, with their simple wooden or metal adjustment slides, can be attached to the cockpit coaming on either side of the tiller. One feels and adjusts the tiller by hand to obtain the necessary rudder angle.

Fig. 1.6.

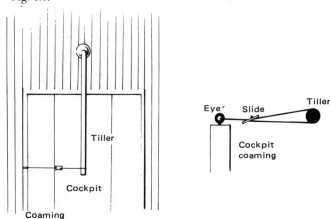

Self steering gear

On long passages self steering gear is of considerable value. In all probability the man who only occasionally intends traversing long distances will decide it is not for him. He cannot justify expenditure upon costly vane steering gear or the equally costly and yet highly efficient electronic device: Tillermate. In passing, it may be remarked here that the efficiency of vane steering varies with the brand purchased and the comments of long distance lone sailors should be sought before buying. Tillermate depends upon electric power and, although battery drain is very small in ideal sea conditions, the more it must work as sea state deteriorates, the greater the drain on accumulators. Unless an owner motor-sails quite a lot, and his engine charges his accumulator, he may be reluctant to use it throughout a sea crossing.

Long before yachtsmen became targets for modern sales techniques, sailing cruisers had to rely upon sheet to tiller arrangements to obtain self steering. It was crude but seamanlike

and efficient. One such method is the utilisation of materials which most craft carry. They are:

(a) A storm jib, a discarded dinghy foresail, even an adapted triangular piece of sail canvas with an area of, say, 20 to 35 square feet.
(b) Four small blocks.
(c) Two sheets made from any adequate line available.
(d) A short length of light shock cord.

Adaption may be necessary in unconventional craft but, for the average sloop rigged yacht, the following unsophisticated arrangement will prove easy to rig and will work well at most sailing angles.

The tack of the adapted staysail is lashed to the foredeck mooring cleat or the stem head. The topping lift for the booming out spar or spinnaker pole is attached to the peak and hauled taut. Two of the blocks are secured in the shrouds, port and starboard, at suitable height and two are secured to the guards rails in line with the tiller. The sheets having been secured to the clew of the sail, they are led aft through the blocks. The weather sheet is tautened to a degree which brings the staysail slightly aback and is secured to the tiller by a clove hitch. This knot is preferable because it is easiest to adjust. To provide counter balance, the shock cord is also secured to the tiller and taken to the guard rail on the leeward side. The operation of this extraordinary cheap self steering device is best described graphically.

Fig. 1.7

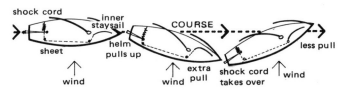

Naturally a slight loss in performance must be expected but long periods of unremitting concentration on compass and sails are tiring and tiresome to many. These people may regard minimally reduced speed as acceptable if they can be relieved of helm duties.

PART 2 INTERNAL FACTORS

Internal fittings generally

Someone wrote: no one thinks of winter when the grass is green. By the same token, visitors inspecting the internal fittings of yachts at a boat show sometimes forget practical considerations. The most important of these is whether a yacht's interior will provide acceptable living conditions in a force 4 breeze 10 miles offshore. Occasionally people are captivated by ingenuity, cunning use of space, decor and sometimes downright gimmickry: bemused by what they see they are temporarily unable to differentiate between practical design and eye-catching living space which is better suited to a caravan.

It will be accepted that the majority of craft, even when manned, spend more time in harbour than at sea. Must it be assumed that this gives the occasional builder license to cater for motionless conditions only, yet use the word seaworthy in advertising pamphlets? Sometimes the strength, occasionally the design of fittings are inadequate to withstand the testing they will receive at sea. Unfortunately, day sailing does not really accentuate inadequacies. Yachtsmen may go to bathrooms ashore before casting off, eat a healthy breakfast so that sandwiches will suffice at lunch time, never attempt to sleep at sea, and practical navigation is generally unnecessary. A mere 24 hours at sea in anything but a flat calm will devastatingly reveal to an owner every design defect in his craft below decks. Better by far he assesses his problems before he sails.

For example, let the case be considered of a 12 stone man who, whatever his experience afloat, is caught off balance by a sudden lurch of his craft. Reflex action will cause him to grab the nearest apparently solid fitment when the alternative is bad bruising or worse. It may be a rack, a shelf, a partition, a table. If the handhold he obtains is inadequately anchored or it lacks the inherent ability to withstand the destructive tug exerted upon it, then if it is not ripped from its mooring, it will be smashed in his hand. For this reason, the best designed sea-going craft have smooth, stout overhead grab rails and thoughtfully placed vertical posts, in addition to the usual handholds provided by hatchways, bulkheads and similar strength members.

When doubts exist the intending voyager should examine all internal fittings of his craft and assess their security, strength and utilitarian value at sea. For example, light section plastics for fittings other than lamp shades is generally unrealistic. One can encounter the use of the same size of screw which would be used for the equivalent task in a house. Few house builders use a screw which is larger than the minimum size required for a specific task: yet it is unanswerable to apply the same principles aboard a sea going craft. Bolting through would appear a logical alternative in some cases. Perhaps the occasional boat fitter leaves these apparently minor decisions to carpenters who have never sailed in their lives.

To continue, a chart drawer whose fastening is of such inadequate type that, the weight of his charts being thrown against it, they are pitched on to the cabin sole amongst all the other odds and ends which might find their way there for a what-the-hell reason is clearly useless. Little better is a twist clip if it is retained by a short screw which allows the clip to work slack. A chart table which demands erection before use, and depends for support upon light metal clips and asinine struts will be rent from position at the first solid lurch of the navigator. Is an advertised bunk merely a narrow 6-foot settee capable of being used as a bunk in port only? Is a firm hand hold or a sound foot support available so that an athwartship table can be used with fair confidence at sea? And if in this latter case the only hand hold offered is the table itself, secured, as it occasionally may be, with fastenings of doubtful security and a foldaway leg, what real value has the table except in port? Does the W.C. compartment or area provide the means by which a person can use the W.C. and hold himself secure when craft movement is lively? These examples should give guidelines along which an owner might direct his thoughts.

There is no implication in these remarks that a yachtsman speedily rids himself of a craft of questionable internal design and construction. It is nevertheless averred that, perhaps finding he owns a craft which fails to meet the standard of seaworthiness essential below decks which he himself may set, he seeks and finds answers to problems which may face him. It might well be

that he decides to stow away a portable table throughout a sea passage. He could determine to remove a settee cushion and resolve to do his chartwork on the level surface beneath. He might exchange drawer and locker fastenings for ones of greater utilitarian value. In the absence of adequate lips – fiddles – to prevent articles from sliding off working surfaces, he could consider the value of damp cloths placed between slippery surfaces and utensils. Here broad guidelines are given but these comments would not be complete without emphasis on toilet facilities. If essential security is not available, one does not ruminate upon the desirability of good hand grips: one fits them or gets them fitted. One only needs to be pitchforked once through a lavatory door to recesses beyond to realise the wisdom of this recommendation. In the last resort, there remains the widely used but seldom mentioned bucket.

Bunks and bunking down

Giving a feeling of security equal to that obtained in a hammock, perhaps the pipe cot is the best type of bunk for use at sea in small craft. It generally comprises two 6-foot pipes between which is suspended slack canvas, the amount of belly in the canvas being adjustable. Pipe cots tend to be found on functional craft rather than on those designed for family cruising. Unless they are bolstered with bedding and clothing, they are most uncomfortable to sit on.

Almost universally provided in modern motor and sailing craft are ship's side bunks with foam filled cushions stretching their length. Except in port, some of these often narrow berths cannot be used as anything but settees, therefore an advertised four-berth craft may have to be re-designated by an owner as a two-berth one in sea conditions. Old fashioned bunk boards were deep boards of bunk length which transformed this type of bunk into a cot. They were the ideal means by which a sleeper obtained essential security necessary for sleep at sea. Although providing restful sleep, they could not be used as settees, except by the most sanguine, and perhaps this is the main reason why one almost never encounters them today.

The modern alternative is the canvas leeboard, standard fittings on some good craft but not on the majority. Such a leeboard is merely a canvas triangle, the base of which is secured to the centre of the inboard edge of a bunk. The apex is attached by a lashing to a point overhead. The base is perhaps 30″ in length. As has been mentioned, security is necessary for proper sleep at sea, therefore with knees on leeboard and buttocks against the ship's side, it may be agreed that these are merely a poor relation to the out-dated bunk boards. The making and fitting of canvas leeboards is well within the capability of most owners.

Quarter berths, those cavernous provisions for sleep which reach beneath cockpits of sailing craft, provide essential security but they have disadvantages. In some they produce claustrophobia but, assuming a yachtsman is not so effected, he may find his head too close to a companionway, a chart table or a galley stove, not to mention the occasional splashes on his face from above to rudely awaken him.

Of course on sailing craft which might well spend a few hours on one tack or reach, one will probably sleep soundly and securely on any lee settee. However, one cannot regard as preposterous the man who, amidst a welter of sail bags, bedding and clothing, curls up in the bows to enjoy a sleep as restful and secure as a bunk of any type can produce.

Galley stoves

Ideally, a galley stove is fitted with gimbals which respond to rolling and has two burners and a grill. An oven beneath, yet integral with, the stove lowers the centre of gravity of the unit and therefore improves gimbal action besides improving cooking facilities. The two-burner Gaz stove whose cylinder is screwed on to the bottom of the unit gives equally improved gimbal action and has the added quality of needing no piping of any sort. Again ideally, the galley area is such that the cook can wedge or belt himself in and hold on too.

At worst, a yachtsman has a stove which folds away and has no gimbals. In such case it may well be that the cook must kneel, sit or poise to tortuously tend pots, plates, boiling water and prepared food. Fortunately all stoves have fiddles, the fixed or adjustable bars which prevent pots from sliding off the stove. Even in moderate conditions at sea, effective fiddles notwithstanding, such a stove may demand that a kettle or pot be held on the stove throughout. Its seaworthiness is questionable.

Food

It may be said that three factors determine the quantity and variety of hot cooked food a crew will eat on passage:

(a) The utilitarian value of the cooking stove.

(b) The degree of security the cook can obtain when preparing a meal.

(c) The ability of the cook to remain below, with a variety of cooking smells, without being violently sick.

For those who realise that they must sail with less than satisfactory cooking facilities and a cook who might prove a useful member of the crew only by remaining in the open air or lying down, there is a satisfactory answer. It is the prior production of good, appetising stews and soups, kept hot in large vacuum flasks. Satisfying hot meals produced in this manner, perhaps heated a little on the stove if necessary, may be interspersed with frequent tasty cold snacks and hot drinks which a skipper himself can produce if necessary. Such an eating pattern is necessary on a long haul, whatever the cooking facilities. Alcohol in any form is generally welcome to most when discomfort is great, but it will be found no substitute for hot drinks.

Warmth

What yachtsman has not wakened to dank, humid, sticky conditions produced by two or three people sleeping aboard during a chilly summer's night? Unless a warm dry day follows so that maximum internal ventilation can be given, everything below decks will be damp and will remain so in the absence of ventilation and warmth. A cabin heater is an effective answer. On an extended passage, at sea and particularly at night, a heater is the means by which shivering is quickly overcome, damp clothes are dried and sleep made invitingly close.

Until relatively recently lack of space, safety considerations and cost have denied all but the owners of large yachts the means to heat a cabin area. Although a yachtsman is now offered many choices of cabin heaters, perhaps the catalytic type has the greatest number of advantages. Stable enough in itself, it can nevertheless roll about the cabin sole, be stood on a bunk, even have petrol poured on it and it still remains entirely safe. The Minicat is adequate for craft up to about 22 feet in length and the Maxicat for those up to about 27 feet. These stoves are reasonable in cost and meet the demands of the most safety-conscious yachtsman. For large craft, catalytic stoves with greater heat output have variable control, are more costly and less handy.

A criticism of these stoves one may encounter is the necessity to carry the highly volatile, special fuel, and methylated spirits to produce ignition. The writer cannot agree that there is any real substance in such argument. Fuel should be carried in a metal can and stowed in a deck or cockpit locker. If a heater well is always filled in the open air, with a funnel, fire risk is negligable. One naturally tends the stove when a small amount of methylated spirit must be poured on its heating surface and ignited, the means by which a catalytic heater is started, but thereafter no other stove can surpass its safety. When filled, this type will burn for up to 18 hours and running costs are low.

Fig. 1.8

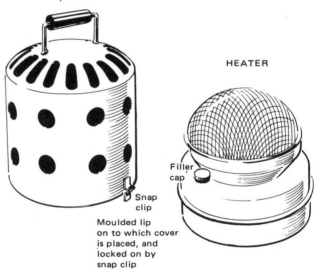

Rubber hot water bottles may seem unseamanlike provisions on a seagoing craft but they often have real value when one is cold and damp.

PART 3 GENERAL FACTORS

Preservation of accumulators

Those who cruise to places with unknown facilities must, in the absence of a generator system divorced from the main engine, be constantly aware of the limited nature of their electrical supplies. Although most motor cruisers and large, well-equipped sailing yachts only casually demand this awareness, for the remainder the need is paramount.

The writer has a distaste for formulae and so the nature of a yachtsman's problems may best be described by him in the following manner. The voltage of a craft's electrical circuits is always known to the owner, and any light bulbs in circuit have their wattage printed on them. An accumulator always has a known ampere-hour capacity so let a large one of 60 ampere-hours be considered. To crudely define ampere-hours, if one drains a current of 60 amperes from it, it will be exhausted after one hour. One the other hand, if a current of one ampere is taken from it the period of life without charging would theoretically be 60 hours. Both states assume a fully charged accumulator. The cruising family will drain an accumulator somewhere between the two extremes quoted.

An owner can roughly calculate the amount of this drain. If he totals the wattage of light bulbs generally in use and divides this figure by the voltage of the electric circuit, he arrives at a figure. The electrical drain from the accumulator is the resultant figure: x amperes. The ampere-hour capacity of the accumulator is then divided by this figure, this quotient, and the final figure obtained is the number of hours for which the accumulator will provide services. Such calculation must assume an efficient accumulator which is fully charged at the outset. In this uncomplicated example it will be noted that no account has been taken of electrical devices given sporadic use, such as extractor fans, fresh water pumps and navigation lights.

Example:
Given:— 12 volt boat circuit. Accumulator capacity of 60 ampere-hours. 4 cabin lights with total wattage of 36.
36 watts divided by 12 volts   = 3 amperes
60 ampere-hours divided by 3 amperes   = 20 hours life.

In fact, due to loss of voltage, lights will dim long before 20 hours is reached.

Defined in this manner, the limited nature of one's electrical supplies may be surprising to some. 20 hours of illumination at idealistic best from a lighting arrangement which cannot be regarded as lavish is good reason for conservation of supplies. Of course an engine fitted with a generator or alternator will generously return to the accumulator its depleted capacity, always provided it has not been so exhausted that it lacks the ability to effectively actuate the self-starter. An owner with starting handle in hand approaches with trepidation a marine engine possessing the kick of a mule and demanding the strength of a gorilla to turn it.

Clearly the moral in this dissertation is never to drain an accumulator unnecessarily. In the crowded conditions in which yachts must often manoeuvre, that the immediate start of an auxiliary engine on a sailing yacht should possess this ability is considerably more important than the artless use of full lighting during a party which lasts into the small hours, or a child's desire to read in bed.

On a craft where no means of charging an accumulator exists, perhaps when secondary motive power is provided by an outboard motor, extravagant use of lighting can only result in all lights dying until the accumulator can be taken ashore to be charged.

Some owners who depend upon a single heavy duty accumulator to start an engine might ponder the desirability of fitting a second one of smaller capacity for electrical services other than the starter motor. A throw-switch being fitted to connect both accumulators in series, when the engine is running

charging of both will take place. Disengagement of the switch in port would ensure that only the smaller accumulator is suffering drain, and the considerable power which the main accumulator must provide to start the engine is assured at all times.

Lighting

It must be assumed here that navigation and internal lights are maintained in proper working order but, for a protracted sea journey, other aspects of lighting must be considered.

Secondary lighting in no way dependent upon the primary source of power is necessary. A secondary electrical source must generally be ruled out as impractical and the usual waterproof torch and handlamp are merely essential adjuncts to primary lighting. If one loses power to feed navigation lights there is, from a practical point of view, nothing the average yachtsman can do about it apart from exhibiting some form of white light if necessary. Therefore this prospect need not be discussed here. In the opinion of the writer the answer to one's problems lies in the common Tilley lamp. Objections may be made about the undesirability of carrying paraffin and methylated spirit, about possible potentially dangerous flare-ups but, if good sense and the advices of the makers are applied to their use, then they produce extremely good illumination for both internal and external use. Elsewhere it has already been emphasised that the drain on accumulators of ordinary cabin lighting is always a depressing reality. What better answer to these problems in port than a Tilley lamp?

There will be those who prefer propane gas illumination for this purpose. The ability of these lamps to produce light is roughly equivalent to that of the Tilley lamp but — not in the open air. They are not designed for this purpose. If the type with the small replaceable cylinders is chosen it will prove an expensive form of secondary lighting. Yet if the yachtsman still thinks that this type of lamp is a worthwhile purchase, let him buy one which will stand on a table as easily as it can be suspended from the deckhead. Propane gas or Tilley lamps all have fragile mantles and glass flame shields, so one must have a safe place to stow one's lamp.

The mechanics of chartwork are difficult enough on a heaving craft on a bright day. If cabin electric lighting does not provide adequate chart table illumination at night a quite unrealistic resolution is to plan to supplement it with a torch. The installation by an owner of a small electric light on a flexible stem, mounted in a suitable position, needs minimal electrical knowledge and is most modest in price. In the absence of proper provision for chart illumination, nothing less will suffice.

Compass lighting, seldom or never used by weekenders, must be checked. Its true value should be established in darkness before sailing, if only to adjust the screen and bracket and clean seldom used electrical contacts.

Finally, the writer makes reference to a special light for use on sailing craft in Chapter 2. Its sole purpose is to produce effective mainsail illumination.

Clothing

Although the reader will no doubt possess sea going clothing to meet his previously modest needs, he may find the following remarks of value.

However sunny and warm it may be in harbour, it will

almost invariably be chilly at sea, even in the lee of the land. Some distance offshore in similar weather it can be downright cold and awareness is accentuated when exposure is prolonged. Night temperatures are inevitably lower than those of the day. Wetness produced by either rain or spray, when coupled with the chill of day or night sea air, can produce misery.

Constant body warmth is achieved by creating and preserving pockets of still air next to the skin, all over. If unsuitable clothes are worn, or if wind can insidiously destroy this essential condition, then coldness and shivering will result. Never should appearance dictate the content of a male or female sea-going wardrobe. People who insist upon wearing cotton T shirts and hip-clinging jeans beneath wet weather gear are best left on shore. They could well be reduced to unwanted trammels during a 12 or 18 hour passage.

Sensible provision for either sex for cruising might comprise two each of the following articles:

Long sleeved woolen vest.
Long woollen underpants, commonly known as Long Johns.
Brushed cotton shirt or blouse.
Polo necked, long sleeved, light woollen jersey.
Corduroy or similar trousers.
Long, floppy, heavy woollen sweater.
Cotton fisherman's smock.
Long silk gloves, long woollen gloves and rubber or plastic
    waterproof ones which will cover either or both.
Absorbant towel for use as a scarf.
Wool socks.
Long, heavy woollen seaboot stockings.
Balaclava helmet.

As an alternative to this considerable but not excessive provision, perhaps at some time in the future cruising men will contemplate a less bulky and more effective alternative. It is the wet suit worn by dinghy sailors who sail the year round. A dinghy man may sometimes protect his suit from possible damage by wearing a shirt and light trousers over it.

Wet suits will provide comfortable, prolonged warmth in bitter conditions. When activity is low, as is frequently the case during long hauls across the sea, their value is greatest. Considerable exertion or movement will quickly produce perspiration – without loss of body temperature – and this, although acceptable to dinghy sailors who can strip off and shower once ashore, might be deemed undesirable by cruising men.

Their value is even greater if a wearer falls overboard. Their slight buoyancy may be defined as a swimming aid. If it is recalled that hypothermia – a lowering of the body temperature – is more likely to cause death in sea water than drowning by asphyxia, an even more important aspect is revealed. As a rough example, in a sea temperature of about 45° Fahrenheit the wearer of a wet suit might have a life expectancy of about 4 hours. Without one it is reduced to perhaps a half hour or less. Summer sea temperatures will lengthen these periods but death by hypothermia remains no less a danger and the best lifejacket available cannot prevent it.

Oilskins come in various materials, qualities, colours and styles. A two piece suit is generally regarded as preferable. The type most likely to preserve dryness of garments beneath is that which has chest high trousers with short braces and elastic

bottoms. Its smock is jumper-like with a hood; it is laced or zipped at the neck, has elastic internal cuffs and a tightening cord round the bottom. The colour should be yellow or red: for safety reasons no other should be chosen.

Seaboots are commonly short with flat soles, or perhaps knee length with lace-up tops. The best of the latter type are expensive but one can swim in them. Those who insist that gym shoes are the only footwear which will give surefootedness and speed of movement on deck are right, but only when the sea is smooth and the weather is pleasant. Otherwise, tight cotton footwear will rapidly produce excessively cold feet and consequent serious discomfort. Whatever type of seaboot is chosen, it should be one or two sizes larger than one's normal foot size. Some experienced cruising men wear common Wellingtons, they being reasonably warm provided they are too large and they can easily be kicked off in the water. Or so it is said.

It is proposed that clothing is kept in plastic bags, fairly strong refuse sacks being useful for this purpose. They have neither weight nor bulk, they are waterproof, they assume any shape desired and in most senses they must be judged preferable to grips, kit bags and canvas satchels.

Crew content

On the average sailing craft a skipper will need at least one other person, male or female, whose competence is near equal to his own. These two should be immune from seasickness except in the worst conditions.

Amongst the remaining crew members there may be those who are potentially useful and the ones who have come along for the ride. The latter may well be good friends and excellent company ashore and yet, through the effects of seasickness, could become one more source of concern for a skipper if they need attention at sea. Children might come into this category, although a seasick child can be less of a problem than a seriously sick adult.

Content of crew in a motor cruiser can be related to the speed of the craft and the length of the passage planned. In many cases it will suffice if the skipper alone has the essential knowledge and experience. Many passengers can readily be taught to steer a course and, so that a skipper obtains breaks for meals and navigation, one of them can be given the wheel, he remaining in effective control of the craft.

Watches

Crew content will determine the length of time any one person should remain at the helm and for this reason fellow voyagers can be divided as follows:

(a)   The competent.
(b)   The potentially useful.
(c)   The passengers.

Except in unavoidable circumstances the 'watch on deck' should be on duty for no longer than 3 hours. The man who considers he will never be able to sleep at sea takes no account of the constant flexing and relaxing of almost every muscle in his body, produced by the movement of his craft. The effect is real. Fatigue overcomes the unfit far sooner than the fit and, having set in, only the flow of adrenalin in the body produced by anxiety or fright will counter it for a while. It has the effect of dulling judgement, blurring awareness and is potentially dangerous. These comments take no account of the pre-occupying and demoralising effect of even mild seasickness.

Where only two competent people are aboard a sailing craft and the remainder, if any, are passengers, the two will have to divide helm duties between them. They may well find that 2 hours is quite long enough as a trick at the helm. Yet they will probably discover that even passengers are of assistance to them if the latter are not seasick, if only to bring and carry and to take the helm for brief spells. Conversation in itself is helpful and minor necessary tasks on deck need not be the planned, timed, controlled movements of the lone helmsman.

Seasickness

Many a long cruise has had to be abandoned due to the effects of seasickness, and so few skippers with crew members of uncertain reaction to the prolonged motion of a craft can be assured that it will not happen to them. For no obvious reason there are those who are totally immune; others who are only sick in bad sea conditions yet not rendered useless; and many who would be seasick in a flat calm.

Few yachtsmen are unfamiliar with the circumstances and conditions which will worsen and ease seasickness, but they may not have encountered a person who is reduced to such a degree of misery and despond that he ceases to care for his own safety, even to discontinuing to react against the movement of a craft. A person afflicted to this degree can produce alarm and concern in others, very much to the detriment of the efficient working of the craft by others not so smitten.

Many palliatives and considerable good advice is offered to sufferers. In this sense, good advice is usually of the type which is either adopted naturally or forgotten, so only medication will be considered here. All seasickness tablets have the same basic beneficial effect and so there is really nothing to choose between them. Rigid adherence to the makers' recommendations remains the most satisfactory guard against the onset of seasickness. It has been remarked by the writer's family that 'Quells' produce unpleasant drying of saliva glands but 'Sea-legs' do not. Their common vague queasiness is made less bearable if they have dry mouths as well.

CHAPTER 2

Navigational Equipment

An artisan's skill is not impaired if he is denied good tools, nor if their number falls short of his wishes: neither is the skill of a navigator. Nevertheless, both will achieve the results they desire with greater ease if they do not have to tolerate these inadequacies. If in addition their natural skills are supplemented by electronic devices designed to assist speed and accuracy, further benefit must result.

There are a great number of navigational tools, instruments and devices now offered to yachtsmen, but here the writer commends only those articles which he regards as either essential or highly desirable. A yachtsman who wishes he had more navigational experience might wistfully reflect that, at the flick of a switch on a very costly instrument, he could obtain continuous, accurate positions in all weathers merely by reading dials. This is true, but at the same time he would remove one of the fascinations of yachting. Most yachtsmen prefer the spices of cruising in their entirety, although perhaps the inner motivation of a few would be the avoidance of a considerable overdraft, no matter what their declarations.

This is one of the reasons why no mention is made here of radar, radio compasses, Decca Navigator and similarly excellent if costly navigational aids. Those who have the good fortune to own any of them should always regard them for what they are: aids to navigation. Never must a seaman consider them as means by which the normal processes of pilotage, navigation and seamanship can be by-passed.

Chart table

The bigger the working top, the easier it is to do chartwork on it. It follows, therefore, that only large motor and sailing yachts have sufficiently spacious interiors to allow builders to make adequate provision. In a small yacht minimal table dimensions might be 18″ x 18″ and, if no secure working top gives this area, alternatives must be considered. It might be the removal of a settee cushion so that charts may be laid on a level surface beneath, or the provision of a ½″ plywood board capable of being slotted over an existing fitment, even if it be a bunk or settee.

A permanent fiddle in the form of a wooden lip at or round the edge of a chart table can be of questionable value. It really needs to have a height of about ¾″ to prevent charts and rulers from sliding off. Yet such a lip often joins with other limits, such as bulkheads, to exasperatingly interfere with the free movement of a parallel ruler.

The tops of chart tables are traditionally highly polished, yet more practical in any small craft would be surfaces which have the texture of flour paper: a markedly matt finish which is not abrasive to charts.

Parallel rulers

There are sundry types of ruler designed for chartwork and each successive Boat Show appears to produce one more. Yet one gains the impression that the old and tried Captain Field's Improved type is still the most widely used.

Fig. 2.1

There are many makes in many sizes, of boxwood, plastics and ebony, and a yachtsman may have to ask himself the question: which? The writer would commend one of boxwood, for its unpolished under surface. A ruler which does not readily slide on a chart is desirable. Its length should be 12″: no more than this because it would be too large for manipulation on a table of limited area: no less because it then ceases to provide a straight edge of sufficient length for practical chartwork. Its hinges must be free and, if they are stiff, they should be worked and worked until they open and close the ruler freely. One has only to try to 'walk' a stiff-hinged ruler across a chart on a schoolroom desk to realise how markedly the effectiveness of the ruler is reduced in consequence.

An alternative ruler is the Douglas Protractor. Of proven value over a great number of years and inexpensive, it has the advantage of gripping a chart surface well and it demands no manipulation once the direction of a course or a bearing has been determined. Totally different in character from Captain Field's Improved, there are advantages in carrying both types.

Fig. 2.2

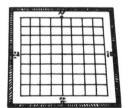

Douglas Protractor

Dividers

Only one type of divider is really suitable for use aboard a yacht. It is the one illustrated.

Fig. 2.3

If no proper provision has been made a yachtsman can easily make this simple requirement for himself. His need is a piece of suitable wood 8″ x 2½″ x 1″ thick. Holes are drilled or gouged as indicated in the following figure.

Fig. 2.4

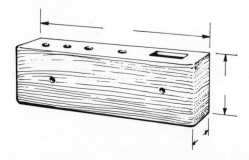

This fitment is screwed to a bulkhead or partition within close reach of the chart table. Less satisfactory alternatives are chart drawers, handy lockers or cubbyholes, a 1″ high wooden retaining lip at the rear of the chart table or even a plastics wall fixture intended for flowers.

It should be 6″ to 8″ long and made of a combination of brass and stainless steel. This instrument might be considered expensive for what it is but one should not settle for less. It can be both opened and closed with one hand, an essential feature in small craft navigation. Straight-legged navigational dividers lack this quality therefore they should be avoided, as must be any type of geometry dividers which have the added disadvantage of damaging charts with their sharp points.

Rubbers

Reeves India Rubber erasers or their high quality equivalents are always provided for use on merchant vessels. Clearly this is because they are the best for use on navigational charts.

Geometry compasses

Any type of compasses, preferably about 4″ long, and capable of drawing pencil circles, is essential for efficient chartwork. This instrument may be used for scribing round lighthouses and lightships their charted ranges; it facilitates the geometrical projection of tidal triangles and can be used for drawing round a danger the minimum range one wishes to close it.

Pencils

The standard chartwork pencil is a high quality article with a 2B lead. The reason is not artless. Without excessive pressure, it produces a line which can comfortably be seen in artificial light and yet it is easily erased.

Protractor

Seldom used but from time to time justifying its presence amongst chart instruments is a 6″ perspex protractor.

Ready use stowage for chart utensils

On a constantly moving craft pencils, dividers and rubbers are items which are frequently needed, yet in the absence of proper stowage adjacent to the chart table they will either be misplaced by someone or they will misplace themselves. Would that all builders give this simple yet essential requirement some thought.

Charts

For a sea crossing the writer would commend both Admiralty and Stanford charts, with Admiralty charts taking precedence. Perhaps the following assessment of both types will provide guidance.

ADMIRALTY CHARTS

Advantages:
(a)   In any scale desired, their coverage in the areas considered cannot be equalled by any other publisher.
(b)   Their detail and accuracy is of a high order and a close study of them gives a mental picture of the waters to be traversed and terrestial features which may be encountered.
(c)   The new type of Admiralty Chart which extensively uses pale colour wash to amphasise depth contour and land demarcation enhances their value to yachtsmen.

Disadvantages:
(a)   Aboard small sailing and motor yachts their folds are exasperating. Intended for use on large vessels, the remainder of yachtsmen must of necessity fold them again and again. These charts do not fold naturally and repetitive folding blurs detail on old creases and quickly reduces their useful life.
(b)   In the absence of a chart drawer some 30″ wide and of proportionate length, Admiralty charts must be rolled up when not in use. Seldom is flat stowage under settee cushions satisfactory. Charts which endeavour to retain their rolled state when needed are unhandy and vexing.
(c)   At the time of writing, only a section of the English Channel is given coverage in the new style charts.

Old style charts for the remainder of waters round the British Isles, for all their excellence, do not lend themselves to easy reading in artificial light in a yacht.

STANFORD CHARTS

Advantages:
- (a) Their flamboyant style and their extensive use of colour wash is particularly helpful to yachtsmen.
- (b) Their built-in folds, 10″ x 5½″, lend them to ready use on any size of chart table and to stowage almost anywhere.
- (c) Plans of yachting ports within the orbit of any Stanford chart are produced upon the face of it, together with abbreviated sailing directions for these ports.

Disadvantages:
- (a) Although complete coverage of the British Isles is planned, at this time adequate embrace is limited to waters round the southern half of the British Isles and West Scotland.
- (b) Sea and coastal features are identical to those produced on Admiralty charts, but land contours and terrestial detail is minimal.
- (c) The publishers never intending to supplant them, these charts are best supplemented by Admiralty charts to ensure total coverage when demanded.

A yachtsman is well advised to take advantage of the qualities of both where possible. As a broad principle, therefore, there is much to be said for first buying Stanford charts for one's cruising ground when they are available, and then supplementing them as considered necessary with Admiralty charts. The writer would, for instance, at least ensure that he had the Admiralty chart of the appropriate section of the French coast when bound for Dieppe, if only to assure that he could obtain from it a clear mental picture of the shape of the hills behind the coastline, and other details which might assist early recognition when a landfall had been made.

All Admiralty chart depots and agents have available for reference the Hydrographic Office publication, NP131, Catalogue of Admiralty Charts and other publications. Nevertheless, it should not be overlooked that in each volume of the Admiralty Sailing Directions there is an outline chart of the area for which the book gives coverage. On the face of this chart is drawn the limits of every Admiralty chart available, together with their numbers. Where doubts exist about the total number of charts required, it is better and safer to have too many charts of an area than too few.

Preservation of charts

In small boat conditions, particularly in wet weather, any chart can suffer damage of a nature which may well demand its renewal before another cruise is contemplated. For this reason many experienced yachtsmen completely cover their charts with clear Contact plastics film. By this means charts are strengthened immeasurably and are made almost impervious to wetness. One is then committed to using Chinagraph wax pencils which produce thick, bold lines. This practice may seem crude when working on a chart at home but in difficult conditions at sea many would aver that it is the only system which is related to reality.

Perhaps for the man who has not cruised extensively before, who wisely chooses a period of settled weather before sailing outward, this system is best not adopted at the outset. Pre-sailing notations which the competent yacht navigator might consider superfluous would necessarily have to be made in a heavy, clumsy style. In addition, a film-covered chart is minimally less easy to read than one which is not.

Publications

The volume of Admiralty Sailing Directions appropriate to a yachtsman's cruising area is an essential purchase when a sea crossing is considered. Three other Hydrographic Office publications provide a seaman with information of such a comprehensive nature and such excellence that, although few yachtsmen appear to do so, one is wise to obtain them:

The Admiralty Tide Tables, Volume 1, British and European Waters.

The Admiralty List of Lights.

The Admiralty List of Radio Signals, Volume 2.

Compendiums of the information contained in these volumes are available, in very limited form, in Stanford's Sailing Companion and Reed's Nautical Almanac. With the H.O. publications in one's possession, either or both of these books provide supplementary information in no way essential to the competent navigator. The remainder of yachtsmen may well find assistance in either of them, depending upon individual need.

Compasses

It is a reality that a steering compass is the most important single item of navigational equipment aboard any type of yacht which is to venture offshore. Few yachtsmen are capable of knowledgeably comparing various brands of compasses and a consequence of this is that, seeking an article of good quality and high precision, one must of necessity choose one amongst the most costly. It may be well to note that although the Henry Hughes 'Sestral' range is generally expensive, its excellence has been proved over a great number of years. In any event, in the absence of a Consumer Association report upon a wide range of yacht compasses, one is well advised never to consider economising when buying a compass. External appearance can be no indication of internal quality. Every compass bowl is sealed and compass cards look more or less the same whether a complete article cost £9.00 or £90.00. Who is to say whether as a consequence of a maker using materials of indifferent quality and mass production techniques, built-in compass error is not present in an attractively priced compass?

At least it is possible to assess the utilitarian value of a compass's external fittings. Binnacles provide compass bowl protection, but it is frequently impractical to use a compass so fitted. Adequate strength of gimbals and bracket then assumes importance. This quality will not be found in fitments made of a combination of light section metal and plastics. An involuntary lurch against such fittings can spring a compass bowl from its mounting: that it can just as easily be sprung back again is inadequate solace to a yachtsman at sea. Any government surplus compass is invariably of high quality but, if such an article has been designed for a different location from that planned the advantages of attractive price and excellent construction may be wholly negated by an inability to comfortably read it both by day and by night at sea.

Whether a helmsman is able to recline in an armchair, whether he must stand straddle-footed while grasping a wheel, or whether he must of necessity repose as best he can in an open cockpit, his compass must be comfortably visible to him from any one of these static positions. If it is not, then over a long period fatigue will occur, which may cause misreading of the compass or even produce errors of parallax. Re-siting, elevating or lowering usually overcomes this kind of problem.

But cockpit steering compasses may produce more complex problems, although most present day builders make sensible provision for siting them. Such a site will, or should be, one from which a helmsman can with comfort keep his eyes roving between compass, sails and horizon. There remains the unconventional yacht where the compass bracket may have been screwed to any convenient surface somewhere near the helmsman. Stating categorically that any position within the well of a cockpit is to be condemned, the writer would comment that a compass moved too far forward cannot effectively be read; yet it must be forward of him and, if the only possible site demands that he looks almost vertically down upon it, then it too is unsatisfactory. A yachtsman with these problems might consider the dual-purpose Sestral 'Moore' compass which can be located high on the after end of the doghouse. It can be read from a horizontal position, it will withstand any buffeting to which it might be subjected, and it can also be used for taking bearings. Although infrequently seen in sailing yachts, this compass has a great deal to commend it.

Hand bearing compasses

The range of hand bearing compasses is considerable, from the tiny ones with which necklaces are provided, to the weighty type which makes one realise that one is grasping a fistful of compass. If choice exists between these two extremes, the latter is to be preferred. Listed below are qualities which the writer himself would seek in one:

(a) Robust construction.
(b) Ability to hunt and hold magnetic North, although lateral movement is rapid.
(c) Proven quality of materials and workmanship.
(d) A compass card graduated in no more than 2° steps.
(e) High magnifaction through integral prisms.
(f) Vertical handgrip.
(g) Illumination for night use.

It is not propounded here that one should speedily replace his hand bearing compass if these qualities are absent in his own: it is suggested to a few that their lack of ability to quickly and accurately obtain bearings might be due to the compasses they use. The Sestral 'Radiant' is a compass, amongst others, which possesses the qualities listed above.

Air bubbles in compass bowls

Not infrequently air bubbles develop in compasses of all types over a long period. Unless they are minimal they can sporadically wander across a course being steered, even linger over the important arc of the compass card and so make steering a course difficult. Any owner can remove such bubbles and none need tolerate them.

A hypodermic syringe filled with ordinary fresh water is needed. In the side of the bowl of all magnetic compasses a tapped screw will be found. If the compass bowl is held so that the screw is uppermost, the bubble will settle beneath it. With the screw removed, water can be injected into the bowl so that a bubble is completely ejected. This bare statement suggests that the operation is easy. Although a large air bubble is quickly reduced, the banishment of a final small bubble needs patience and care. The syringe is essential, it being virtually impossible to pour water through the vent.

Compass deviation

No yachtsman should attempt a sea passage without certain knowledge whether or not deviations are present in his steering

Dual Purpose Compass

Steering Compass

Fig. 2.5

compass. The amateur who has taken no steps to ascertain this essential knowledge is well advised to enlist the services of a compass adjuster. Many are available round our coasts and most yacht chandlers and boatyards know how a local one can be contacted.

It often occurs that a craft has been swung for deviations shortly after delivery but, although she may be a few years old, she has not been swung since. If no structural alterations involving ferrous metal, and no potentially magnetic equipment has been since added in the vicinity of the steering compass, then one may cautiously say that swinging again is unnecessary. This cannot be said of craft wholly made of ferrous metal, in which type of craft the molecular structure of the metal can insidiously change over a period, causing changes in compass deviations.

Listed below are the generally accepted conditions which must be fulfilled before it can be said with reasonable certainty that no deviations are present in a magnetic compass:

(a) No permanently positioned ferrous metal is within 4 feet of it.

(b) No radios or other electrical equipment capable of producing a magnetic field is within 5 feet of it.

(c) No hand bearing compass is given sea stowage within 4 feet.

(d) No ferrous loose gear is within 3 feet.

(e) Twin electric wiring near the compass is twisted to neutralise its magnetic properties.

This is quite a formidable list of conditions and it must be borne in mind that measurements must be taken directly from the steering compass, whether or not GRP, wooden, brass, copper or alloy bulkheads and partitions intercede. To answer a question before it is asked, there is no material available to yachtsmen which will provide an effective barrier between a magnetic compass and magnetic materials.

A law of magnetism states that the strength of a magnetic field varies inversely as the cube of the distance from its source. If one can comprehend its import, this law is useful knowledge to a yachtsman. The writer is aware that over-simplification of a complex subject can contain potentially dangerous pitfalls but, to assist comprehension, it may be helpful if a crude example of the application of this rule is attempted. Let it be assumed that a butane gas bottle is given stowage which is 1 foot from a steering compass and the effect of this is to introduce 8° of deviation on certain headings. If the distance between bottle and compass is increased to double this distance, 2 feet, the deviation is reduced, not by half but to a mere 2°. At 3 feet deviation will still be present but of such a minute amount that no yachtsman could regard it. In this example there is useful intelligence which is related to the conditions listed from (a) to (d). The minimum distances quoted can be reduced slightly in the knowledge that deviations incapable of being measured are perhaps being introduced into a compass but – as these distances are increasingly reduced, deflection of Compass North from the magnetic meridian is increasing at an impressive rate.

It is always assumed that deviations do not exist in hand bearing compasses. This assumption is valid so long as they are used sufficiently far away from potentially magnetic materials and, poised in the open with compass in hand as one invariably must be, it is reasonable.

Sounding equipment

The excellence of transistorised, battery-operated echo sounding apparatus now available to yachtsmen at a cost which is incredibly cheap, bearing in mind the service it performs, makes it one item which no amateur yachtsman can afford to be without. Although it cannot be argued it is vital equipment without which one cannot sail, the fact that it gives instantaneous and continuous soundings from 1 foot up to 60 or 100 fathoms causes the writer to regard it as highly desirable equipment on any cruising yacht. Even the cheapest of sets are both reliable and efficient and so there is little to choose between them.

In common with any other piece of sophisticated man-made equipment, echo sounding sets can develop malfunction and therefore a hand leadline remains a sensible provision in all craft. Like over dependence upon an auxiliary engine in a sailing craft, total reliance upon echo sounding apparatus is unwise.

Distance recorders

A means of measuring distance run is a navigational necessity for long range cruising and sea crossings. Although the writer readily allows the estimable qualities of modern electrical equipment produced for this purpose, for leisurely family cruising he favours a trailing log for its very simplicity. At sea one can do very little about a failure in advanced electronic devices. In addition, when distance recorders of this type depend upon the free running of an underwater impellor, and that is slowed or stopped if a wispy piece of seaweed fouls it, the log is rendered useless until the weed can be removed. .

The turning of a trailing log line is produced by a rotator at its end. Through tiny but robust reduction gears within a taffrail clock, the rotation is translated into miles and tenths of distance run on the clock. If the rotator is fouled by weed, the cessation of spinning of the line and governor is quickly detected and removal of the foreign matter is merely a case of handing the log line. A few regular drops of light oil on the gears of these logs and they will give trouble free continuous running for years.

Walker's 'Knotmaster Mk. 111A' is the best known of these logs and this type can be hired. It will operate accurately at speeds between 2 and 20 knots.

Speed recorders

It must be said that, unless a speedometer is required for use in conjunction with full instrumentation in a high performance sailing craft, in no way can it be justified for navigational purposes in a cruising yacht. In such a craft carrying only essential equipment the information these instruments impart provides interest but little else. Translation of the information imparted by a distance recorder will give the same intelligence at no extra cost.

Clocks

Provided there are wrist or pocket watches aboard a craft, a bulkhead clock cannot be regarded as essential equipment. Nevertheless, for convenience of navigators it must be regarded as highly desirable. A bulkhead clock which is fitted with an alarm is quite the best. The alarm can be set to warn a skipper when a shipping weather bulletin is due; and how many weather forecasts have been missed in the absence of a warning device? It also precludes the necessity of someone being condemned to twilight sleep to ensure that a departure in the small hours occurs as planned. Of course, a bedside alarm clock brought from home for a cruise will serve the same purpose.

Barometer

All cruising yachtsmen must of necessity take an interest in elementary meteorology. No short term forecast of immediate weather trends can be made without observation of three weather features: first, cloud formation; second, wind direction and force; third, barometer reading and tendency. It follows, therefore, that a barometer is essential equipment.

It might be argued by some that shipping weather bulletins possess such a degree of reliability, and are broadcast with such frequency, that yachtsmen are effectively relieved of the necessity of assessing future weather. One would counter such argument by stating that even the finest meteorologist can be proved wrong in a forecast; that his forecast might be right for one section of a forecast area, yet wrong for another. The man who is actually experiencing weather is best able to judge whether a forecast is valid or whether he would be wise to retain reservations and attempt a forecast himself. An essential tool for this latter endeavour is a barometer.

Course indicator

To calculate the course to steer to counter the effect of a tidal stream one must generally indulge in chart geometry in conditions which are in no way conducive to accuracy. Young's Course Indicator, available from many yacht chandlers, will relieve the yachtsman of this requirement. These rigid, perspex,

Fig. 2.6

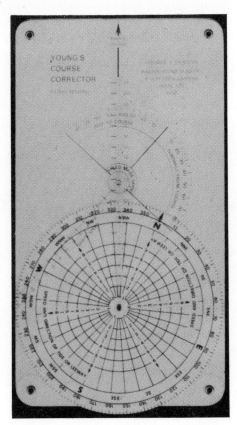

weatherproof instruments can, in a matter of seconds, give the course to steer to counter the effect of a current upon one's intended course.

This time factor alone makes the device highly desirable: some will regard the total removal of the possibility of geometric error as of equal value. Add to these assets the fact that it can be manipulated in an open cockpit in the rain and Young's Course Indicator becomes a worthwhile purchase.

Radio direction finding

No doubt unwittingly in most cases, British yachtsmen accept as normal the fact that they have at their disposal a system of marine radio beacons which give a sea coverage second to none in the world. It is equally as natural to them to accept that modern technology presents for their consideration small, lightweight, relatively cheap radio direction finding receivers. Yet these two facts make D/F sets designed for use aboard small craft highly desirable equipment when a short sea crossing from a British port is planned.

Basically there are two types: those which give bearings relative to the boat's head and those which give magnetic bearings. The latter are recognisable by their integral magnetic compasses and for the amateur this type is to be preferred. The reason is uncomplicated: with immediacy it gives to the mariner a magnetic bearing which he can lay off on his chart. Sets giving relative bearings demand that the steering compass be read at the moment each bearing is taken and then the relative bearing must be applied to the direction of the boat's head to achieve the same result which the other type of set produces directly.

Sets of the type recommended vary in price from about £35.00 for Electronic Laboratories 'Seafix' to over £200.00 for the Brookes and Gatehouse 'Homer'. In the high price ranges one is paying for quality, precision, design and durability, therefore one may expect high quality of incoming signals from them, coupled with fairly sharply defined 'nulls'. It must be emphasised that the finest sets will produce disappointing results in the hands of a novice, thus it is important that whatever set is chosen no opportunity is missed in practising taking bearings, even in port when signals can be heard. Lack of practice produces the following pitfalls: a coarse tuning touch when infinite lightness is demanded; an inability to distinguish weak signals from others which are audible and from inherent and unwanted 'fuzz'; an arc of no-signal many degrees greater than an arc produced by an experienced operator. The 'Seafix' set will meet the needs of most yachtsmen and, if performance is related to price, it must be regarded as a good purchase. These sets can be hired.

Some small transistor radio sets of foreign origin are surmounted by pivotal aerials and, in crude definition of the term, they can be called direction finding sets. They will produce relative bearings from a coarsely graduated scale on top of the set, always assuming it is possible to precisely secure the set so that bearings are related to the fore and aft line of the craft. It is improbable that a practised operator could obtain worthwhile results from these sets.

Sextant

Contrary to views expressed from time to time in the yachting press, the opinion must be expressed here that there is no navigational necessity for the provision of a sextant on a motor or sailing yacht whose owner's only intention is to voyage in the confined waters under consideration.

Those rare individuals who are familiar with celestial navigation can, on occasion, remove doubt by taking a sight of a celestial body when information from other sources is lacking. For the remainder, who are unquestionably the majority, a sextant will serve two useful purposes. Firstly, to obtain distance off a terrestial object of known height: a lighthouse, for example. Second, to fix position by horizontal sextant angles between charted terrestial objects which demands excursions into geometry. The practical yachtsman may agree that these two methods of fixing position are not sufficiently valid reasons for carrying a sextant, however valuable either navigational exercise may be regarded. The first method is valuable indeed: the second is perhaps best left to the ardent exponent of seldom used navigational practices.

Finally, one must comment that a sextant is a delicate and often a very valuable instrument. Every time it is removed from its case it is put at risk in a small craft. This risk is very much greater when it is in the hands of an inexperienced navigator. One must ask oneself: do the navigational advantages obtained through possession of a sextant justify their purchase? The writer suggests that they do not.

F.P.H. Distance-Off Estimator

'Distance off by vertical angle' was a common method of fixing position at sea before the advent of radar. It was big-ship practice which did not lend itself to adoption aboard small craft. A sextant was a pre-requisite, but all big ships carry sextants. The method was uncomplicated. A terrestial object of known height would be selected – a lighthouse, a promontory – and a vertical angle taken of it between sea level and its upper extremity. By reference to a widely published table, 'Distance off by vertical angle', the angle would be transposed into a range. A compass bearing of the object being taken at the same time, it was simply a matter of laying off the bearing and, to this bearing, the distance off would be applied. So a position was obtained.

The F.P.H. Distance Off Estimator adapts the same principles, yet precludes the use of a sextant. As ranges are read directly from the instrument, reference to tables is unnecessary. Sturdy in construction, it cannot develop malfunction because of its very simplicity: it demands no critical venier adjustment and will withstand the rigours of navigational processes aboard a small craft. For yachtsmen it will produce ready and valuable information in all weathers in a matter of seconds and therefore is regarded by the writer as a desirable item of equipment.

Station pointer

Those yachtsmen who, for one reason or another possess a sextant might consider a station pointer a worthwhile purchase. It is an expensive instrument which, given the precise horizontal angles between charted objects a sextant will provide, will produce an exact position. As explained fully in Stanford's Sailing Companion, a square of greaseproof paper will produce the same result and therefore purchase is unnecessary.

Light for sail illumination

The illumination of a white mainsail is a good method of drawing the attention of ships to one's presence at night. However, unless it is bright, bold and eye-catching it might well fail in its intention. This degree of illumination cannot be obtained from a torch or handlamp. The writer commends the use of a car lamp giving a diffused light and purchaseable in any car accessory shop. Wired into a boat's electrical circuit and fitted with a flexible lead of adequate length, it can be kept at hand below decks and ready for use. When sail illumination becomes necessary the helmsman need only reach for the lamp to produce radiant evidence of one's presence.

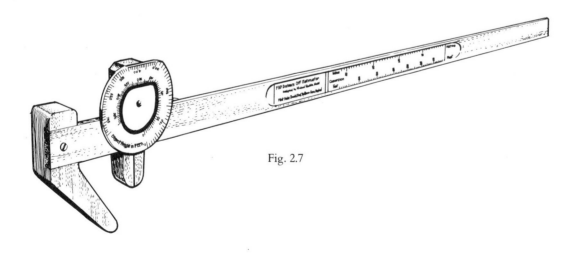

Fig. 2.7

CHAPTER 3

Working The Tides

Every 12 hours and 25 minutes the vast central area of the North Atlantic Ocean is raised about 4 feet. Up-down-up-down, with the regularity of a metronome, countless millions of tons of water are lifted and allowed to settle again. Interesting? It is more than interesting. It is phenomenal.

Each upheaval and subsidence creates a ripple of gargantuan proportions. Outwards from some central point, like the effect produced by dropping a pebble into a still pool, the undulations spread outwards to spend themselves on distant shores. One upheaval, producing a single massive ripple, will release a whiting from a pool high on the beach at Scarborough, cause a coaster anchored in the Gironde River to swing without option in a different direction and alter the course of a piece of driftwood in Chesapeake Bay for the thousandth time.

This is a gross yet fairly accurate simplification of the tidal phenomenon. No matter. It serves to emphasise natural forces in the form of tides which British yachtsmen must live with, or take to the inland waterways in exasperation.

One of these ripples or surges is in fact a tidal oscillation. The sea rises above its normal level, falls back below it and returns to normal again. Just as waves steepen on a gradually sloping beach, so does a tidal wave steepen as the sea bed rises from its cavernous depths to the continental shelf and later the shallower areas of sea bed as coastlines are approached. The slight rise in mid-Atlantic becomes about 10 feet in Belfast Lough, 13 feet in the Solent, 26 feet in the Channel Islands and an impressive 36 feet in the Severn estuary.

It follows that where vertical movement of the sea level takes place, lateral flow must occur. It produces the tidal streams we know, flowing first one way and then the other in the seas surrounding our coastlines.

The behaviour of tidal streams

Beyond the knowledge that tidal ebb and flood produce familiar patterns of water flow in the entrance to a river or harbour, and in open water, some yachtsmen's knowledge is lacking. This lack denies them the ability to take advantage of favourable streams, and avoid the strength of adverse ones. Thus, they are unlikely to make progress on passage equal to that of more knowledgeable yachtsmen.

Learning from authoritative books helps but ideally, local knowledge of tidal stream behaviour such as is possessed by fishermen is desirable yet unattainable. A wider knowledge of tidal behaviour will, however, lessen their disadvantage.

Let the reader imagine an empty North Sea and the effects of a decision to fill it from flood gates stretching from the Shetlands to the Norwegian coast. The water will fill the deeper sea valleys

first and, approaching higher levels, its flow in the vicinity of coastlines becomes almost predictable. Meeting a promontory, is it not reasonable to expect the water flow to be deflected to seaward, accelerating as compression and deflection occurs when the headland is encountered? It follows, therefore, that any craft off that headland will be carried offshore when tidal flow is brisk.

Fig. 3.1

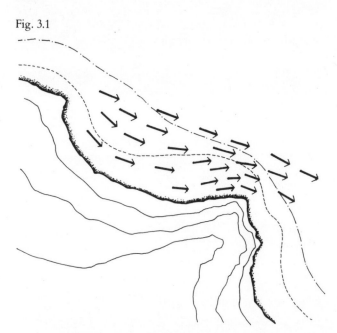

In a bay beyond, the rising water needing to flow into it to achieve its natural level, it is similarly reasonable to expect a tongue of tidal current to curve into it. A craft sailing coastwise will undoubtedly be set inshore, not to the same extent as she would be set out off the headland but still by a perceptible amount. The flow into the bay will follow the curvature of the coastline, tending to take the path at least resistance which will be where the greater depths occur. A gradually sloping beach producing extensive shallows will tend to be overlooked and so an eddy, a reverse current, may well be generated. It would be gentle but nonetheless real.

The probable flow of tidal water into a bay which reaches in the reverse direction to the tidal flow is more or less self-evident. Clearly, multi-directional eddies must occur which a yachtsman on passage would do well to avoid in the interests of forward progress.

Fig. 3.2

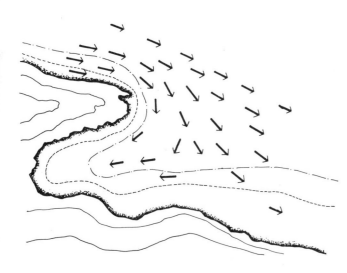

Fig. 3.4

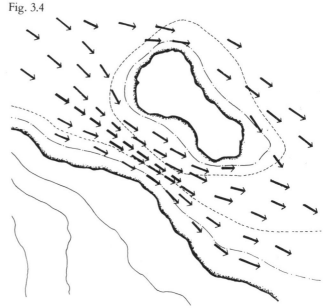

Fig. 3.3

Fig. 3.5

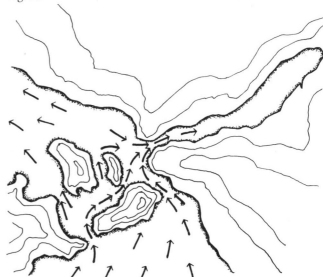

An island or islet off a coast generally produces a funnelling of water in the strait between island and mainland. If the mariner studies the breadth of the strait, its varying depths, the distance the island extends to seawards and the contours of adjacent coasts, he might well arrive at conclusions published in handbooks he has not read or does not possess.

Although by no means can one state that it is an absolute rule, deeper areas of water can be said to have been produced by centuries of scouring by tidal flow or currents. They are often the areas which the flow favours, therefore it is reasonable to assume in many cases that the stronger flow is likely to be encountered in the deeper seabed valleys, whether they are in narrow straights and waterways, or in the open sea around our islands.

Funnelling effects, producing formidable races, occur on the west coast of Scotland. But let one reflect that water levels in a loch many miles in length and of considerable breadth must match the rising and falling levels of the open waters to seaward.

If the relatively narrow entrance is interrupted by islands big and small then the reasons for funnelling become self-evident.

The author is aware that a study of tidal stream atlasses and the Admiralty Sailing Directions will indicate that there are so many inconsistencies of tidal flow inshore as to apparently negate anything written here. Why, for instance, do double high waters occur in the Southampton Area which, from a practical point of view, cause high water levels to be maintained for some three hours? Why do tidal streams flow in a southerly direction throughout most of the tidal cycle on both the east and west coasts of Portland Bill? That they do is the prime reason for the existence of the treacherous Portland Race to the south of the Bill. In fact the vagaries in direction of shorelines, the aimlessness of depths offshore and astronomical effects more subtle than the gravitational effects of the moon alone, often combine to confute every practical calculation attempted by seamen.

Nevertheless, it must be averred that such basic, practical

thinking is often of use to those whose tidal current charts do not give the detail they desire. The shortest course is not always the best one: distance added to avoid the strength of a stream frequently shorten passage times: and in the absence of local knowledge, avoidance is from time to time just a matter of common sense.

Fig. 3.6

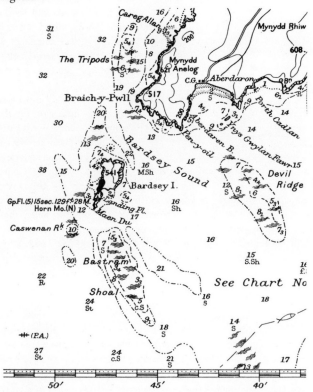

Overfalls

A study of the charts of all our local seas will reveal the frequent appearance on them of the Admiralty indication of overfalls. The lumpy, white capped, swirling appearance of overfalls sometimes give the impression that thousands of tunnyfish are gambolling madly just below the surface. Waves bob up and as quickly disappear. Some overfalls are inocuous and, apart from making life a little uncomfortable on a small craft, can be crossed with safety. Others by their very intensity must be avoided, particularly in heavy weather when they can be *lethal* even to large, well-found motor cruisers and sailing yachts. As a broad principle, therefore, the insignia on a working chart of an area of overfalls is sufficient reason for giving it a fairly wide berth.

Conflicting tidal currents, irregularities of coastlines and sharply undulating areas of seabed are mainly responsible for their occurence. The two latter factors are constants: only the tidal currents vary, both in direction and velocity. For these reasons overfalls usually occur at certain states of the tide, so one must not be dismayed if no evidence of overfalls is found in an area where they are indicated on the chart. Again it is the Admiralty Sailing Directions to which one must refer to obtain full knowledge of these generally unpleasant and occasionally extremely treacherous phenomena.

Offshore tidal streams

In the stretches of sea which surround our coasts, tidal flow is far more regular and, broadly speaking, tidal atlasses give most of the information the yachtsman needs. However it is well to appreciate that most of the predictable effects described above can be duplicated in open waters, but on a much larger scale. For instance, where the seas narrow one can expect and will experience acceleration of tidal currents. The stretch between the Isle of Wight and the Cherbourg peninsula is not an apparent case but it is nevertheless real.

Open water tidal flow

In narrow channels one is well used to tidal flow in one direction, the decrease in velocity until it comes to a standstill and the following reversal. Although in its broadest interpretation, this is also what happens in sea areas, it is rather more subtle. In fact the streams never cease to have velocity at any state of the tide. They have a circular pattern. For example, a north easterly flow of the main stream diminishing, it may swing slowly round to east, southeast, south and eventually commence the reverse flow. The velocity may well have decreased to a mere quarter or half knot as it circles round from one main direction to the other, but it is perceptible and contributes towards making the effective countering of tidal streams by yachtsmen, always a problem at the best of times, that little more difficult.

Fig. 3.7

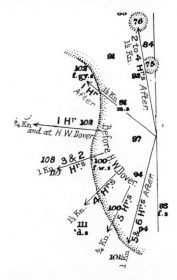

The effect of wind upon tides and tidal streams

When wind blows over water, friction must occur. The resulting reduction in wind velocity at sea level is of no consequence to the mariner; the wind he feels is that with which he must contend. That this same friction produces a surface current in the direction in which the wind is blowing concerns him very much. The strength of a current so produced will vary directly with the period during which the wind remains steady in direction, the extent of the sea area over which it blows and, of course, the strength of the wind itself. Realisation that every famous ocean current throughout the world is generated by an unvarying combination of these conditions lends point to these remarks.

It must not be expected that a light southerly breeze blowing in the Irish Sea for a few days will produce a perceptible current flow northwards. But let that same wind have the force of half a gale and a surface current would, if it were measurable in those conditions, make itself apparent in one's courses. In such foul weather, when choice exists, the average yachtsman remains in port until the gale has blown itself out, and then sails for his destination. He must not expect that a current so produced will die with the wind, and seldom will it have a velocity in excess of one knot. It will probably flow for twelve hours or more after the weather change, and so some allowance for it in his courses would be a seamanlike action. Such currents are superimposed upon existing tidal streams, and so an almost predictable disruption of the latter occurs.

Strong winds will in general raise the sea level to leeward. A strong onshore wind piles up the water on the shore and produces high water levels greater than those predicted; a strong *offshore* wind produces the reverse effect. A similar wind blowing along a coast tends to generate waves perhaps many miles long which travel along the coast. Where the crest of such a wave appears, the sea level will be raised, to be followed by a lowering when the trough passes. The sheer unpredictability of such surges makes them of academic interest to the mariner; that they exist in certain conditions is useful knowledge.

The banking of water in rivers and estuaries having long tidal reaches is common with an onshore wind. Many yachtsmen who berth their craft in such waters will be familiar with high water levels exceeding predicted levels by two feet or more, being attained before the predicted times, and a prolongation of these upper levels. In similar waters, offshore winds can deter tide levels from achieving their predicted heights. The existence of such winds might prevent one from removing a craft from a mud berth at high water, although tide tables predict heights which should make it possible.

The effect of barometric pressure upon tides

In many nautical publications one encounters reference to the effect of barometric pressure upon tidal heights. Perhaps river pilots with considerable local knowledge can on occasion take into consideration this fact. The average seaman does not because he cannot, therefore the subject is best left unexplored. In any case, the minimal change in sea level so produced is of no real consequence to the average yachtsman.

In all cases, having determined as best he can the probable depths of water he will encounter in a locality, his sounding apparatus or leadline must dictate whether safety or danger lies ahead.

Tide tables

That yachtsmen, like the remainder of the human race, are beasts of habit is in no way better emphasised than in their choice of tide tables. Most sail in one locality and so the give-away tide tables often produced by local tradespeople meet their needs. That these abbreviated booklets have shortcomings is well known and so, perhaps a little too often, they are expanded to meet needs. Predictions for port adjacent to each other are often near enough to use this device. Slightly extended excursions coastwise by yachtsmen who see no reason to buy comprehensive tide tables may produce anxieties, yet in the main they manage. To make a sea crossing, even to make an extended coastal cruise,

full tide tables are essential.

Above all other publications, the writer commends to the reader the Admiralty Tide Tables. Volume 1, European Waters, is the volume which meets his needs. Its excellence cannot be exceeded and the information frequently required by the yachting fraternity for small ports, havens and reaches demands less calculation in them than in other comprehensive tables.

A number of yachtsmen appear to regard the annual purchase of Reed's Nautical Almanac as being as vital to the boating scene as a calendar is to the home. Those who do carry it have, in this expansive compendium of nautical intelligence, complete tide tables for the British Isles and the continent. Yet much of its other content is abstract cockpit reading for the average yachtsman.

Another alternative remains: Stanford's Sailing Companion. In a largely successful endeavour to simplify tidal data for the amateur seaman, a practical system is adopted. Dover high water predictions are published for a two-year period, and for almost every yachting port in the British Isles and on the near continent a sufficiency of tidal information is given. From this latter information one can, by mentally applying it to the Dover predictions, obtain the high water time and height for any of the listed ports. This system is based upon the realistic belief that, given high water information, the yachtsman himself can and will estimate the rest. Like Reed's, this book gives much more information than that of tides alone and so choice between the two becomes a matter of individual need.

The use of tide tables

Before entering any tide tables to extract information, two factors must be borne in mind. Firstly, the information given in them is not an indesputable portent of fact; as explained earlier, sundry factors can disrupt times and heights but never the basic pattern. Secondly, it is neither seamanlike nor necessary to calculate tidal predictions with mathematical exactitude. The nearest half hour and the nearest foot are invariably sufficient for yachtsmen's needs. Tide tables give seamen precisely calculated predictions; it remains for them to interpret them practically and to take soundings when ever depths are in doubt.

Standard ports

In comprehensive tide tables Standard Ports are those for which complete predictions are given. There are very few of them. Usually they are ports widely used by shipping and infrequently by yachtsmen, so seldom can the latter enter tide tables and immediately obtain the information they seek.

Secondary Ports

All ports other than Standard Ports are known as Secondary Ports. Yachtsmen use them most of the time. For these ports 'constants' are given. Constants are time intervals, and heights, each of them being prefixed with a plus or minus sign. As every Secondary Port has one of the Standard Ports as its parent, it is simply a matter of applying the constants to Standard Port predictions to obtain the intelligence required.

Tidal stream information

For those who intend ranging far in home waters, no publisher produces tidal stream information superior to that

Fig. 3.8   Fig. 3.9

ENGLAND, SOUTH COAST — DOVER
Lat. 51° 07' N. Long. 1° 19' E.

TIMES AND HEIGHTS OF HIGH AND LOW WATERS

FEBRUARY

m Ft.	Time		m Ft.	Time		m Ft.	Time
5·9 19·4	0421		5·8 19·0	0027		2·3 7·6	0257
1·7 5·6	1144	1	1·8 6·0	0613 16	5·1 16·7 1	1020
5·5 18·0 F	1708		5·4 17·8 Sa	1309	2·3 7·6 F	1529
			5·0 16·5	1903		2242
2·0 6·7	0014	2	2·0 6·5	0153 17	2·4 7·8 2	0355
5·6 18·4	0541		5·6 18·4	0740	5·1 16·6	1118
2·0 6·5 Sa	1301		1·9 6·3 Su	1445 Sa	2·2 7·3	1640
5·3 17·4	1835		5·4 17·8	2019	5·2 17·1	2349
2·2 7·3	0137	3	2·0 6·6	0327 18	2·1 6·9 3	0520
5·4 17·7	0709		5·6 18·5	0848	5·3 17·3	1239
2·0 6·7 Su	1431		1·8 5·9 M	1604 Su	1·9 6·3	1816
5·3 17·5	1958		5·7 18·7	2117	5·5 18·1	
2·2 7·1	0309	4	1·7 5·6	0432 19	1·7 5·7 4	0119
5·4 17·7	0826		5·9 19·5	0959	5·6 18·3	0658
1·9 6·3 M	1555		1·5 4·8 Tu	1657 M	1·6 5·2	1419
5·5 18·0	2105		6·1 20·0	2202	5·9 19·2	1944

304   ENGLAND, SOUTH AND EAST COASTS

No.	PLACE	POSITION		TIMES AT STANDARD PORT				HEIGHTS IN (METRES) AT STANDARD PORT			
	STANDARD PORT	Lat. N.	Long. W.	High Water at		Low Water at		MHWS	MHWN	MLWN	MLWS
65	PORTSMOUTH	(see page 17)		1000 and 2200	0500 and 1700	0000 and 1200	0600 and 1800	4·7	3·8	1·8	0·6
	SECONDARY PORTS			TIME DIFFERENCES (Zone G.M.T.)				HEIGHT DIFFERENCES			
	Chichester Harbour										
68	Entrance	50 47	0 56	+0005	−0010	+0015	+0020	+0·2	+0·2	0·0	+0·1
68a	Bosham	50 50	0 52	+0020	+0005	★	★	+0·4	+0·2	★	★
68b	Itchenor	50 48	0 52	+0015	0000	◇	◇	+0·4	+0·2	0·0	0·0
68c	Dell Quay	50 49	0 49	+0025	+0010	★	★	+0·4	+0·2	★	★
69	Selsey Bill	50 43	0 47	−0005	−0005	+0035	+0035	+0·6	+0·6	0·0	0·0
70	Nab Tower	50 40	0 57	0000	+0015	+0015	+0015	−0·2	0·0	+0·2	0·0
72	Pagham	50 46	0 43	+0005	−0015	+0025	+0025	+0·8	+0·7	0·0	0·0
73	Bognor Regis	50 47	0 40	0000	−0020	+0035	+0030	+0·8	+0·7	−0·1	−0·1
	River Arun										
74	Littlehampton (Entrance)	50 48	0 32	0000	−0020	+0035	+0035	+1·0	+0·8	−0·1	−0·1
74a	Littlehampton† (Norfolk Wharf)	50 48	0 33	+0005	−0015	+0040	+0130	+0·8	+0·5	−0·2	+0·1†
74b	Arundel	50 51	0 33	+0120	◇	◇	◇	−1·6	−1·6	◇	◇
81	SHOREHAM	(see page 22)		1000 and 2200	0500 and 1700	0000 and 1200	0600 and 1800	6·2	5·0	1·9	0·7
75	Worthing	50 48	0 22	0000	+0015	+0010	−0005	−0·1	−0·2	0·0	0·0
81	SHOREHAM	50 50	0 15	STANDARD PORT				See Table V			
82	Brighton	50 49	0 08	−0010	−0010	−0005	−0005	+0·3	+0·1	0·0	−0·1
83	Newhaven	50 47	0 04	−0010	−0015	0000	0000	+0·4	+0·2	0·0	−0·2
84	Eastbourne	50 46	0 17	−0005	−0010	+0015	+0020	+1·1	+0·6	+0·2	+0·1
89	DOVER	(see page 27)		0000 and 1200	0600 and 1800	0100 and 1300	0700 and 1900	6·7	5·3	2·0	0·8
85	Hastings	50 51	0 35	0000	−0010	−0030	−0030	+0·8	+0·5	+0·1	−0·1
86	Rye (Approaches)	50 55	0 47	+0005	−0010	◇	◇	+1·0	+0·7	◇	◇
86a	Rye (Harbour)	50 56	0 46	+0005	−0010	◇	◇	−1·4	−1·7	◇	◇
87	Dungeness	50 54	0 58	−0014	−0014	−0011	−0021	+1·3	+0·8	+0·3	+0·2
88	Folkestone	51 05	1 12	−0020	−0005	−0010	−0010	+0·4	+0·4	0·0	−0·1
89	DOVER	51 07	1 19	STANDARD PORT				See Table V			
98	Deal	51 13	1 25	+0010	+0020	+0010	+0005	−0·6	−0·3	0·0	0·0
102	Ramsgate	51 20	1 25	+0020	+0020	−0007	−0007	−1·8	−1·5	−0·8	−0·4
103	MARGATE	(see page 32)		0100 and 1300	0700 and 1900	0100 and 1300	0700 and 1900	4·8	3·9	1·4	0·5
102a	Broadstairs	51 21	1 27	−0020	−0008	+0007	+0010	−0·2	−0·2	−0·1	−0·1
103	MARGATE	51 24	1 23	STANDARD PORT				See Table V			
104	Herne Bay	51 23	1 07	+0034	+0022	+0015	+0032	+0·4	+0·4	0·0	0·0
105	Whitstable	51 22	1 02	+0042	+0029	+0025	+0050	+0·6	+0·6	+0·1	0·0

★ Dries out at low water.
† Tidal heights inside Littlehampton Harbour are affected by the water coming down the River Arun; the tide seldom falls lower than 0·7m above datum.
◇ No data.

HEIGHTS IN METRES

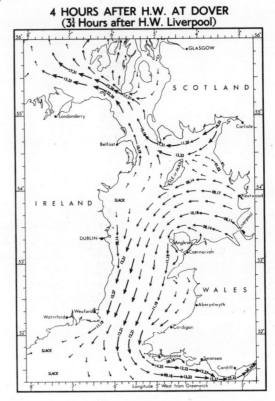

4 HOURS AFTER H.W. AT DOVER
(3¼ Hours after H.W. Liverpool)

published by the Hydrographic Office. Yachtsmen might wish that detail inshore was given more emphasis but in no way would such comment detract from its over-all value.

Admiralty Tidal Stream Atlases

The requirements of yachtsmen who cruise in open waters are almost entirely fulfilled by a series of 11 slim booklets of convenient size. They are entitled Pocket Tidal Stream Atlases and their coverage, indicated on the face of each atlas, is as indicated below.

On the 13 pages of each booklet, identical charts of every area are produced. In each, tidal stream information is related to HW Dover and so almost any tide tables can be used in conjunction with them. The tidal flow for each hour of the tidal cycle, from 6 hours before high water to 6 hours after, is successively superimposed on the chartlets. Both spring and neap rates being given, computation of rates between these two extremes may be mentally solved, or determined from simple data contained therein.

Admiralty Sailing Directions (Pilots)

Within the text of every volume of the Admiralty Sailing Directions very considerable information is given about tidal streams for every port, harbour and coastal stretch to which a volume makes reference. This information is frequently so complete as to be exasperating to the reader. Although it is a good fault, it tends to make tedious reading for areas where no particular difficulties arise. However when the need is great for every item of information one can glean, its value is immense. The Channel Islands area and the west coast of Scotland come to mind.

Admiralty charts

On many large scale Admiralty charts, tidal stream information identical to that already described is published in a wholly different and less satisfactory manner. The Standard Port, not necessarily Dover, to which the information is referred is always printed above a block of tables. Heading each column of tidal stream data is a lettered symbol and the position, in terms of latitude and longitude, on the chart where an identical lettered symbol will be found. In each table will be found tidal stream information which may be expected in the vicinity of the lettered symbol within the body of the chart.

Fig. 3.10

Tidal Streams referred to H.W. at LIVERPOOL

Hours	Ⓐ 53°19'.0N. 3°58'.4W. Dirⁿ	Rate(kn) Sp.	Np.	Ⓑ 53°29'.0N. 3°49'.8W. Dirⁿ	Rate(kn) Sp.	Np.	Ⓒ 53°42'.8N. 4°01'.0W. Dirⁿ	Rate(kn) Sp.	Np.	Ⓓ 53°05'.5N. 4°44'.5W. Dirⁿ	Rate(kn) Sp.	Np.
Before H.W. Liverpool 6	124°	0.4	0.2	000°	0.2	0.1	237°	0.2	0.1	002°	0.3	0.2
5	114°	0.8	0.4	098°	0.8	0.4	082°	0.8	0.5	002°	1.4	0.8
4	127°	1.1	0.6	102°	1.6	0.9	084°	2.0	1.2	002°	2.1	1.2
3	134°	1.2	0.6	106°	1.7	1.0	083°	2.6	1.5	002°	2.2	1.2
2	146°	0.9	0.5	105°	1.3	0.7	087°	1.8	1.0	002°	1.5	0.8
1	164°	0.6	0.3	098°	0.6	0.4	092°	1.1	0.6	002°	0.7	0.4
H.W.	241°	0.3	0.2	Slack			174°	0.2	0.1	182°	0.3	0.2
After H.W. Liverpool 1	296°	0.7	0.4	280°	0.6	0.4	260°	1.0	0.6	182°	1.3	0.7
2	311°	1.1	0.6	277°	1.1	0.6	166°	1.6	0.9	182°	1.9	1.0
3	317°	1.2	0.6	280°	1.5	0.8	270°	2.1	1.2	182°	2.1	1.2
4	318°	1.0	0.5	287°	1.4	0.8	271°	1.8	1.0	182°	1.7	0.9
5	337°	0.5	0.8	282°	0.9	0.5	265°	1.2	0.7	182°	0.9	0.5
6	315°	0.1	0.0	313°	0.3	0.2	253°	0.8	0.4	002°	0.1	0.1

Hours	Ⓔ 52°41'.2N. 5°56'.6W. Dirⁿ	Rate(kn) Sp.	Np.	Ⓕ 52°53'.7N. 5°50'.6W. Dirⁿ	Rate(kn) Sp.	Np.	Ⓖ 53°03'.6N. 5°44'.5W. Dirⁿ	Rate(kn) Sp.	Np.	Ⓗ 53°19'.3N. 5°54'.5W. Dirⁿ	Rate(kn) Sp.	Np.
Before H.W. Liverpool 6	024°	1.0	0.6	025°	1.7	0.9	026°	2.3	1.3	002°	1.1	0.6
5	025°	2.4	1.3	025°	3.5	1.9	025°	3.5	1.9	002°	2.0	1.1
4	025°	3.2	1.8	025°	3.9	2.2	025°	3.6	2.0	002°	2.1	1.2
3	025°	3.0	1.7	025°	3.4	1.9	025°	3.0	1.7	002°	1.7	0.9
2	025°	2.1	1.2	025°	2.0	1.1	029°	1.7	0.9	002°	0.9	0.5
1	027°	0.8	0.4	025°	0.4	0.2	177°	0.3	0.2	002°	0.1	0.1
H.W.	200°	0.6	0.3	205°	1.5	0.8	205°	2.5	1.4	182°	0.9	0.5
After H.W. Liverpool 1	204°	2.3	1.3	205°	3.4	1.9	206°	3.5	1.9	182°	1.9	1.0
2	205°	3.2	1.8	205°	3.9	2.2	206°	3.5	1.9	182°	2.2	1.2
3	205°	3.3	1.8	205°	3.4	1.9	206°	2.8	1.5	182°	1.9	1.0
4	206°	2.4	1.3	205°	2.2	1.2	206°	1.7	0.9	182°	1.1	0.6
5	207°	1.1	0.6	205°	0.6	0.3	206°	0.3	0.2	182°	0.2	0.1
6	014°	0.4	0.2	025°	1.0	0.5	028°	1.2	0.7	002°	0.7	0.4

This style may be regarded as helpful in the sense that there, on the face of the chart, tidal stream information is available. It often involves searching for a lettered symbol, and small boat sailors usually lack the time for methodical, quiet searches. Again, unless one's eyesight is above average, reading the tables with ease usually calls for the use of a magnifying glass. Finally, it gives tidal streams in precise locations and often these locations are widely spaced. What, some may ask, happens to tidal streams in between? From other points of view, none of these adverse comments are entirely fair and the system has two values: it provides tidal stream information when the mariner has none other and it occasionally gives guidance in localities for which imprecise indication is given in tidal stream atlases.

Reed's Nautical Almanac

Reed's Nautical Almanac has the virtue of giving in large scale and some detail tidal stream information about areas which frequently pose anxieties for the navigator. For this limited purpose, if the same boldness of presentation adopted by the Hydrographic Office were used, the writer might use Reed's but does not.

The yachtsman who plans a sea crossing with the assistance of this volume is doomed to disappointment: he will find no chartlets of sufficient size and clarity to assist him in his sea crossing. He is unable to draw lines across tidal stream charts of good size and say: well, from departure point to destination, these are the streams I must counter. Apart from the useful items of local tidal stream intelligence produced within the text, this

volume can only be regarded as supplementary to and no substitute for Hydrographic office publications.

Stanford charts

The tidal stream information given on these charts is valuable in that it is included on working surfaces. On each chart its coverage is equivalent to that of the navigational area of the chart. The style of presentation is almost identical to that of Reed's and, for the weekend yachtsman, can be regarded as entirely adequate. For a sea crossing, in the opinion of the author, the Hydrographic Office publications remain of superior value.

Countering the effects of tidal streams

Here it must be assumed that the reader is familiar with the geometric means by which the effect of a tidal stream may be countered in one's course. It is not always appreciated to what extent the course of a small craft of moderate speed can be effected by tidal currents and the following diagrams will serve to emphasise it.

Fig. 3.11   Fig. 3.12

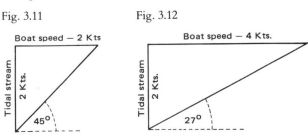

Fig. 3.13

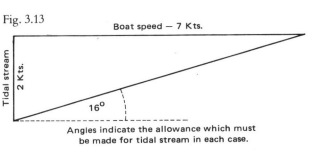

Angles indicate the allowance which must be made for tidal stream in each case.

Perhaps (a) and (b) are the most interesting. When a boat's speed through the water is a mere 2 knots, common enough when the wind is light, the course to counter the effect of a similar stream is vastly different from the direction in which one wishes to go. On the other hand, the fast motor cruiser of 25 knots might well decide to ignore streams of this velocity. In the case of the majority of craft it may be said that the tendency is usually to under-estimate the effect of a stream and so, with a stream athwart the course, unless the strength is assessed realistically and accurate calculation made, one may easily find oneself down-tide.

Notations on tidal stream atlasses

It is assumed here that the reader possesses the appropriate Hydrographic Office Tidal Stream Atlas and that, across each of the 13 chartlets, he has drawn his courses across the sea.

He will find it of great assistance during passage if, before he sails, he notes on each page the times, hour by hour, to which each will apply. For example, let us say that the times of HW

Dover which will occur during his intended passage are 0118 and 1336. The first chartlet in each atlas is entitled '6 hours before HW at Dover'. On that page will be marked in pencil the times 1918 and 0736, both of which times are 6 hours before the quoted Dover times. Thereafter each page will be marked with successively later times.

Fig. 3.14

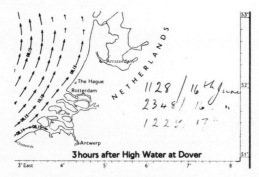

3 hours after High Water at Dover

This system has the considerable merit of allowing the navigator to refer to his tidal stream atlas at any time during passage and immediately obtain the flow of tide he is experiencing. It is always sensible to make these jottings for a period considerably in excess of the ETA at one's destination. One never knows what delays may occur.

Systems of countering tidal streams

The man who has never crossed to a continental coast may wonder with what frequency he must adjust his course to counteract the ever-changing strength and direction of tidal streams. Undoubtedly when he has made a few trips abroad he will adopt his own methods and this might well be because most men and women who make such passages are individualistic. Certainly this would explain why the man who seeks advice on this subject may obtain a variety of positive assertions, depending upon the number of yachtsmen he asks. Here the writer will make his own positive assertion.

On short sea passages not exceeding (say) 30 miles, in areas where streams are not inconsiderable, hourly intervals are desirable. For passages of greater length, yet not exceeding 100 miles, 2-hourly intervals are sensible. Until one knows quite a lot about deep water navigation, these intervals should not be increased.

The reason is this. One wishes to hold to one's course line as nearly as possible. DR positions are considerably easier to calculate if it can be reasonably assumed that a DR must be on the line drawn on the chart. The accuracy of a DR position assumes importance when DF fixes are being attempted, and by using the above techniques, time spent poring over a chart in a bucking craft is reduced.

To lend emphasis to these recommendations, let another system be examined. A yachtsman calculates the means strength for the whole period of a north-going stream and makes a single calculation of course adjustment for the 6-hour period. The track of his craft during the period will appear as follows:

Fig. 3.15

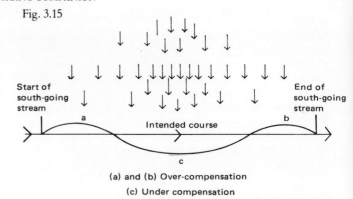

(a) and (b) Over-compensation

(c) Under compensation

He will be over-correcting during the beginning and end of the period, and under-correcting for the remainder of the time.

If during a 12-hour period he decides that the north-going stream is countered effectively by the reverse flow and so there is no case for making any allowance throughout the complete cycle, his course over the ground will probably be this:

Fig. 3.16

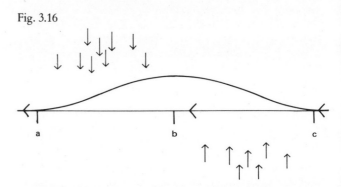

The inexperienced voyager with a sailing craft will, on occasion, meet a situation where the angle of the wind in relation to his desired course entirely precludes his ability to make regular allowances in his courses. It may be that he could head for his destination on a close reach, and to make these recommended tidal allowances would require him to tack from time to time. The author has a distaste for beating on extended passages, unless the occasion demands it. Again he will reiterate that one cruises for the pleasure of one's crew as well as oneself. Achievement and exhileration often a positive delight to a skipper, might well be misery to one's crew. So: in these circumstances it is proposed that he adopts the following more sophisticated method of course correction and go. He may experience increased naviational anxieties as a consequence but this is insufficient reason for deferring the passage.

Young's Course Indicator

Tidal triangles are an essential feature of chartwork if one is not to guess the amount of adjustment necessary to a course. They are time consuming, difficult to draw, in small craft conditions they are prone to faulty projection and the most experienced make slight errors in them.

The author commends to any deep-sea yachtsman Young's Course Indicator. Made in sturdy plastic and impervious to rain and sea water, by manipulation of a dial and cursor, these triangles can be solved with immediacy and accuracy, even in a wet cockpit. Of equal value is the fact that the chance of personal error is reduced to a minimum, and the possibility of faulty projection assumes negligable proportions.

At the time of writing Mr. Walter Young, the inventor, is in the process of improving this instrument. It will retain its present valuable qualities and, in addition, rpoduce DR positions. This feature has its greatest value when working to windward on a sailing craft. Chartwork in these conditions is intricate, difficult and prone to human error.

Danger of experimentation without knowledge

Let is be assumed that the described method of course correction is adopted by a yachtsman for his first couple of passages. It is probable that he will thereafter seek to emulate the apparently easy, ofttimes artless, methods of others. It is, as indicated earlier, argued by a few that there is little point in making course corrections at regular intervals throughout a period of 12 or 13 hours at sea. Clearly, they aver, for all practical purposes one full tidal stream in one direction will be cancelled out by the following reverse stream. The answer to this asservation is: near enough is not good enough. Even meticulously planned sea passages can present unwanted head-scratching, and to make this assumption is to invite it. Some bold, self-styled nomads will sail off into the blue, laughingly deriding the sensible techniques of more knowledgeable and responsible yachtsmen. Others act similarly through sheer ignorance of navigational processes and of what may befall them as a consequence of their shortcomings, even though the latter may be only a mid-sea muddle after some hours on passage.

Described below is a single-correction technique used by many experienced yacht navigators. The reader is adjured to adopt it in course of time. No system can produce faultless landfalls every time, but wisdom dictates that to load the dice in one's favour is to more nearly approach this desirable yet unattainable goal. The method which follows is as responsible as that described earlier, yet it has much more to commend it to owners of low-powered motor cruisers and sailing craft generally.

The single-correction technique

A single course to steer to one's objective is determined prior to departure. In brief, it entails estimating the duracton of passage and, for successive hours during this period, the various tidal sets and drifts are extracted from one's tidal stream atlas. Using the departure position as a datum, these sets and drifts are laid off in sequence on the working chart. From the final projection a position is determined: and it is from this position that the course line is drawn to one's destination. Fig. ? best defines the technique. Given an accurate estimation of passage duration — the reader should mark well this requirement — no better calculation of the course to steer to counter tidal streams can be made.

Advantages

(a) One course is steered throughout. No imagination is needed to assess this advantage to all yachtsmen. The motor cruiser owner has his chartwork at sea considerably reduced. That and more is offered the

sailing man. It markedly reduces sail work. This yachtsman will reflect that, in the conventional method of course correction earlier described, depending upon the wind slant, it may not always be possible for him to lay every course demanded by that system. Indeed, it occasionally may be only a tail wind which will give him the ability to do so.

(b) Sailing time is reduced. At, say, 15 knots and more this advantage is small but the slower the speed of a craft through the water, the more marked is this advantage. In the demonstration figure in which the craft is making 4 knots, the sailing time is 12 hours 20 minutes. Using the conventional method of course correction it would have been 13 hours.

Disadvantages

(a) It cannot be used if insufficient searoom is available on both sides of the course line. Shoals, islands and shorelines sometimes intercede to preclude its use. Using this system it is common for a craft to be carried 7, even 10 miles, to port or starboard of a course line.

(b) Some may find it unsettling to allow one's craft to 'wander' in the manner described. Good results from D/F fixes may be questioned and DR positions create dismay. Provided the yachtsman's mind is attuned to the manner in which he may expect his craft to progress towards his destination, it is suggested that these objections have little substance.

Explanation

The single-correction technique demands careful pre-passage planning and it must be fully understood so that, if mid-passage course adjustment must be made — usually required if speed through the water alters — one may carry it through with assurance. A studied estimation of duration of passage is a prime requisite and, to make it, three factors must be taken into account:

(a) The distance from point of departure to destination.

(b) The probable speed through the water. This constituent, simple enough to estimate by the owner of a motor cruiser in most cases, is difficult in sailing craft. For this reason some of the racing fraternity and other experienced yachtsmen may make these entire calculations several times, to ensure that the correct course to steer is known as soon as speed through the water is established.

Some sailing yacthsmen with limited offshore experience use their auxiliary engine from time to time if the wind is fitful, so that the speed for which calculations have been made is maintained. Naturally deplored by purists, this practice reduces navigational uncertainties and is probably wise for those who adopt it. And there is he whose intention is to maintain his ETA at his destination, to lessen fatiue and to carry through carefully laid voyage plans. And why not?

(c) An assessment of the broad effects of tidal streams which will be encountered. This is necessary to be able to judge whether they will shorten or lengthen the passage. Clearly, streams which are mainly favourable will shorten sailing time, and vice versa. Those partially athwart the course line could have helpful or deterrent components in them.

And so, using these factors, duration of passage is estimated.

To facilitate the later task of determining the set and drift of the tidal streams for each hour of the passage, the following device is proposed. A once-folded piece of plain paper will produce a straight edge, a ruler upon which one can write. It must be of sufficient length to reach from departure position to destination on the chartlets of one's tidal atlas. The paper ruler is then marked to give hourly intervals of indication of position. Naturally, estimated speed and passage duration give the number of marks and supporting notations to be made. These intervals, although they will not indicate high quality dead-reckoning positions on the sundry pages of a tidal atlas, will nevertheless produce sufficiently accurate information for one's purpose.

The correct page of the tidal stream atlas from which to comence extracting sets and drifts will, of course, be that which coincides in terms of time with the expected time of sailing from the departure position. And hte position from which to draw one's first projection of set and drift is the departure position on the working chart. Thereafter, page by successive page, the paper ruler readily indicating on each the correct set and drift to use, the various directions and rates are progressively connected on the chart. From the terminal position of the final set and drift drawn, the course is laid off to one's destination.

Again it is emphasised that this course to steer is accurate for a passage of predetermined duration. And this duration wholly depends upon the accuracy of the estimaed mean speed through the water. Hence a wrong assessment of speed will cause one to over- or under-correct for tidal steams during passage.

Unwanted possibilities will now be introduced. Let is be assumed that a yachtsman has made only one assessment of duration of passage and, very shortly after leaving his departure position, he realises that his assessment is inaccurate because speed through the water is faster or slower than envisaged. At this early stage it is a simple matter to add to or substract from the hourly projections of tidal streams on the chart, and so he can re-draw his course. This new course will then be related to his reappraisal of duration or passage. Hourly DR positions, supported where possible by reliable D/F fixes, remain essential throughout the passage.

As will be realised, at any stage of the passage weather conditions could change, thereby upsetting carefully laid voyage plans. In addition, even if the weather remains remarkably consistent throughout, it is well within the bounds of possibility that a good D/F position might indicate a position markedly different from one's DR position. Either occurrence could demand that the yachtsman re-draws his tidal projections from the position reached, so that he may decide what course adjustment should be made. Depending upon conditions and the distance still to be sailed, he might decide to revert to the old and tried method of course correction to which reference is made earlier.

To sum up, notwithstanding the mildly dolesome aspects which have been described here in full, this method of course correction for any slow craft in tidal waters has almost everything to commend it. It is proposed that a man with a couple of short sea crossings already to his credit should gird his loins and adopt this system. It is improbable that he will revert to drawing tidal triangles when a passage offers him this alternative.

CHAPTER 4

Safety Equipment and Safety Aspects

It is generally known that there are no statutory regulations which require pleasure craft under 45 feet in length to carry safety equipment. The Department of Trade and Industry, in consultation with yachting organisations having considerable knowledge of potential dangers at sea, have made recommendations for the benefit of owners. Their counsels are published in a pamphlet: 'How Safe is your Craft?' and its content is produced below.

It is foolhardy to disregard any part of these recommendations. Although expenditure on certain items required for deep water sailing is inescapable, it is stressed that expensive and little used equipment can often be hired at a moderate price for the period during which it may be required. For this reason, lack of funds is no argument to support a decision to sail under equipped, and therefore in an unseaworthy state. It is fair to say that, in the final analysis, people who own craft capable of making a sea crossing, and plan to make one, cannot be so impecunious that they cannot meet the extra expenditure involved.

Certain aspects of the D.O.T. advices engender misgivings in the writer's mind and his thoughts are produced in this chapter, together with other comments which have a bearing upon safety. The intention is not to duplicate the content of authoritative books devoted to the subject of safety, which the reader would be wise to study.

How Safe is your Craft?

The safety of *your* craft and the people on it is *your* responsibility. Accident-free sailing depends on having a boat that is sound, well equipped, and suitable for the particular use you are going to make of it. It depends, too, on you and your crew having enough experience (including the ability to swim) and adequate knowledge to operate your boat in all kinds of conditions. In fact it means being prepared always for any eventuality.

There will, of course, always be risks involved. But the responsible boat owner insures against these by carrying proper and sufficient safety equipment.

A report on safety appliances for pleasure craft up to 13·7 metres (45 feet) in length has recently been submitted by a group of people actively concerned with recreational boating. This booklet is based on the recommendations made by this group. Keep it to hand and use it each time before sailing to check that your craft is furnished with the recommended equipment necessary for your safety and that of your crew. This way only will you get full enjoyment from your boat.

The recommendations have been made with sea-going craft

particularly in mind. You, your crew, and your craft, should always be equal to the worst conditions you might expect to meet.

Craft operating in inland waters may be subject to the requirements of local and water authorities. Some craft might be sailing under organised club rules and these would call for certain standards of equipment to be carried. Where there are no local requirements or specific safety needs, use the recommendations as a guide. Needs will vary. Much will depend on the size and type of your craft, on where you will be sailing and the conditions at the time.

There are legal requirements for pleasure yachts of 13·7 metres (45 feet) in length overall and over. They must conform to the safety equipment regulations laid down in the Merchant Shipping (Life Saving Appliances) Rules 1965 and the Merchant Shipping (Fire Appliances) Rules 1965.

All craft are required, by law, to be equipped with adequate navigation lights and means of giving sound signals to conform to the International Regulations for Preventing Collisions at Sea.

Recommended safety equipment for sea-going pleasure craft of 5·5 metres (18 feet) to 13·7 metres (45 feet) in length overall

PERSONAL SAFETY EQUIPMENT

Safety harness – to BSI specification. One for each person on sailing yachts. One or more on motor cruisers as may be needed when on deck.

Wear a safety harness on deck in bad weather or at night. Make sure it is properly adjusted. Experience has shown, however, that a harness can be dangerous if you go overboard at speeds of 8 knots or more.

Lifejackets – of Department of Trade and Industry accepted type or BSI specification. One for each person.

Keep them in a safe place where you can get at them easily. Always wear one when there is a risk of being pitched overboard.

RESCUE EQUIPMENT FOR MAN OVERBOARD

Lifebuoys – two at least.

One lifebuoy should be kept within easy reach of the

helmsman. For sailing at night, it should be fitted with a self-igniting light.

Buoyant line – 30 metres (100 feet) minimum breaking strain of 115 kilos (250 lb)). This too should be within easy reach of the helmsman.

OTHER FLOTATION EQUIPMENT FOR VESSELS GOING MORE THAN THREE MILES OUT, SUMMER AND WINTER:

Inflatable liferaft – of Department of Trade and Industry accepted type, or equivalent – to carry everyone on board. It should be carried on deck or in a locker opening directly to the deck and should be serviced annually; OR

Rigid dinghy – with permanent, not inflatable, buoyancy, and with oars and rowlocks secured. It should be carried on deck. It may be a collapsible type; OR

Inflatable dinghy – built with two compartments, one at least always kept fully inflated, or built with one compartment, always kept fully inflated, and having oars and rowlocks secured.

It should be carried on deck. If the vessel has enough permanent buoyancy to float when swamped with 115 kilos may be stowed. In sheltered waters a dinghy may be towed. Check that the tow is secure.

FOR VESSELS GOING NOT MORE THAN THREE MILES OUT IN WINTER (1 NOVEMBER TO 31 MARCH):

Inflatable liferaft or alternatives, as above.

In sheltered waters the summer scale equipment, listed below, may usually be adequate. Liferafts may not be necessary on angling boats operating in organised groups when the boats are continually in contact with each other.

FOR VESSELS GOING NOT MORE THAN THREE MILES OUT IN SUMMER (1 APRIL TO 31 OCTOBER):

Lifebuoys – (30-inch) or **Buoyant seats** – of Department of Trade and Industry accepted type. One for every two people on board.

Lifebuoys carried for 'man overboard' situations may be included. Those smaller than 30-inch diameter should be regarded as support for one person only.

GENERAL EQUIPMENT

Anchors – two, each with warp or chain of appropriate size and length. Where warp is used at least 5.5 metres (3 fathoms) of chain should be used between anchor and warp.

Bilge Pump. Efficient compass – and spare.

Charts – covering intended area of operation.

Distress flares – size with two of the rocket parachute type.

Daylight distress (smoke) signals. Tow-rope of adequate length.

First-aid box – with anti-seasickness tablets.

Radio receiver – for weather forecasts. **Water-resistant torch.**

Radar reflector – of adequate performance. As large as can be conveniently carried. Preferably mounted at least 3 metres (10 feet) above sea level.

Lifeline – also useful in bad weather for inboard lifeline. **Engine tool kit.**

Name, number or generally recognised **sail number** – should be painted prominently on the vessel or on dodgers in letters or figures at least 22 centimetres (9 inches) high.

FIRE-FIGHTING EQUIPMENT

For vessels over 9 metres (30 feet) in length and those with powerful engines, carrying quantities of fuel – two fire extinguishers should be carried, each of not less than 1.4 kilos (3 lb) capacity, dry powder, or equivalent, and one or more additional extinguisher of not less than 2.3 kilos (5 lb) capacity, dry powder, or equivalent. A fixed installation may be necessary.

For vessels of up to 9 metres (30 feet) in length, with cooking facilities and engines – two fire extinguishers should be carried, each of not less than 1.4 kilos (3 lb) capacity, dry powder, or equivalent.

For vessels of up to 9 metres (30 feet) in length, with cooking facilities only or with engine only – one fire extinguisher should be carried, of not less than 1.4 kilos (3 lb) capacity, dry powder, or equivalent.

Carbon dioxide (CO_2) or foam extinguishers of equal extinguishing capacity are alternatives to dry powder appliances. BCF (bromo-chloro-difluoro-methane) or BTM (bromo-trifluoro-methane) may be carried, but people on the boat should be warned that the fumes given off are toxic and dangerous in a confined space, and a similar notice should be posted at each extinguisher point.

Additionally for all craft:

Buckets – two, with lanyards.

Bag of sand – useful in containing and extinguishing burning spillage of fuel or lubricant.

Your craft should have been designed and built with the object of keeping fire risks to a minimum, but a check may be made on such 'built-in' precautions by referring to the Home Office pamphlet 'Fire Precautions in Pleasure Craft' (HMSO, price 12½p).

Recommended safety equipment for pleasure craft of less than 5·5 metres (18 feet) in length overall

Craft of less than 5.5 metres (18 feet) in length overall cover a wide variety – from dinghies and motor cruisers to boats for sea-angling trips, diving and water ski-ing. All are limited in the amount of equipment and the number of people they can carry and there are separate recommendations for them given on the following pages. For deep-sea sailing more than three miles from base and for cruising follow the recommendations, as far as possible, for craft of 5.5 to 13.7 metres (18 feet to 45 feet).

Never overload. The number of people or the amount of equipment a boat can carry is generally shown on a plate fitted by the builder. Sea-angling vessels should be more restricted and the following scale is recommended.

Craft of		
4.9 metres (16 feet) to less than 5.5 metres (18 feet):	**4 persons**
4.3 metres (14 feet) to less than 4.9 metres (16 feet):	**3 persons**
3.7 metres (12 feet) to less than 4.3 metres (14 feet):	**2 persons**

Sea-angling from craft of less than 3.7 metres (12 feet) in length is hazardous.

Owners who are going to be at sea more than three miles from base, or whose craft are designed for cruising, should, as far as possible, follow the recommendations for craft of 5.5 metres to 13.7 metres (18 feet to 45 feet).

It is recommended that other craft in this category shall carry the following unless taking part in organised club events with specific safety equipment required.

PERSONAL SAFETY EQUIPMENT

Lifejackets – of Department of Trade and Industry accepted type or BSI specification. One for each person on board.

Alternatively, in sheltered waters, one buoyancy aid, of the Ship and Boat Builders National Federation approved type, for each person on board. Always wear a lifejacket or buoyancy aid when there is a risk of being pitched overboard.

RESCUE EQUIPMENT

Lifebuoy – one, and a 30-metre (100 feet) **buoyant line** (minimum breaking strain of 115 kilos (250 lb)), where practicable.

Alternatively, one Department of Trade and Industry accepted rescue quoit. A second lifebuoy should be carried on motor cruisers and, where practicable, on other craft.

GENERAL EQUIPMENT

Anchor – of sufficient size and with a long enough mooring line or cable, according to the type and size of craft and the possible areas of operation.

A spare anchor and tow-line of 18 metres (10 fathoms) advisable, especially for sea-angling trips.

Efficient bilge pump, and a **bailer** or **bucket** with lanyard (even if the yacht is fitted with a self-bailer).

For powered craft, the bilge pump should be fixed. On other craft a portable bilge pump which can draw water from the sea may be useful for fire fighting.

Paddle or **oar with rowlock** – one at least: two if practicable.

Distress signals – two at least. Even in sheltered waters adequate distress signals should be carried.

Compass – for motor cruisers, angler's craft, dinghy cruising and racing.

First-aid kit.

Water-resistant torch.

Radar reflector – or adequate performance. For craft engaged in sea-angling and cruising in the open sea.

Radio receiver – for craft engaged in sea-angling and cruising in the open sea.

Engine tool kit.

FIRE-FIGHTING EQUIPMENT

One fire extinguisher of not less than 1.4 kilos (3 lb) capacity, dry powder (where fuel is carried), or two if galley is also fitted.

Carbon dioxide (CO_2) or foam extinguishers of equal extinguishing capacity are alternatives to dry powder appliances. BCF (bromo-chloro-difluoro-methane) or BTM (bromo-trifluoro-methane) may be carried, but people on the boat should be warned that the gumes, given off are toxic and dangerous in a confined space and a similar notice should be posted at each extinguisher point. A blanket or rug soaked in the sea may also be effective in fighting fires.

Bucket – with lanyard, one, (which may be that used as a bailer).

Your craft should have been designed and built with the object of keeping fire risks to a minimum, but a check may be made on such 'built-in' precautions by referring to the Home Office pamphlet 'Fire Precautions in Pleasure Craft' (HMSO, price 12½p).

ADDITIONAL SAFEGUARD

Yachtsmen making a coastal passage in UK waters are strongly advised to contact the local HM Coastguard station to complete a Coastguard '66' Passage Report Form. This ensures that the Coastguard Service has full particulars regarding the craft, occupants, its equipment and intended voyage, for use should search and rescue action be needed. At his destination, the yachtsman reports his arrival to the nearest Coastguard station. **There is no charge for this service.**

Reprinted from the booklet "How safe is your Craft?' with the permission of the Controller of H.M. Stationery Office and the Department of Trade and Industry.

Copies of the booklet can be obtained from: **Information Division, Room 306, Department of Trade and Industry, 1 Gaywood House, Great Peter Street, London SW1P 3LW.**

The necessity of a liferaft

A liferaft is a self-inflating rubber dinghy with an integral canopy. It is fully equipped with emergency packs containing essential survival gear. A 6-man liferaft is the size of a fully packed kit bag and may be packed in a neoprene valise or a fibreglass container. With its lanyard secured to one's craft, it only needs to be thrown over the side to become a fully inflated liferaft within seconds. Sizes vary from the 4-man to the 20-man type. A type approved by the D.O.T. is the only satisfactory insurance against shipwreck. The smallest of them costing hundreds of pounds, plus the essential costly annual survey charges, cause many yachtsmen to seek alternatives, which the D.O.T. offer in their recommendations. In the opinion of the author, there is no alternative for use in sailing craft under about 30 feet in length.

One may ask what point there is in buying a very expensive article which may be required only two or three times a year. There is no need to. Liferafts can be hired for a relatively small sum. At the time of writing, a 4-man liferaft can be hired for a fortnight for less money than the average cost of its annual service.

The use of an inflatable tender as a liferaft

The recommendations for the use of inflatable dinghies as liferafts should in the opinion of the writer, be qualified. What sailing craft under about 30 feet in length can carry a partially or fully inflated rubber tender on deck in such a manner that it does not constitute a serious hazard to crew members who must work the craft? Perhaps the reader has seen a small sailing craft whose owner has accepted this advice. If an inflatable dinghy is lashed on deck forward of a cockpit, visibility ahead is non-existent unless the helmsman remains standing throughout his trick, and any movement forward is rendered precarious. It could be argued that the adoption of this practice increases risk, and so it increases the need for the very article which produces this state of affairs. It is anomolous. Some aver that a loosely inflated rubber tender carried below decks is a safer alternative than that suggested by the D.O.T. The writer must disagree with such argument, yet reiterate that these craft should carry a proper liferaft.

Most motor cruisers of any size can adopt the recommended alternatives to a liferaft. A partially or fully inflated rubber tender, even a rigid dinghy, can be lashed abaft or on top of the wheelhouse: perhaps on deck forward of it if deck space and visibility permits. Hazards to the crew on this type of craft are considerably less than on those which depend upon the wind for propulsion.

Lifebuoys and their stowage

Lifebuoys should be carried in racks attached to guardrails or bulwarks, and should be within easy reach of watchkeepers. There are plenty of neat stainless steel or canvas racks available in which a lifebuoy enhances the appearance of a craft and looks most efficient but, apart from providing secure stowage, what real value have these racks? Let us evaluate this so-called ready-use stowage and assess what is likely to occur if a crew member falls overboard when a craft is moving at 5 knots.

Crew reaction	Time factor
Stunned realisation of incident	1 second
Decision making	1 second
Movement towards lifebuoy rack	2 seconds
Detachment of lifebuoy light from clip	1 second
Hefty upward tug to release lifebuoy from rack	2 seconds
Swing back and heave lifebuoy towards swimmer	2 seconds
Total	9 seconds

It may be agreed that 9 seconds is a minimum period for this evolution and it takes no account of the possibility of stumbling, clumsy action due to excessive haste or the tail of a main sheet befouling one's feet. Taking into consideration the unstable platform from which the lifebuoy is thrown, the lifebuoy may hit the water some 15 feet abaft the transom, leaving the person in the water about 60 feet to swim to reach it. As in the case of the writer, perhaps the reader will regard these as sombre, startling certainties. The latter calculations are supported by experimentation and they indicate that, except on a sailing craft carrying a full racing crew, the traditional racks for the stowage of lifebuoys only have value when a craft is idling through the water, a time when calamity is less likely to occur.

The author's answer to these frightening possibilities is a home made, quick-release rack. At this time it has no equivalent on the market, although it appears possible that it may be available in the future. It is best described in sketch form.

Fig. 4.1

The rack may be attached outboard of the pulpit or taffrail and lanyards are lead forward on both guard rails within reach of the helmsman, be he in a cockpit or a wheelhouse. One slap on a lanyard and the lifebuoy immediately drops into the water, with its light attached. The helmsman is then free to manoeuvre his craft towards the swimmer. Although it may seem fantasy, again experimentation indicates that, given a 30 foot craft and a reaction period of 3 seconds for the helmsman, a person who fell overboard on the foredeck could find a lifebuoy bobbing up alongside him.

There are two obvious objections to such an arrangement. Firstly, the lifebuoy can be accidently dropped into the water by inadvertant tripping of a lanyard. This did not happen on the writer's craft throughout a busy season. Second, situated outboard as it must inevitably be, it could be buckled by careless manoeuvring in a confined haven such as a marina.

Certainly it is adaptable to transom or quarter fixing on most types of sailing or motor craft. It is a matter of giving satisfactory leads for the lanyards to positions within reach of the helmsman. Construction of the rack needs no expertise and it can be made for pennies.

An improved commercial version of this rack will be available through yacht chandlers early 1976.

Anchors

Deck or hawsepipe sea stowage for a bower anchor, with chain permanently shackled to it, must necessarily be adjudged safer than any alternative on short sea routes. The modern dished, or sunken, foredeck provides quite the safest and best sea stowage. There are those who, immediately the possible need for an anchor diminishes, stow their anchors below. Certainly when a foredeck is uncluttered by an anchor, surefootedness when working with headsails is greatly increased. Sea stowage of an anchor below decks is only acceptable if discipline and self-discipline is exercised. Approaching a port, it is an irritation to retrieve the anchor from its stowage below and, having brought it on deck, to shackle it to the cable once again. It is too easy, too simple, to take a chance and gamble on the fact that an anchor may not be needed. Leaving the anchor below can become a habit: it can be shifted from a ready-use position to a locker and in time it can be fouled by odd pieces of rope and little used paraphernalia. Sooner or later a manoeuvre will go wrong and an anchor will be needed in a hurry. Where an anchor quickly let go would have saved the day, grounding, collision or similar mishap becomes a probability.

Some may consider a kedge and warp in a handy cockpit or wheelhouse locker is reasonable provision against an unexpected occurence. Firstly, a kedge seldom has the holding power of a bower anchor and second, locker stowage is seldom very handy in practice.

Safety harness

A number of Trans-Atlantic single handers have been quoted in the yachting press as saying that they did not wear safety harness throughout their extraordinary feats of seamanship. If such statements are coupled with one's own observations, the inevitable conclusion must be that harness is regarded by the majority of yachtsmen much in the manner that seat belts are regarded by motorists.

Any prudent and experienced skipper will insist that safety harness is worn by all crew members on deck, (a) at night at all times, with particular emphasis on the lone helmsman, (b) at all times when, due to sea conditions, movement is tricky and potentially hazardous.

It is well to bear in mind that an experienced yachtsman and seaman subconsciously uses hands and feet to counter every movement of his craft. With his conscious mind he can concentrate upon work in hand. The inexperienced person cannot possess this ability born of long association with the sea and consequently he is at greater risk.

Knife

If a sea-going craft has no knife aboard it can only be because it has unwittingly been left ashore. But merely to have a knife aboard is insufficient in the interests of safety. A knife can be needed, open and immediately within reach, at unpredictable times even in fine weather. If it is not it can spell the difference between normality and an accident. A sheath knife worn on a belt or a lanyard round the waist is the answer. A closed clasp knife in a pocket, or in handy stowage in the wheelhouse or cockpit, is not.

Ideal for a yachtsman's purpose is a Green River knife, a sheath knife of a type used by sailing ship men and still available today. It is workmanlike and unpretentious, having a total length of perhaps 7 inches, including simple wooden handle. It can be bought with or without 'pricker', a tiny marline spike in the same sheath. The pricker is a very handy article when bottle screws, turnbuckles and shackle pins are tight.

Radar reflectors

It is generally known that radar reflectors are important items of equipment in yachts at sea in home waters. What is less well known is precisely why this is the case. That this lack of knowledge exists is apparent on a considerable number of cruising yachts in the size of reflectors used and the positions in which they are worn.

Today merchantmen of all shapes and sizes are fitted with radar sets and it is quite common for very large ships to carry two. The general practice is to operate radar continuously in our waters, both by day and by night. The plan position indicator, which is the circular viewing screen, tends to receive quite a lot of attention from watchkeepers, in many cases rather more than the horizon receives from a lookout. This latter point is important to yachtsmen generally.

Fig. 4.2

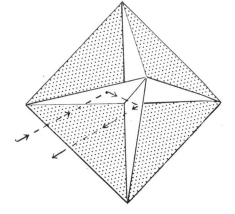

A flat, hard surface, such as metal or rock, which presents itself at right angles to a radar transmission will produce an echo which is easily picked up by the radar set's receiver. The reflected signal will appear as an illuminated blob on the watchkeeper's screen.

Solid objects which are presented at an obtuse angle to radar transmissions will cause some to skate off and only a few will be returned to the radar receiver. It may be said, therefore, that the intensity of the visual response on a radar screen will vary directly according to the angle at which the reflecting surface is presented to transmissions.

Fig. 4.3

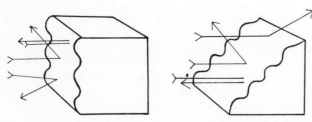

The larger the reflecting surface, the greater the expanse of the echo, the illuminated blob, on the screen. It necessarily follows that the smaller the reflecting surface, the more difficult it will be to detect its presence on a screen which may well have other perhaps expansive echoes to detract the eye. Absorbant materials such as dry wood, the foliage of trees and canvas will tend to absorb transmissions and from them little or no response should be expected.

These sundry facts emphasise the need for a yachtsman to purchase the largest radar reflector practicable for his craft, these reflectors being so designed to produce maximum response no matter from which direction a radar transmission emanates. But possession of a large radar reflector is insufficient. Another weakness of radar must be explained.

Sea waves will return echoes just as effectively as any other similar reflecting surface and, because a great number of waves may be present on the sea, a similarly large number of echoes will be visible on a radar screen. This mild saturation of the screen is known as sea clutter. It is non-existent on a smooth sea, it may extend two or three miles in a moderate sea and, when a high sea is running, it might well extend to six or seven miles.

A large reflector is virtually useless at a height very little elevated above a yacht's deck level. Certainly it will return an echo in smooth water but then so will one's hull in these conditions. The futility of a reflector so worn is highlighted when waves are present. The speckling sea clutter on a radar screen will effectively hide the steady response of a radar reflector which has an elevation minimally above the height of the waves themselves. Yet let the large reflector be high on a mast and a small, steady echo will be returned. Except in bad sea conditions it should be detectable at a range beyond the extent of sea clutter. How high is high? Let us say a minimum of 15 feet above deck level, and that every foot above this elevation increases the value of the reflector as a safety device.

Of course few motor cruisers can achieve such a height by virtue of their design but owners may gain solace from the knowledge that their craft are highly manoeuvrable. On a sailing craft there is only one practical place for a radar reflector: on a halliard or stay high up the mast. On a sloop-rogged craft an inner halliard on the spreader lends itself to this purpose. Few owners appear to like this position, perhaps due to the possibility of damage to headsails from the usual sharp edges of reflectors. These edges may be covered with an adhesive tape of a type which will not blow away and, if particular attention is given to the corners, the objection is overcome. To prevent spinning, the reflector must be shackled or frapped to a shroud or stay. Finally, the connecting points provided by the makers are provided to ensure maximum response from the reflector. To hoist one peak uppermost may have aesthetic appeal to some: gratifying appearance is wholly negated by the very necessity of indicating one's presence by all means possible to big ship mariners at sea.

Fire extinguishers

One must guard against fire extinguishers which, although efficient for use against a car fire in the open air, many give off toxic gases when used in a confined space. Powder extinguishers tend to be favoured because they do less harm to articles undamaged by a small and containable fire. Wise stowage for them is one forward and one aft for it cannot be known which side of a fire below decks one might be if an outbreak occurs. For this same reason it is folly to stow anything over a forward or after hatchway. Although seldom regarded as such, in the final analysis they are escape hatches.

Distress flares

Distress flares and rockets are quite expensive and they have a limited life. Hopefully one may never require them but foolish is he who seeks to economise on items such as these. Manufacturers produce them in sealed packs and that known as the offshore pack contain the very minimum of rockets and flares for a sea crossing.

The packs are provided with means of hanging them on a hook, and hooks provide the best stowage for them, readily available but out of the way. The method of igniting them should be ascertained during a quiet period in port, because the moment when they may be needed is most unlikely to be conducive to reading directions, however simple and clear.

Radio receivers for reception of weather forecasts

Bad weather can be lethal for any type of craft and a radio's ability to receive weather reports for shipping makes it an item of safety equipment.

One can encounter yachtsmen, indeed professional seamen, who never listen to weather reports. Given a barometer and a reasonable experience of weather, they argue, why should they subject themselves to anxiety when a forecasted gale may not materialise? Why adopt voyage tactics based upon a weather forecast when subsequent weather indicates their plans were based upon an inaccurate premise? But pray, how often is the professional forecaster seriously in error? The wise cruising yachtsman ignores such arguments and never fails to obtain shipping weather forecasts.

Meteorologists are experts in their field, yet with the tools at their disposal they must interpret elemental phenomena and then give their considered opinion of what future weather might be. Predictable tangibles are denied them. Nevertheless, they are infinitely better equipped for the task, both in information and knowledge, than the professional seaman, not to mention the amateur. So a race was won because a weather report was not obtained. A lucky coincidence. Shall the authentic case be quoted of a liner's Master who, a boastful believer in this asinine dogmatism, disastrously sailed through the centre of an Indian Ocean cyclone?

One's radio, be it a portable transistor set or an expensive fitting, must be capable of tuning to BBC2 on 200 Khz., 1500 metres, the long wave as it is commonly known. Four times during every 24 hours the shipping forecast is broadcast. It is always wise to note the forecast for areas to the westward of one's own, because weather systems tend to move in an easterly direction. Not infrequently it will be found that present weather in, say, Fastnet will be the future weather in Lundy.

Radio telephony

In the event of disablement or shipwreck, a radio capable of transmitting a distress call to ships and shore stations, on one of the international distress frequencies, is by far the most efficient means of drawing the attention of others to one's plight. This fact has been emphasised by the Royal Yachting Association whose ability to speak with authority on such matters is real.

At the risk of upsetting those with technical knowledge, it appears to the writer that radio telephony sets fall into three categories. The price range of each category tends to accentuate their fundamental differences. A factor which is noticeable is the reluctance of technical sales representatives to be specific about the potential ranges of sundry sets. No doubt there are valid reasons to support this disinclination, yet it is unhelpful to a yachtsman who may be contemplating a considerable cash outlay for a set which will meet his specific requirements.

1. Portable sets which can be used on 2182 kHz only, an international distress frequency. One of the least sophisticated of these is the cheapest 'Callboy' set with an output of less than a watt which, in terms of transmitter power, means that its range is severely restricted. Costing about £100, its range is variously described as 40 miles or more in good radio conditions and 10 miles in bad. In the seas around our shores, many may consider such ranges as being quite acceptable with shore and ship stations in relative profusion around them at most times. These sets can be hired.

    'Callboy' sets and their equivalents are available which have an output of 2.5 watts, giving ranges of perhaps 30 to 100 miles and more, but their price is near £200. A refinement in these sets is a two tone alarm which is intended for use to indicate to shore and ship stations that a distress call follows.

2. The VHF radio telephony set with 8, perhaps 12, press button, crystal controlled channels. The majority of the crystals being tuned to useful ship and shore stations communication frequencies, and that for distress purposes, spare crystals can be tuned to any other desired, which might include one of a friendly craft or a mariner. Telephone link with the Post Office telephone system is possible through shore stations, those talking to each other necessarily having to adopt RT jargon.

    Typical of these sets is the 'Seavoice' which, with aerial

and fitting, might cost £250. Some of these sets cost considerably more. Like any other VHF set, 'Seavoice' will only give line-of-sight communication. That is to say, if a straight line cannot be drawn from aerial to aerial, possibility of communication is considerably lessened. It follows, therefore, that the greater the height of aerials, the greater the range of radio contact. Ranges of about 50 miles are commonly quoted, although they are frequently more. Notwithstanding, a range of 50 miles should meet the needs of all voyagers whose intentions are modest.

3. The radio telephony set having wide capabilities on the intermediate frequency band, even to the extent of having a natural conversation with one's family at home. The 'Sailor' and its equivalents can cost £800 and often much more. As an example of their essential versatility, they are often fitted on coastal and fishing vessels.

Clearly this subject resolves itself into a matter of that which a yachtsman may demand, often leavened by that which he can afford. Purely in terms of safety, the first category could well meet most yachtsmen's needs.

Whilst recognising that one can make provision for safety to an excessively expensive degree, before a reader dismisses all thoughts of radio-telephony he should cogitate upon the following not unknown circumstances.

An experienced yachtsman sails with his wife who lacks expertise. All decisions, evolutions and risky tasks are carried out by him. If he has a heart attack or suffers any other form of disablement, his craft being offshore, his wife will be in serious difficulties. Yet if she could speak to a shore or ship station her dilemma would be immediately reduced and, given a little time, overcome.

SAFETY RELATED TO CRAFT AND ENGINES

Seaworthiness

A craft which is in all respects ready for sea is seaworthy. In this simple statement the three important words are: in all respects.

The author must assume that the reader already owns a craft capable of undertaking a sea passage and able to withstand the rigours of weather to which she may be subjected. Any yachtsman who has doubts about the sea-going qualities of his craft should seek professional, or at least knowledgeable, advice. There are pleasure craft afloat of all types which would be death traps in a nasty sea offshore.

Yet fulfilment of this prerequisite is not in itself sufficient. Any of the following circumstances present on a craft would render her unseaworthy:

Inadequate, inexperienced or incompetent crew.

Absence of a full range of charts for the intended passage.

Inadequate cooking facilities.

Incomplete safety equipment.

Safety equipment which is defective or is not readily available.

Sails with undetected flaws in them.

An unreliable or neglected power unit.

This list could be extended considerably but it gives guidelines to a true state of seaworthiness. If one bears in mind that craft have foundered through the failure of a single item, the inadequacy of which could have been found before sailing, appreciation of the full meaning of seaworthiness is better achieved.

Safety and propulsive power

It may be agreed that the well found, properly manned sailing yacht is the most reliable sea transport for yachtsmen generally. However, this generalisation loses some of its substance if a yachtsman's only intention is to sail from a British port to make a short sea crossing. Shipping abounds in our waters and weather changes are common. Lee shores are never very far away, yet neither are havens in which small craft may take shelter. Total reliability of propulsive power *at all times* gains ascendency and therefore, from the point of view of safety and assuming a seaworthy craft in all cases, the writer regards sundry types of craft as follows:

The most reliable and safe:	The motor cruiser with twin diesel engines whose power units are maintained properly.
Next in order:	The motor cruiser with two inboard or outboard engines maintained in similarly excellent order.
Third:	A sailing craft with a good auxiliary engine.
Fourth:	A motor sailer.
Fifth:	A sailing yacht with no secondary means of propulsion.
Sixth:	A motor cruiser with a single inboard diesel engine.
Seventh:	A motor cruiser with a single petrol inboard or outboard engine.
Eighth:	A twin engined motor cruiser whose engines are old and are given scant attention.
Ninth:	A single engined motor cruiser, whether the propulsive unit is inboard or outboard, and it is similarly neglected.

One may well disagree with this order but, whatever rearrangement is made, common ground will be found in one single fact: the more man relies upon mechanical devices, the greater the need to ensure that, so far as possible, they will function as their designers intended for protracted periods. In the absence of essential maintenance, the simple sailing craft is considerably more reliable.

The following reflections have led the writer to determine the above order:

(a) A diesel engine is generally regarded as the most reliable marine power unit. Two of them must inevitably be more reliable than one because, if one fails, a yachtsman does not lose all propulsive power.

(b) The yachtsman with two good power units can with confidence and with no particular regard for direction of wind and sea, head for a distant destination. If inclement weather is forecasted during passage, he can if necessary alter course for the nearest haven.

(c) Outboard engines, what ever the claim of makers, tend to be regarded by yachtsmen as temperamental. Some inwardly sigh with relief when they start and wonder whether they are going to cough to a halt when they are working.

(d) Under sail alone, few motor sailers have the ability to claw off a lee shore in a manner equal to that of the majority of craft purely designed to sail. In the event of engine failure in either type of vessel, the sailing craft must therefore be judged safer.

(e) The sailing craft with no auxiliary engine, an obsolescent breed invariably owned by highly competent sailing men, must be assessed as being safer than a craft which depends upon machinery for propulsion, when that machinery is inefficient and unreliable.

Susceptibilities of motor cruisers

A weakness in motor cruisers is their engines, particularly as they become older. Age in itself does not imply unreliability but if, over a period of years, an engine is neglected or inadequately serviced, then sooner or later it will fail. Improper function is not the only cause of engine failure as is explained later in this chapter but the result remains the same. The records of the RNLI relating marine casualties in recent years lend substance to these remarks.

Water in the fuel

Nothing will more effectively cause sound engines to cease functioning than water reaching diesel fuel injectors or petrol jets. A common cause is condensation in fuel tanks and a simple means of preventing this occurring is to keep fuel tanks topped up, particularly during winter.

Grit and sludge in fuel tanks

Grit and sludge lying quietly in the bottom of a fuel tank, even in ordinary sea conditions, can be disturbed in a rough sea. Fuel filters can become choked, perhaps fuel lines too, and so the engines they feed stop through fuel starvation. This single occurrence is one of the most common causes of engine failure.

Few owners have the ability to diagnose every engine fault. Those who have will need no advice on this subject and so, not only will they ensure that their engines have been properly serviced at the commencement of a season; they will be certain that their fuel tanks and lines are clean as well. The man who relies entirely upon boatyard servicing may not, through ignorance, give any instruction beyond that of engine service. He will expect instant reaction to his finger on the starter button at all times, but he is vulnerable. Experiencing engine failure and having exhausted his battery using the starter motor, or perhaps himself in his repeated endeavours to start his engines by hand, he can only call for help.

Certainly boat designers do nothing to assist yachtsmen with this problem. Some fuel tanks demand engine removal and subsequent tank removal, before inspection can be achieved. Others have no inspection plates or drain cocks. It seems that in builders' endeavours to produce sleek, attractive craft, too often engines are ingeniously inserted into tiny, barely accessible compartments and fuel tanks are hidden away. Fuel lines and filters, difficult enough to dismantle by an experienced mechanic in port, become articles which can be seen but not handled by a yachtsman in a heaving craft. A north east coast fishing coble usually has its marine diesel engine in a box which sits proud on the bottom boards. The wisdom in such unattractive design is obvious. What is the answer to the problems of some yachtsmen? Certainly it is not to just hope that the worst is unlikely to happen. Money might well be the unwanted amalgam. Money to pay for boatyard charges for cleaning a fuel tank. It is often the price of having to accept modern design.

The fuel tanks of outboard engines

Craft fitted with outboard engines generally use petrol with which an oil additive must be mixed. It will be a precise mixture, perhaps 30 or 40 to 1, and the blending must be complete. Such craft have only to lie at moorings for two or three weeks and the additive will sink to the bottom of the tank. When one attempts to start the engines, the petrol with the excessively high oil content at the bottom of the tank is drawn into the carburettors and complete engine failure results. Until the proper mixture is achieved and the plugs cleaned, perfect engines will not start.

The obvious answer to this problem is the vigorous stirring of fuel remaining in a tank before the engine is started. Small tanks can be picked up and handled like a cocktail shaker for a minute or so.

Outboard engines served by two or more tanks

In this case a less apparent risk exists. An owner may board his craft, knowing that he has one full tank and one which needs topping up. The latter is filled before sailing, the fuel content is effectively mixed during the process and, with this tank connected to his engine, he commences his voyage. At sea a considerable while later, he decides to change over to the other fuel tanks and at that point his engine dies. The probable fault has already been described and even moderate motion up to that point has been insufficient to effectively produce the fuel mixture in the untouched tank the engine demands.

Engine failure in bad weather

If engine failure occurs in a motor cruiser in a rough sea, the craft should not be allowed to broach to and lie in the trough. She will then be at her most vulnerable and serious damage could result.

An effective answer to this is a sea anchor, an item of safety equipment which should be regarded as essential on all sea-going motor cruisers. A drogue of this type will prevent a craft from lying near athwart to wind and sea, the condition to be avoided. She may well respond to the brake by yawing widely, perhaps wildly, but in the main wind and sea will be held on an ahead bearing.

Excessive dependence on auxiliary engines in sailing craft

It sometimes occurs that a sailing craft arrives off a port and, when sail is about to be removed, the engine will not start. Possibly the tide is bearing her inshore and a ferry has just assumed control of the channel. Contrary to the reaction of some in these circumstances, all is not lost.

It is well to reflect that one invariably extricates oneself from these unsettling predicaments, and upon how sailing craft managed in the days before auxiliaries became commonplace. It is sensible for a relatively inexperienced sailing skipper to be just a little daring from time to time. He might try taking his craft into port under reduced sail when the weather is clement. Sailing competence is near complete when he regards his auxiliary engine as a helpful but somewhat superfluous fitment.

CHAPTER 5

Keeping Out Of The Way Of Shipping

Imagination may be the plaything of poets but to ordinary citizens it can be a curse at times. Especially is this so for those of us who, perhaps for the first time, are planning something containing risk. For it is fear of the unknown, to paraphrase a better known writer, which makes cowards of us all. More things than brass bedsteads go bump in the night. Most people have their own particular daymates, if they are prepared to be honest with themselves, based largely upon imaginary dangers.

The yachtsman planning to cross the narrow seas for the first time may well feel qualms. He pictures his tiny craft on the open water with no land in sight. In his imagination he sees massive merchant ships cutting mighty swaths across the sea, while helpless in their paths sails a very anxious yachtsman. It is, of course, himself. How can he possibly avoid them all? Their radar sets may not divulge his presence; their watchkeepers may not have the keen eyes he wishes they had. Do they even care about his presence? 'Better to back a good big 'un than a good little 'un', the saying goes. Well of course a merchant vessel of any size is a good big 'un if she collides with a yacht. Her paint is barely scratched, but the good little 'un is lucky if she remains afloat – hardly a comforting thought. It has to be said that a decision to make a short sea crossing can be complicated by sufficient problems without those which are largely imaginary.

There is one fact which is so obvious that it can be overlooked. In the wide open spaces off our shores there is a great deal more sea than ship. At sea when the possibility of collision appears to exist, the probability of this occurring is small indeed. Naturally this assumes reasonable seamanship on the part of a yachtsman. He must sail away from our shores to prove for himself these truths. He will not really believe them until he does. It is illogical that the same people who might be deterred from making an overseas adventure by thoughts of collision at sea will drive on our motorways with verve, and with no disquiet whatsoever. Yet the chances of them being involved in a disastrous car accident are considerably greater than those of being embroiled in a similar catastrophe at sea. Surely this contradiction occurs simply because in deep waters the amateur yachtsman is in an unknown or, at the least, an unfamiliar environment. What ever his degree of intelligence and moral courage, he may fail logically to consider the true probabilities of collision at sea. By comparison with the risks on our roads they are small.

Here follows no dissertation on the Collision Regulations: in this volume it must be assumed that the reader has some knowledge of them. If he seeks interpretation of the Rules, his needs are met in Stanford's Sailing Companion. There follows comments on sundry aspects on the subject of how yachtsmen can best avoid craft in general and merchant ships in particular.

A comparison

If one is asked to imagine the problems of a long distance lorry driver who encounters youngsters on bizarre cycles on the road, one can find room for sympathy. He is the professional who plies the road for a living and his experience is vast. They are the artless amateurs who are a potential hazard to him. He has forgotten more about road law, road lore and road manners than the youngsters have ever learned. If he had his way cycles generally would be confined to cycle paths.

It may not be pleasant for yachtsmen to compare themselves with such youths on cycles but, if they seek perspective in this troubling question of yachts v. merchantmen, they might try.

Whatever hair raising stories are recounted by yachtsmen, any realistic approach to this subject must be based upon the premise that no merchantman's watchkeeper wishes to put at risk his DTI certificate, his means of livelihood. He might artlessly, irresponsibly do so, but not intentionally. To the first-shaking yachtsmen who shout 'Bloody murderer' at the bridge of a large ship one would say this: if the outcome of an encounter was death to a yachtsman, the Master he addressed would be unlikely to be found guilty of culpable homicide in a court of law. Neither would his counterpart on our highways in similar circumstances. Negligence, probably; failure to obey the Rule of the Road, almost certainly: but not – murder.

Master's of merchant ships have problems ...

The numerical explosion in the number of yachts at sea has produced a situation which Masters and watchkeepers of merchant vessels do not like at all. They gain some solace from the knowledge that, more often than not, yachts are encountered during the summer months in fine weather. However, they know that even in daylight a tiny yacht may not be seen in sufficient time for them to adequately turn their vessels. Waves, particularly white crested ones, make yacht-spotting difficult; reduced visibility adds to their trials. So a yachtsman experiences anxieties! He might spare a thought for those of a watchkeeper. Most are no less fearful of running down a tiny yacht than the lorry driver is of knocking down a cyclist.

All merchant ships are sluggish on the helm and mammoth ships although very manoeuvrable for their size, are no better. Understandably, the professional seaman is mistrustful of the amateur at sea, hence if choice exists he will give a yacht of any type a wide berth. He does not always have freedom of action, due for instance to the proximity of other vessels invisible to the yachtsman. Similarly, he may show a vertical black cylinder by day, or three vertically-disposed red lights at night, to indicate to other vessels that he cannot deviate from his course due to his considerable draft which could be about 55 feet. Yet occasionally another may with complete confidence pass so close to a yacht that her helmsman has a temporary spate of nerves.

Darkness exacerbates the situation. A watchkeeper, high on the bridge of a merchantman, wonders whether he is suddenly going to see the tiny navigation lights or the illuminated sail of a small craft whose skipper, through ignorance, has left action on the see-and-be seen code far too late. Consider the alarm of the watchkeeper. The author speaks with feeling, having suddenly sighted a poorly illuminated mainsail, obviously that of a crossing yacht, a point on the port bow of a large vessel at a range of about a mile. And a mile at sea on a big ship is the equivalent of 100 yards on a highway.

Obviously all remarks made here relate to properly run merchant ships on which efficient watches are maintained. They are the majority. Nevertheless, even in home waters where all kinds of navigational hazards are present, one can from time to time encounter a vessel on which an inefficient watch is being kept, although the master down below might be unaware of it. It is generally produced by the slackness of individual watchkeeping officers, thus the standard of watchkeeping can vary from watch to watch, as well as from ship to ship. Typical of the slack watchkeeper would be he who, with radar switched on and auto-pilot engaged, from time to time leaves the warmth of the chartroom to view the radar screen and scan the horizon, with the radar claiming priority. The latter comment is worth a mental note on the part of a yachtsman.

Remarks in the preceding paragraph will give cold comfort to the yachtsman, whatever his competence. He must of necessity assume that the watchkeeper on an approaching merchant ship may be careless and irresponsible, although there is a likelihood that he is both competent and efficient.

... and so do yachtsmen

Articles in yachting magazines which assail the International Regulations for the Prevention of Collision at Sea appear from time to time. A common attack of yachtsmen is on Rule 18, the 'Steam and Sail' rule. It is said that the Rule has no meaning in modern sea conditions when tiny sailing yachts encounter huge merchantmen; the only wise course for the skipper of a sailing yacht to adopt is to keep out of the way of all large, on-coming merchantmen and never to wait until it is decided that evasive action is not being taken by the other. Certainly this is a wise and seamanlike course and, what is more, the Collision Regulations uphold such a decision.

The Rules have been drawn up by men of experience with a vast knowledge of sea conditions. It is suggested here that the Ministry of Trade and Industry do not counter attacks made by yachtsmen on Rule 18 because they realise that the attackers do not interpret the Rules correctly. Had modern conditions produced an anomoly in them there is little doubt that it would have been corrected before now, and certainly in the new Regulations. There are myriad variations in the circumstances and conditions which can produce risk of collision at sea and for this reason any Rule within the Steering and Sailing Rules – Rules 11 to 18 – must always be read in conjunction with others.

A classic case

A yacht is under sail making 3 knots. A large and fast merchant vessel is sighted from her some 5 miles away. The yacht skipper considers that risk of collision exists. He has no means of knowing whether the watchkeeper on the merchantman has sighted his craft and foremost in his mind is the knowledge that within 20 minutes or so the big ship could be upon him. If sighting of his yacht by the merchantman occurs when the range has been decreased considerably, then it could pass him at least dangerously closely because the merchantman may be slow to react to rudder movement. He recalls that blindspots can extend as much as 2 miles ahead of some ships and thereupon he goes about, perhaps assisting the power of his sails with his auxiliary engine and moves sharply out of the danger zone.

Let us now seek, step by step, the support for an action which is seamanlike within the Rules. Rule 18 states:

'A power-driven vessel shall keep out of the way of ... a sailing vessel.'

This must be read in conjunction with Rule 17(a)(i) which states:

'Where by any of these Rules one of two vessels is to keep out of the way, the other shall keep her course and speed.'

Clearly this sentence, by itself, considers simple circumstances. They might be when the sailing vessel is a large schooner and the visibility is excellent. Very wisely, it requires a mariner not to deviate from his course, or alter his speed, during the period when another vessel must take action to avoid him. But the Rule goes on to state:

'When, from any cause, the vessel required to keep her course and speed finds herself so close that collision cannot be avoided by the action of the giving way vessel alone, she also shall take such action as will best aid to avoid collision.'

In effect, responsibility for the avoidance of collision is now divided between the large merchant ship and the tiny sailing yacht. How close is close? The yachtsman considers that 5 miles is close enough when the merchantman could be doing 15 knots and may not have even seen his diminutive yacht. If this reasoning is not considered sufficiently conclusive, one must regard the content of Rule 2(b) which states:

'In obeying and construing these Rules, due regard shall be had to all dangers of navigation and collision, and any special circumstances, *including the limitations of the vessels involved*, which may render a departure from these Rules necessary to avoid immediate danger.'

Well, that is proof positive that the yachtsman has the authority and the right to speed off at a tangent if he considers it good seamanship to do so, but the Collision Regulations contain a stern warning to those who disregard the Rules lightly. It is in Rule 2(a).

'Nothing in these Rules shall exonerate any vessel, or the owner, master or crew thereof, from the consequences of any neglect to comply with these Rules or of the neglect of any precaution which may be required by the ordinary practice of seamen, or by the special circumstances of the case.'

In conclusion, it must be remembered that when a yachtsman does decide to disregard Rule 17 which requires him to keep his course and speed, an efficient watchkeeper on a merchantman, sighting his yacht at a good range and deciding to take avoiding action, experiences anxiety when the craft he must avoid suddenly alters course. The yachtsman's action can still be justified in the knowledge that, if this is the case, that same watchkeeper will change his avoidance tactics. He is alert to existing dangers.

Don't thrash your nerves if you don't have to. ...

A large vessel pointing at a yacht at any range can produce qualms, and the cries of alarm from well-meaning family members do nothing to assist a skipper in arriving at a cool decision. Unless that large vessel is under a mile away, or unless one's yacht is becalmed at greater range with an auxiliary engine which will not start, there is no true reason for excessive anxiety.

Consider the following figure. It is only in position (a) that the yachtsman may have to decide upon avoiding action. If the yacht is in position (b), in the 8 minutes it will take for the merchantman to reach that position, he has moved 0.37 miles away from the vessel's course line. In position (c), although the vision of the merchant ship remains daunting, no danger exists. None.

Fig. 5.1

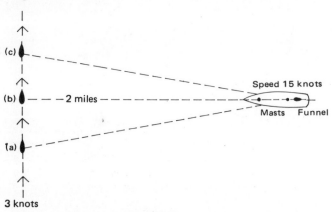

The Rules make reference to vessels being end on or nearly end on. This is highly descriptive. The fact that a vessel is coming towards one is reason for taking notice. Yet what is infinitely more important is the precise angle of her fore and aft line to her bearing from the yacht. Her masts and funnel usually provide this information by day but, at ranges over 3 miles, it might require a pair of binoculars to determine. Without this angle, no reasoned decision can be made as to whether avoiding action is necessary or not

Fig. 5.2

Positiveness, purpose, predestine action

'Any action taken to avoid collision shall, if the circumstances of the case admit, be positive, made in ample

time, and with due regard to the observance of good seamanship.'

So says an extract from Rule 7. Like so many paragraphs in pages and pages of any type of regulations, this one can be read without its considerable importance being absorbed. Yachtsmen will contribute vastly to their safety in accepting the fact that within the Rules no sentence is used unnecessarily, no simple instruction can be ignored, no cautions may be disregarded. This particular sentence demands emphasis for the consideration of those whose knowledge of the Rules is sketchy.

Yachtsmen may alter course to take evasive action, either because they are required to do so or because they decide that, whatever they *should* do, their common sense tells them to clear a potentially dangerous area. The decision having been made, the alteration must be bold, thereby leaving the other vessel in no doubt of the action upon which they have decided. There is much to commend a practice adopted by many experienced seamen. It is to allow one's craft to swing beyond the calculated course of evasion. One's intention having thus been boldly declared, the helm can be eased and the craft allowed to swing back to the required course. Potentially dangerous is the man who artlessly alters course a mere couple of degrees. He knows what he is doing, but has the other fellow correctly assessed his intention? Is the minimal alteration just careless helmsmanship and no alteration has been made? Is his intention to play Chicken, a dangerous game in which few seamen will indulge? Through inexperience, is he delaying avoidance action far too late? Or has the helmsman wined too well? Whatever interpretation is made by the other, he is forced to take an action which might not otherwise be taken. The history of marine casualties shows clearly the damage and loss of life which have resulted from flouting the content of the simple sentence quoted above.

Risk of collision – present or not?

'In determining risk of collision such risk shall be deemed to exist if the compass bearing of the approaching vessel does not appreciably change.

So reads one of the most important sub-sections of Rule 7.

Time to carefully watch the compass bearing of an approaching vessel from the cockpit or wheelhouse of a yacht seldom presents itself. To do so in many cases might be to invite a

Fig. 5.3

Throughout, compass bearings between both vessels remain constant.

close-quarters situation which would have otherwise been avoided. Obviously most yachtsmen are going to take avoiding action immediately it is decided that risk of collision *might* exist. Possibility will be regarded as reality.

These comments are in no way intended to detract from the wisdom or importance of the preliminary quoted above. One might reflect that its substance is mainly directed towards naval and merchant ships generally. One can never afford to ignore it, provided one has time to exercise its wise counsel.

The overtaking vessel

The large, fast merchant vessel coming up from astern is an overtaking vessel: so is the large, fast sailing yacht overtaking a slow motor cruiser. Both must obey Rule 13 which states unequivocally that all overtaking vessels must keep clear of the overtaken until they are *finally past and clear.*

This almost subversive approach does not tax the nerves to the same extent as one from another direction. Combined approach speeds are lessened. Pressure on thought processes is reduced. If risk of collision is present, danger is no less real.

Disobeying Rule 13, because in most cases it is difficult to determine whether one's craft has been sighted, an alteration of course of 2 or 3 points will remove a yacht from the path of an overtaking vessel. Justification for this action can be obtained from Rule 2.

See and be seen

In daytime

None can make his craft more apparent to a lookout than she already is, short of adopting methods which would border on the ludicrous in a yacht. There remains a highly important means of drawing the attention of merchantmen to his presence: the use of a radar reflector. What are considered to be important comments on this subject are made in chapter 4.

So long as merchantmen continue the practice of using radar in our waters both in daytime and at night, in clear and thick weather, the radar reflector remains the means by which a yacht can be detected at sea, even though she is not readily discernible to an alert lookout.

By night

Observations already made about radar reflectors have equal substance here. Adequate illumination when necessary remains an evident need. The wattage of electric light bulbs in navigation lights tends to be misleading. Clearly, watt for watt, a white navigation light will have considerably more luminosity than that of a coloured one. Hence the motor cruiser which, by the Rules, must carry a white light in addition to her green and red side lights, is much more likely to be seen at good range than a sailing craft which must carry green and red side lights only. In these remarks there is an implied recommendation that, wherever possible, the wattage of navigation lights be increased. Short of completely renewing all one's navigation lights, this is often impossible.

The owner of a motor cruiser will obtain some satisfaction from these comments: the sailing man will not. For the latter, worse follows. His sidelights, low placed as they commonly are, will be seen by an approaching vessel only intermittently, due to the intercedence of waves and swell. Even a merchant vessel's large and powerful sidelights are visible to the naked eye only at about 5 miles range on a clear night: at what diminutive range may a yachtsman expect his own tiny sidelights to be seen? In present day conditions no yachtsman can rest content with this degree of illumination. One must seek within the Rules for additional lights to display.

In Rule 25 one finds the authority for sailing craft to carry additional lights. It is in sub-section (c) which reads as follows:

'In addition to the lights first listed in paragraph (a) of this Rule, two all-round lights in a vertical line, exhibit at or near the top of the mast, where things can best be seen, the upper being red and the lower green, but these lights shall not be exhibited in conjunction with the combined lantern permited by paragraph (b) of this Rule (which refers to sidelights carried at the masthead). Both lights ... shall be visible at a distance of at least 2 miles.'

This may well be fine on a large ketch or schooner which carries batteries or auxiliaries capable of providing the electrical demand of these additional lights. Inescapable are two facts. First, the average owner of a small yacht is either unwilling to have such lights fitted, or he cannot afford to do so. Secondly, both are coloured lights which, although of greater value than his sidelights, remain short range lights in practice.

The Rules, however, are nothing if they are not comprehensive. In Rule 36 one obtains authorisation to exhibit a light in addition to the prescribed lights. It reads:

'If necessary to attract the attention of another vessel try to make light or sound signals that cannot be mistaken for any signal not housed elsewhere in these Rules, or may direct the beam of her searchlight in the direction of the danger in such a way as not to embarrass any vessel.'

Undoubtedly the white hand flare, with its brilliant incandescence, is by far the best means of drawing the attention of other craft to one's presence – always assuming that watchkeepers on other craft are keeping an efficient lookout in the minute or so during which the flare burns. Perhaps this is one reason why it is difficult to find a cruising yachtsman who adopts this legal and effective practice. Another might be the cost of white hand flares.

Sundry devices have been used by experienced sailing yachtsmen to attract the attention of large vessels to their presence. None are authorised by the Rules and yet one must allow that all have merit:

1. Illumination of the mainsail. If this is carried out, it must be done effectively and early, if possible some miles before an approaching vessel is in one's vicinity. It is stressed that a torch or hand lantern is ineffectual for this purpose. A brilliant, diffused white light, on a wandering lead specially carried for this purpose and connected to a craft's main circuits, is a practical answer.

2. Some yachtsmen switch on their masthead electric riding light. In a 'See and be seen' code, this has considerable merit. The light is at a height which ensures that it is constantly visible. Its whiteness and brightness, coupled with the telltale evidence produced by a radar reflector, should attract the attention of a merchant vessel if anything will. One will recall that a single white light at sea may belong to a variety of craft. A stern light of a vessel of any size; a tiny craft

under oars or sail; a vessel at anchor under 150 feet in length; the single masthead light of a small coaster whose side lights are not yet visible. The very fact that a single white light can be any of these, and others, is a good reason for a watchkeeper on a large vessel to be wary of it. And awareness on his part is all the yachtsman seeks.

3. It is not unknown for a yachtsman to lash a Tilley lamp to his pushpit rail and turn in for the night. The author reflects that, in the absence of extraordinary confidence and steely nerves, he would have to be excessively tired to do this in home waters.

The Tilley lamp is intended to deceive approaching merchantmen. Most of them are only too familiar with the bobbing white lights of Portuguese fishermen, Grand Bank dories and cobles on the East Coast. Illegal, no doubt: adopted, frequently. Fishing craft may have nets or lines extending outwards and merchantmen do not like them at all.

Finally, there is no call for a yacht to carry lights of any description unless other craft are in its vicinity. Owners of sailing yachts may frequently enjoy the comfort of knowing that the limited life of their batteries is not being shortened. The chances of them colliding with other unlit yachts, even during Cowes Week in the English Channel, are remote indeed.

Blind spots

Blind spots on merchant vessels have always been present; it is only their extent which has increased on some ships in recent years. If a yachtsman wears spectacles he will live with blind spots; again, driving a car, he will be well aware of the areas of the road he cannot see. It is similarly evident to him that those who are in control of a craft of any size, more or less confined to one position as they invariably are, must be subjected to blind spots too.

The wide variations in blind spots on ships, almost all of which are predictable by yachtsmen, make only one extreme type worthy of mention here. It is produced on a vessel with the bridge right aft, a common enough sight at sea these days. She may be trimmed by the stern so that her bows are lifted above their normal height; or she may have a high deck cargo which reaches the whole length of her foredeck; or she may be normally trimmed but of massive dimensions with high bulwarks round her bluff bows.

Such a vessel's blind spot may extend 2 miles or more ahead of her. This fact, although a matter for the concern of yachtsmen, must be held in perspective and the following points are made here:

1. In the open sea any vessel must be assumed to be steaming at full speed. That may be as much as 20 knots and so time is not on a yachtsman's side. Assuming good visibility, he who finds himself in such a vessel's blind spot has allowed his craft to approach her far too closely. One readily allows that there are a number of variables in any such situation but, although dogmatism here is unrealistic, the fact must be emphasised. This advice is particularly directed at those yachtsmen who, uncertain of the action they must take to avoid the large vessel, leave far too late avoidance action which will be clearly apparent to an alert watchkeeper on a large vessel.

2. A yachtsman believing himself to be in this vessel's blind spot, for whatever reason, he will scurry off at a tangent, using every means at his disposal to clear the danger zone. He may gain some small solace in reflecting that the dimensions of his craft are minimal. Even though he passes very close indeed to the massive bows of the merchantman, a nerve-wracking experience in itself, the dangerous swath she cuts across the vast expanse of sea is extraordinarily narrow in fact.

Caution in the vicinity of focal points of shipping

Bowling along with a ship in sight which is obviously going to pass miles clear of one's yacht, it can be startling to see her alter course, and her new course immediately indicates that a collision course with one's craft is a real possibility. So many of these cases are predictable and so, in certain circumstances, it is wise to regard the distant, apparently inocuous ship with caution.

The headland, lightship or shoal around which a vessel is steaming is the usual answer. It may be Flamborough Head, South Stack or Hartland Point. Evidently, when sailing in the vicinity of any focal point, the yachtsman can calculate for himself where he may reasonably expect vessels to alter course, whether they are one or ten miles from the shore.

Thick weather

Firstly, let it be said that the only craft likely to hear the diminutive sound of a yacht's fog signal are other yachts; perhaps small fishing craft. Secondly the large radar reflector, hoisted as high as possible, is the yachtsman's best means of assisting merchantmen to keep out of his way.

Where sea lanes exist, they should be avoided when possible. If this is not feasible, they should be crossed at right angles with all possible despatch. When sailing in an area which can be regarded as a sea lane because the customary tracks of coastal traffic cross it, again it should be cleared. These tactics reduce the likelihood of meeting shipping and so they reduce risk. Reduce but not remove: ships may be encountered anywhere, proceeding in any direction.

A small 'echo' on a radar screen, produced by a radar reflector, cannot be recognised as that of a yacht. Watch-keepers on merchant vessels must assume that such an echo could be a tiny coaster or tug, a fishing craft, even a yacht. Large echo, large ship: tiny echo, tiny ship. It is logical to assume that, provided the echo is located, they will keep out of the way.

Usually there are two watchkeepers on the bridge of a vessel in fog and the radar screen is being constantly studied. The ability of an alert watchkeeper to detect a small echo will, to a considerable extent, be dictated by the state of the sea. A rough sea produces a mass of small echoes, constantly appearing and dying, amongst which the small, constant echo is difficult to detect. A smooth sea, even one with moderate waves upon it, produces near ideal radar conditions. Clearly, the confidence of a yachtsman that his craft has been located must vary directly with the state of the sea.

Nagging doubts in a yachtsman's mind may be threefold:

(a) Has the echo his radar reflector can produce been spotted?

(b) Is an on-coming merchantman fitted with a radar set? These days almost all but the tiniest vessels are.

(c) Even though such a vessel has a radar set, is it

functioning? Has it gone wrong? This possibility cannot be ignored but it is an unknown quantity. It may be said that radar sets are remarkably reliable these days and they obtain frequent servicing.

To these questions the author would respond: with reservations about the state of sea, the dice are loaded in the yachtsman's favour but utmost vigilance remains paramount.

One's ears strain to hear the distant and perhaps approaching fog signal. From the single repetitive note of the syren of an oncoming vessel a yachtsman must decide:

(a)   Her bearing which, vague and indeterminate as it will inevitably be, is perhaps best determined by using a hand bearing compass.

(b)   Her range, which is a matter of serious guesswork.

(c)   Her rate of closing, a factor which has to be assessed from the changing volume of the note.

(d)   And from an appraisal of the foregoing factors, her probable course and speed.

Although the volume of a vessel's fog signal may increase gradually, if its bearing is altering it will almost certainly pass. clear. Danger exists when a fog signal remains steady in direction and increases in volume. Faced with these ominous portents, a yachtsman's action can only be to sail away at right angles to its direction with all possible speed. The fact remains that the bearing of an on-coming vessel which will pass close but clear will appear to remain steady in direction until the latter stages of approach, and then it will alter rapidly.

It will be seen that precipitate action in every case where increasing volume and steady bearing conditions appear to exist might project a yachtsman into danger, instead of moving away from it. To wait until it is decided that real danger exists is nerve testing, yet essential.

Let the reader mark this well: Rules 11 to 18 of the Collision Regulations, which are those directing how one vessel should keep out of the way of another, do not apply when vessels are not in sight of one another. In these conditions broad directives are given. A power driven vessel is required to proceed at a moderate speed, a phrase open to misinterpretation, even deliberate flouting, in the manner which is prevelent on our motorways. Every power driven vessel should stop its engines (but not necessarily its forward motion) when a fog signal, the position of which is not ascertained, is heard forward of her beam. Vessels fitted with radar are, with certain reservations, permitted to proceed at a speed not quite so low as others which are not so fitted.

Avoidance tactics in conditions of low visibility are wisely left to the good seamanship and judgement of individuals in charge of vessels. They may manoeuvre in any manner they deem fit. But – the short and sweepingly comprehensive contents of Rule 2, previously quoted, have absolute ascendency in these conditions.

It is readily allowed that these comments give no specific assistance to yachtsmen who have the misfortune to encounter large vessels in thick weather. The thinking yachtsman will readily appreciate that no one can do so. Let him obtain some solace from the opening paragraphs of this chapter, and the fact that good sense and reasonable courage will invariably extricate him from real danger.

CHAPTER 6

Passage Making

PART 1 GENERAL OBSERVATIONS

The Men Who Sail

Successful passage making is mainly achieved through a combination of good seamanship and what is called the ordinary practice of seamen. If seamanship is loosely defined as wide sea experience combined with good common sense, and the ordinary practice of seamen is accepted as being the manner in which a good seaman would conduct his vessel from one place to another, particularly in relation to other vessels which may be encountered, then the first sentence is no longer obscure.

Yet when discussing passage making with experienced yachtsmen it would seem that many of them are at variance with each other on this uncomplicated demand. It is fairer to say disagreement often occurs on techniques; not on the broad principle. It is suggested here that dissent, if it occurs, is produced by the manner of men expressing opinions. Wisdom, knowledge, perception, experience, caution, courage, daring. Each of these qualities, and the innumerable permutations of all of them, will lead each skipper to approach the same passage problems differently. So if one seeks advice it is well to gauge the character of he who offers it. The writer, presenting the reader with this latter insurmountable difficulty, nevertheless presumes to propound to yachtsmen with inshore experience only, principles and techniques for passage making which he considers sensible for them.

The avoidance of unwarranted risk

A part of seamanship is to recognise and to avoid unnecessary risks. Although excessive caution can bring problems in its train, the cruising man can never be adjudged wrong to err on the side of prudence. Numerous examples could be given: two follow. (1) Rounding a headland quite sensibly at two miles range when, to one's irritation, another craft can be seen close inshore, thereby cutting down distance to the sailed. (2) Deviating grossly to avoid an on-coming merchant vessel when subsequent events indicate that a slight alteration would have been adequate.

The Inability to Sail

It would be interesting to know the number of occasions on which amateur yachtsmen have been unable to commence a sea crossing due to adverse weather conditions. Certainly the number is much greater than one would at first surmise. In yachting the best philosophy is that which accepts with equanimity what may be described as a non-event.

An unwillingness to take unjustifiable risks is wise and a

decision not to proceed will probably be right for the man who makes it. One man's safety can be another man's risk – and a fig for another's disparaging assessment of one's decisions.

Test the Sea Conditions Sometimes

Let it be assumed that future weather is doubtful and that a decision has been made to await the next shipping weather bulletin. The forecast is obtained but unsureness remains. The wind gusts across moorings in an unsettling manner, although some degree of hope was given by the weather man. It is sometimes advantageous to break moorings and see what the wind and sea conditions are outside. The intention must be to turn round and return if one does not think it wise to commence a passage, but just occasionally one obtains a reassuring surprise.

Desirable features of Motor Cruisers

The speed, the ability to complete an intended voyage and the predictability of the average motor cruiser demands that a skipper takes advantage of the navigational opportunities these qualities present. They are not reasons for complacency, no grounds for attempting a passage with less than adequate navigational knowledge. Rather should one's craft's qualities be regarded as desirable bonuses upon which to capitalise. The running fix, the 4-point bearing, doubling the angle on the bow, the challenging line of soundings, the reduction of uncertainties when calculating a DR position; all are means by which a motor yacht's position can be obtained; means which are often denied the sailing man.

PART 2 PRE-SAILING CONSIDERATIONS AND ACTIVITIES

A Sound Passage Technique

As a general principle, it is good seamanship to make a sea passage from feature to feature, rather than from port to port. When ports have features, such as lighthouses, cliffs or promontories in the vicinity, one is fortunate. Where features in a port area are minimal one should head for an adjacent feature – a lighthouse, a lightship, a headland – within comfortable sailing distance of the port, fix position from that and then proceed portwards with assurance.

Planning an Arrival

Few mariners would wish to enter an unfamiliar port during dark hours without the assistance of a pilot. Tortuous searching for close range unlit buoys, barges, piles, small craft and other hazards, all of them innocuous and friendly by day, can be a tense, nerve-wracking process at night. Risk is involved and one never takes risks with craft and lives when safer options are available, hence entry to a port in daylight is more sound.

It being so much easier to pinpoint distant shore features, such as the light of a lighthouse, by night than in daytime, it must always be adjudged preferable to plan to be about 10 miles off a distant shore an hour or two before dawn. One can then berth in daylight and, if unforeseen delay during passage occurs, many hours of daylight remain to render such delay of no great import.

Of course on a short sea passage, say one of 20 or 30 miles, one plans to both sail and arrive in daylight, making an early start to ensure that ample daylight remains in case of possible poor progress or other unforeseeable delay. Clearly, the shorter the sea passage, the less likelihood there is of one's position being in doubt and a faceless, vague coastline ahead in the latter stages of the passage holds less imponderables. One can almost guess where, in the haze, one's destination lies. Uncertainty of position inevitably increases directly as the distance one must sail is extended, hence the value of a pre-dawn arrival.

There are those who are of the opinion that the deep water hazards produced by merchant ships are best faced in daylight, and that this factor outweighs navigational uncertainty as a distant coast is approached. These are usually experienced yachtsmen and, for them, this technique is right. When passages in excess of 50 miles are to be made, they may well make a pre-dawn departure and proceed with a degree of assurance which is not general amongst yachtsmen.

The Time Factor

To owners of both motor and sailing craft, time in hand during a passage is always of value. It is common to experience delaying factors whilst still on moorings and for sundry reasons to make slower progress than planned. There is much to be said for deciding to break mooring somewhat earlier than the time careful calculation indicates. It is, after all, a simple matter at sea to delay arrival at a distant destination: it is often impossible to make up lost time.

Attitudes towards a Return Passage

To voyage to a foreign shore demands a return passage. Detailed planning usually takes place for the outward passage and the return is given little emphasis. In a foreign port, time margins can artlessly be reduced to negligable quantities. Commitments at home sometimes cause yachtsmen to sail homewards in conditions which are anything but inviting. Skippers themselves are not keen on undertaking such a return passage and passengers will inevitably dislike it intensely. A two or even three day margin is a wise provision and so, with options entirely open, a skipper may elect to sail homewards when the weather is suitable, which may well be somewhat earlier than his crew or passengers had hoped.

The application of variation

The vast majority of yachtsmen who cruise in our waters work magnetic, which is to say that they use the magnetic compass roses on their charts and not those which give true direction. This is a practical system because it precludes the necessity of making calculations with variation. Here it is proposed that they work magnetic using a more simple, less time consuming method which requires no reference to compass roses at all. All compass roses are irritating things at best when one is wedged against the heave and wallow of a small craft, and yet precise direction from them must be obtained in the interests of reasonably accurate navigation.

The proposed method demands the proper use of Captain Field's Improved parallel ruler. This instrument has compass graduations from 0° to 360° etched boldly upon its edges and they have to be used. It also requires magnetic meridians drawn upon all working charts, to replace the true meridians which are printed upon them by publishers. It will be recalled that true meridians are the vertical lines drawn at intervals upon charts and they indicate the direction of true north: magnetic meridians would be, if they were printed on charts, similar lines slightly angled so that they indicated the direction of magnetic north. The method resolves itself into two components, both of which will be described separately.

The alteration of charts

Bold lines, drawn in waterproof ink, are superimposed upon existing true meridians. The direction in which to draw these lines can simply by obtained by taking the direction of magnetic north from existing magnetic compass roses on the chart. One must be careful to ensure that the lines, which must be thicker than those already printed, are not artlessly drawn across important chart detail. A tiny gap in them can be left where desirable.

Fig. 6.1

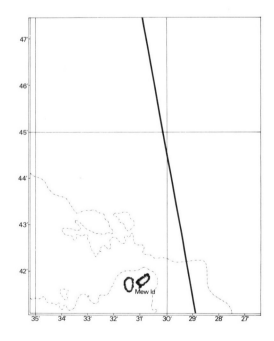

These lines being produced, one has a magnetic datum from which to work; lines upon the chart which indicate magnetic north.

The full use of Captain Field's Improved parallel ruler

An index point is always imprinted on the lower edge of the ruler. Its appearance is as indicated.

Fig. 6.2

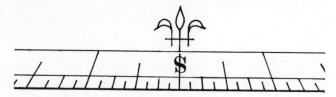

With the ruler closed and this point placed upon a meridian, the ruler is turned until the desired direction on the upper edge also coincides with the meridian; in this case, the magnetic meridian. The ruler will then indicate magnetic direction and can be moved to any position on the chart.

Fig. 6.3

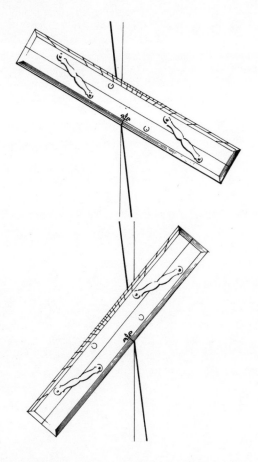

Note

If one invariably uses a Douglas Protractor, or if a yachtsman decides that for a specific chart exercise he will use one in preference to his Field's ruler, it must be remembered that the essence of the Douglas Protractor is the compass graduations imprinted upon its periphery. The advices contained under the previous sub-heading have, therefore, near equal substance in connection with its use.

The application of compass deviation, where necessary

On craft where deviation is known to be present in the steering compass, it must be assumed here that a deviation card produced by a compass adjuster is displayed in the vicinity of the chart table. Upon it deviations may well be produced in a manner somewhat akin to the following.

North
010°   3°W.
020°   4°W.
030°   4°w.
Etc.   5°W.

The application of this information to magnetic courses demands accurate thought processes if a quite inadmissable mistake is not to be made in the course to steer. It is suggested that notations alongside these cryptic advices be made, so that even simple mental calculations are rendered unnecessary. It will be agreed that a skipper usually has distractions enough and any device which renders computation superfluous is of value. The following type of deviation card should assist him considerably.

North
010°   3°W.   Add 3°   Steer 003°
020°   4°W.   Add 4°   Steer 014°
030°   4°W.   Add 4°   Steer 024°
Etc.   5°W.   Add 5°   Steer 035°

If one adopts the practice of the writer, he will extract the magnetic course to steer from his chart in the manner previously described and then mentally apply the deviation correction from his more informative deviation card. Of course, one must interpolate if a course falls between the typical 10° steps of a deviation card but this presents no difficulty; it demands no real thought.

It is the course to steer which is the overriding issue in the vast majority of cases, and others of lesser consequence should not be allowed to befog it. Finally, it is emphasised that anything – *anything* – which contributes to the reduction of precise chartwork calculations is of value to the cruising man, provided it does not detract from accuracy.

Pre-sailing Chartwork

Certain notations should be made on charts before sailing, giving information which is of value and is time saving at sea. They are:

(a)   Scribed arcs round each lighthouse and lightvessel which have as their radii the probable visual ranges of their lights. Any such arc will tell the navigator at a glance when he is within range of a light, even though in daylight it is unlikely that it will be visible to him at the indicated range.

(b)   Lines indicating the limits of shipping lanes, and the direction from which shipping may be expected. Where the limits of published shipping lanes cease, they may be extended by the navigator because the tracks of the majority of ships are predictable to some extent. This is valuable information which must not be sought at sea when one may lack the time, the comfort and the opportunity.

(c)   Lines on small scale charts which indicate the limits

Fig. 6.4

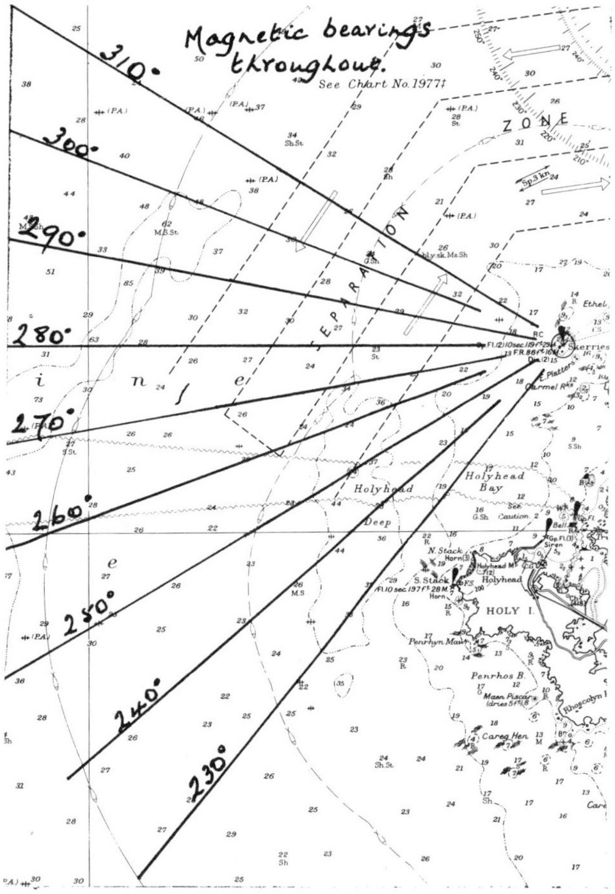

PART 3 SOUNDINGS AND LIGHTS

The Importance of Soundings

For the intelligence they impart, so long as one is at sea, regular soundings should be taken. They remain the oldest and most valuable of all precursory warnings of the danger of grounding. They can on occasion confirm or refute the indications of a doubtful bearing, support the evidence of a fix, aid the calculation of a DR position and even by themselves give valuable information to a navigator.

The Effect of Tides on Charted Soundings

It is invariably known, but not always taken into consideration, that tides often render charted soundings inaccurate. At most times the depth of water exceeds that indicated. When coasting this feature gives a valuable safety factor but offshore, when soundings are required to give some indication of position, it can be misleading. For example, if one is 'feeling' for a 20-fathom line and it is high water, an error of 3 or 4 fathoms could result. It would produce inaccuracy in any estimation of position attempted by this means. It is not propounded that calculation of height of tide be attempted, because it is not possible to do so. Nevertheless mental adjustment of chart datum to the nearest fathom upwards can be made by quick reference to the state and height of tide on the nearest coast.

Lighthouses

Although it may be said that lighthouses are the most easily identified navigational aids, a lighthouse new to the observer may be unidentifiable at long range in daytime. The charted height of a lighthouse merely gives the height of the light's focal plane above MHWS. It does not indicate whether the lighthouse is diminutive and high on a cliff, or of more traditional appearance at sea level. This type of information, of considerable value to the mariner offshore who is trying to resolve his position, will be found in the Admiralty List of Lights, often supported by more detail in the Admiralty Sailing Directions.

Lightvessels

Lightvessels can be difficult to recognise in daytime from other vessels which may be in the vicinity. On small craft it would be unwise to expect to identify one at a range in excess of 5 miles. It is their characteristic topmark, the vertically disposed barrel-shaped lantern on a structure amidships, for which one must scan the horizon.

of other larger scale charts to which one must transfer at the first opportunity.

(d)   When it is planned to utilise certain marine radio beacons it is worth taking the time to draw magnetic bearings on the small scale chart upon which one will work, at 10° intervals outward from the position of the beacons in the manner shown below. The lines terminate at the nominal ranges of each beacon. As is evident, this eliminates the necessity of drawing DF bearings at sea.

The new Stanford DF charts adopt this principle. Unfortunately, at the time of writing, only the central area of the English Channel is so charted, therefore most yachtsmen must draw these bearings themselves.

(e)   Finally, the intended course together with a notation of the initial magnetic course to be steered.

Pre-sailing Notations on Tidal Stream Atlasses

Attention is here drawn to chapter 3 and to the manner in which one should mark tidal stream atlasses so that, throughout a passage and without the necessity of calculating time intervals from Dover or other Standard ports, one can immediately refer to the correct tidal stream chartlet.

PART 4 UNDER WAY

Sailing Craft and the Wind that Blows

Unless a short, hard beat achieves a worthwhile object, and one's passengers have the stomach for it, it is generally preferable to sail off the wind a point or two. In other words why fight the wind when one can go along with it? One cruises for pleasure: not achievement. If the two go hand in hand, one is fortunate. Leaving all options open, the correct mental attitude should be: we hope to reach X-land; if we cannot we shall cruise elsewhere; wherever we are able to go, we should have an enjoyable sailing holiday. There are times of course, when one *must* beat. There are others when, although option exists, one decides that a long beat with its inherent discomfort is preferable to the alternative, whatever that might be.

During the weeks before a summer cruise it is very easy to become almost obsessed with reaching a certain port across the sea and desirable alternatives are not considered. If the wind is unhelpful on sailing day, dolorous reality can lead to temper, frustration and even to sailing in conditions which logic indicates is an undesirable course.

Motor-sailing

Expertise in handling craft under sail varies with individuals and with the amount of experience they have had. One gazes with admiration at a craft being worked up-wind under sail in a narrow waterway, later to be berthed with quiet assurance at her moorings. Many are not in this category and the writer sees no reason why a skipper should not at any time start motor-sailing if to do so gives him assurance in conditions which are difficult. Such a policy may well be scornfully condemned by a few. No matter. When propulsion under sails brings pleasure and achievement, well and good. When certain manoeuvres demand of a skipper greater ability than he possesses, either in restricted waters or offshore, for the safety of his and other craft there are strong reasons for him to commence motoring.

Working to Windward

The trying task of keeping a DR plot when circumstances demand tacking to windward out of sight of land is frequently baffling to the inexperienced. It is probable that he will abandon it in despair. Precision of projection is needed. By its very intricacy it is prone to personal error and it must usually be carried out in a craft pounding heavily. Radio direction finding would appear a feasible alternative, yet it must be remembered that DF navigation must be regarded as supplementary to and never as a substitute for traditional navigation.

In Stanford's Sailing Companion a full explanation of the chartwork involved will be found; fortunately, there is an alternative. Young's Position Finder, a sturdy plastic instrument with a dial and cursor, will solve these tiresome triangles in seconds. It only remains for the navigator to plot on his chart the course and speed made good on each tack. It is a valuable instrument and a practical one too.

Leeway

Leeway is the most elusive of all factors with which a seaman must contend. Much has been written about its causes and effects and repetition here is unnecessary. It may be said, however, that it is better to over-estimate leeward drift than to underestimate it. Although it may be considered the act of a novice, there is one sound method of assessing the amount of leeway being made by any small craft. It is the *placing* of pieces of paper in the water over the transom. They remain visible for some distance astern and make it possible to fairly assess the angle between them and the fore and aft line of the craft. This angle is the amount of leeway the craft is making.

Leeway in Craft under Power

Leeway is not a factor which can be disregarded on a motor cruiser. Assuming moderate breezes, in all probability leeway will be negligable when the wind is within a couple of points of ahead, and when it is on most points abaft the beam. With the wind on any other bearing its effect has to be considered and, if necessary, due allowance made. Naturally great speed can reduce leeway to a negligable quantity whatever the direction from which the wind emanates. Again, minimal top hamper on a craft capable of any speed other than a very low one will produce the same effect. A large displacement can have a like advantageous effect in moderate conditions. It will be seen that there are a considerable number of variables when motor cruisers are being considered. Individual owners must determine for themselves the propensity of a craft to make leeway in certain conditions.

The order of using Charts

In many good navigational publications it will be read that one must always use the largest scale chart of any area. Of course one must, for one's own safety but, when sailing away from a shore and visual contact is lost, it is often sensible to change to a smaller scale chart which may well show both departure point and destination. Perspective is obtained. If one is checking DR positions with soundings of a helpfully contoured seabed, it will be better to retain the large scale chart as long as possible, for on it soundings will be both more prolific and more precise.

DF bearings are invariably difficult to lay off at sea and, provided a Stanford DF chart is produced for the area in which one is sailing, it should be obtained and used. These charts, whose lattices preclude the necessity of using parallel rulers, remove most of the navigator's difficulties in plotting DF bearings. They are plotting charts: not navigational ones. The navigator must therefore transfer positions so obtained from the DF chart to the navigational one. It is worth reiterating here; whenever a position is transferred from one chart to another, the transferred position must be doubly checked.

Approaching a distant coast, one must again transfer position from the smaller scale chart to the larger scale coastal one as soon as one reaches its limits. If an even larger scale chart is available as the coast is more nearly approached, one must in turn transfer to that one.

The Frequency of Calculating Position

The frequency of fixing position in open water on any type of craft is mainly dictated by the speed of the craft. The higher the speed, the more frequently one must either put a fix or note a DR position on the chart. For example, at speeds between 5 and 10 knots, hourly intervals will usually suffice. At speeds greater than those quoted, the intervals should be decreased. At lesser speeds the reverse applies. It is generally better to choose precise intervals for fixing position when possible. This practice gives ready information about speed being made good without the necessity of making calculations.

When either departing from or approaching a coast, the frequency of obtaining positions will be dictated by circumstances but generally intervals must be shortened.

Chart Notations on Passage

If charts are not to become an unrecognisable plethora of pencil lines and notations within a few hours of sailing, a precise system must be adopted. Fixes must be ringed; times must be written against every bearing, fix, DR position and adjustment or alteration of course; with these times the log reading must be noted. There is a generally adopted code, described in Stanford's Sailing Companion and other publications, of chart notations and one should not only learn them; their use must be a natural habit. In fact, all these notations of events should be recorded in the log book but, unless one has a large, experienced crew, log books are too often written up at the end of a passage and so they tend to become someone's private odyssey. For this reason chart notations assume great importance.

The use of Back Bearings

Sailing away from a shore with an empty horizon ahead, the value of back bearings, which are those taken over the stern, are sometimes overlooked. Making due allowance for tidal stream and leeway as one may well be doing, the frequently taken bearing of a terrestial object astern will indicate positively whether the allowances being made are adequate. So long as such an object is visible, bearings of it should be taken. Then when it is lost to view and one is sailing on DR only, allowances will have been adjusted to ensure that so far as is practicable, the course being made good is the desired one.

Night Navigation

Night navigation is very much easier than those who have yet to attempt it believe. At night, in clear weather, lighthouses, light vessels and light buoys can be pinpointed at greater range and with accuracy much better than in daylight hours. These advantages frequently offset the disadvantages of being able to see unlit features ashore. The masthead lights of merchant vessels foretell the sundry directions in which they are heading somewhat earlier than the visual appearance of the vessels themselves by day. Where a total distaste for night navigation exists, most of the passages described herein can be conducted in daylight hours, always provided one is prepared to sail at or before dawn.

Motor Cruisers v. Merchant Vessels

At sea when the collision regulations demand that one vessel must keep out of the way of another, in no sense does the small power craft have ascendency over his vastly bigger protagonist, the merchantman. The latter is met on equal terms and every Rule applicable to power-driven vessels within the regulations is equally applicable to the captain of a power cruiser. As explained in chapter 5 it remains wise and considerably more safe if a merchant vessel is allowed to continue untrammelled on its ponderous way.

Comfort at Sea in Motor Cruisers

It may well occur that the course line of a motor cruiser to a distant port brings wind and sea right on the beam. Excessive rolling and consequent discomfort results. There is much to be said for making two legs of a course, the first bringing the wind about a point forward of the beam and the second a similar amount abaft the beam. At least in theory, one cancels out the other and distance added is minimal.

PART 5 LANDFALLS

Arrivals Offshore in Daytime

When approaching a coast from seaward during daylight hours one endeavours to identify distant land as soon as it is sighted. Imperfect identification of hills and coast lines, common enough when skylines are vague, can lead to a wrong assumption of a boat's position. An alteration of course, wrong in itself, can result and this can later lead to total mystification. It is generally best to continue one's course, taking regular soundings, until absolute identification of shore features is obtained. A good fix being achieved, one can then decide one's future actions.

Approaching a Port in Sailing Craft

It is generally wise to hold up to windward when nearing a port, it being easy to drop downwind at the latter stages of an approach, yet difficult to claw to windward from a downwind position in what may be unfamiliar and shallow waters. If a tidal stream has greater strength than the wind, the craft should be held up-tide for similar reasons.

CHAPTER 7

Introduction To Passages

Samuel Taylor Coleridge is perhaps best remembered for his smoking of pot and The Rime of the Ancient Mariner. Had the particular slant occurred to him in one of his less opium shrouded moments, he might have given his famous Rime the sub-title, 'How not to sail in uncharted waters'. If only the central character of this underrated work had known something of nautical practices and had had a little common sense, how much easier his lot might have been. He would not have sailed into waters where there was every chance of becoming becalmed, he would have had a reserve water supply and he would not have mistaken an albatross for a pheasant. Years bought him knowledge the hard way. In seafaring, as in other skills, there are certain simple do's and don'ts which can save everyone quite a lot of trouble. This information is of course available to anyone who seeks it. One of the objects of the following section is to save the reader, in his voyaging, from wallowing in that Sargasso Sea of uncertainty which beset Coleridge's hoary hero. The writer has attempted to provide, in succint form, relevant data and important features applicable to the sundry passages outlined. In no sense does it seek to supplant, or even to supplement, the wealth of information on every nautical topic which may be found in Admiralty publications in particular and others in general. Rather does it pluck out from the plethora of words in print the important aspects of a passage. It remains for the yachtsman to pass from index to text of Admiralty publications to broaden his knowledge and deepen his appreciation.

Sea crossing are, in the opinion of the writer, rendered safer, less arduous and more enjoyable to the majority when their distances are reduced to practical minima. For example, if bound from Shoreham, Sussex to Guernsey in the Channel Islands, the writer would consider working westward along the English coast, thereafter to make the channel crossing from the Needles, Isle of Wight, or even from Poole Harbour. Of course, vastly experienced yachtsmen ply any waters they choose, proceeding directly if the venture interests them and the broad principles of seamanship are not set aside. Because they may choose to do so, it does not mean that the following advices contain elements of doubtful seamanship, or indeed that different tactics need be adopted as experience increases.

The passages which follow have the appearance of a series of short, sharp swoops across the seas surrounding our shores. This is quite intentional and they are so arranged for the following reasons: firstly, crossing our seaways roughly at right angles reduces the distance to be traversed to a practical minimum; second, the shorter the distance sailed out of sight of land, the less likelihood of dead reckoning positions being seriously in error;

third, sea lanes are generally crossed with maximum despatch. If in addition one can select a route or a course line which takes maximum advantage of natural and man made navigational aids, so much the better.

Voyages, unlike mystery tours, are generally undertaken to get from one place to another. Few families would wilfully undertake a long and arduous passage in order to reach a distant destination just for devilment. Rather would they prefer short passages, from haven to port to anchorage, to attain their planned objective. Fatigue is considerably lessened but the sense of achievement remains. The skipper who adopts these tactics is more likely to retain as his crew the same family members and friends. He has recognised that most itinerants are best treated gently at sea.

In each of the passages which follow there is a sub-title, 'Passage advices'. These describe briefly the manner in which the writer himself would conduct such a passage. Perhaps each passage would best be further sub-titled, 'One Man's technique'. Nevertheless all of them are supported by facts and information which no yachtsman can afford to disregard. Technique in this sense is a matter of a yachtsman of good common sense and with a knowledge of the sea utilising to his best advantage the sundry intelligence with which he is presented. There are, however, many roads to the same goal.

Finally, the writer emphasises that no two passages are ever identical, even though both are, shall we say, conducted by a ferry plying between Portsmouth, Hampshire and Ryde on the Isle of Wight, both being made within a few hours of each other. Identical passages extended beyond these minimal limits increase dissimilarities in proportion. For this very reason it is impossible to give precise passage instructions. The yachtsman must do his homework, glean every item of useful information available, and then sail. From the point, the best actions, like the best words, must be put in the best order to achieve the harmony of his passage. For the yachtsman, fresh horizons are the pointers to new landfalls and in preparation, assiduous planning and knowledge of the elements with which he must contend lies the secret of success.

Prevailing winds

Within the text of each passage the frequency of winds at various observation stations has been given. In each case the stations nearest to each passage have been used. Observations for the month of July have been chosen, they giving a fair indication of wind patterns for the summer months generally. Where wind frequency from any one direction is recorded as 10% or less, it has been included here under the heading 'Other'.

These observation stations are on land and so one can only say that their findings are a good guide to that which may be expected 20 or 30 miles away at sea. Nevertheless, they give useful information to all mariners, particularly to those under sail.

British observatories generally publish two series of observations, one during the forenoon and one in the afternoon. It must be borne in mind that afternoon observations have in them elements of sea breezes produced by the heating of the land when the sun has considerable altitude. The effect can be to deflect an existing breeze on a coast to a somewhat different direction, to accelerate an onshore breeze or to diminish an offshore one, to produce wind when it would otherwise be calm, although many miles offshore effects of this nature are non-existent. For this reason it may be said that morning observations are a better guide to the prevailing winds that those taken during afternoons.

The intensity and visual range of lights

A relatively new Hydrographic Office practice is to publish luminous ranges against navigational lights on their charts. Luminous range is a measure of a light's intensity; it is the range at which it would be seen assuming good visibility and that the curvature of the earth did not intercede. It is, shall we say, the theoretical range a light would be seen from a low-flying aircraft. It is left to the mariner to calculate from tables at what geographical (visual, in other words) range he will see a light and, assuming good visibility, this will entirely depend upon the height of his eyes above sea level.

Within the text of each passage which follows, the main visual navigational aids likely to be encountered are produced. Against each one will be found its luminous range, as published in the Admiralty List of Lights and Fog Signals. In addition, its geographical range is given, assuming a height of eye of 2m. This height, roughly 6'6", is considered to be a fair average of heights of eye of yachtsmen in sailing and motor craft alike. This is the range which a yachtsman may scribe round a lighthouse, a lightvessel or a Lanby buoy and say to himself – it is this range at which I should see this light, assuming the visibility is good.

These two ranges, luminous and geographical, when produced side by side as they are, give a yachtsman additional information. Let the reader ponder this fact: a light having a luminous range well in excess of its geographical range will, on a clear night, have the ability to produce a pronounced loom on the horizon, although the light itself is at too great a range to be seen. It is entirely feasible for a seaman to take bearings of such a loom far beyond the visual range of the light. Excellent examples are provided by Trinity House lightvessels. Their luminous ranges are commonly 22 miles, yet a yachtsman with a height of eye of 2m. will see them at a mere 10 miles.

Conversely, when the geographical range of a light exceeds its luminous range and both are relatively short, there is clear indication that the light has low intensity, low penetrability, and loom from it will be non-existent. Finally, it will be appreciated that, what ever the geographical range of a light, it will be the light with the high luminous range which has the power to penetrate haze and light fog at a range far in excess of that with a low one.

Traffic separation routes

All traffic within the lanes of the separation routes should be proceeding in the direction as indicated by the arrows. Craft crossing these lanes must do so at right angles or as near thereto as possible. Such action:

(a)   keeps crossing time to a minimum, and
(b)   leads to a clear encounter with other vessels within the lanes; i.e. the normal Steering and Sailing Rules apply to both vessels.

When sailing within the limits of the inshore shipping zones, it is important to note that craft will be encountered sailing in any direction.

On the following charlets, and on his working chart, the reader must note that, where any 'guide course line' crosses a traffic zone at any angle other than at a right angle, immediate steps must be taken to disregard the guide line and a new course set to cross the area of the lanes as quickly as possible (see (a) and (b) above).

CHAPTER 8

Outward Passages

PASSAGE NO. 1: LIZARD HEAD TO BREST, VIA CHENAL DU FOUR

Wind direction and frequency in percentages.

	S	SW	W	NW	N	NE	Calm	Other
Falmouth, 0900	–	14	18	19	13	–	4	32
Falmouth, 1500	26	20	12	14	–	–	1	27
Ushant	–	16	19	17	14	12	4	22
Brest	–	19	19	14	13	13	8	24

Main visual navigational aids

	Luminous range in miles	Visual range in miles Height of eye 2 metres
Lizard LH	29	20
l. Vierge LH	29	21
Le Four LH	18	14
Kermovan, front, LH	23	12
St. Mathieu Ldg. Lts. (158½°)	30	18
St. Mathieu Ldg. Lts. (158½°)	28	18
Kereon (Men-Tensel) LH	17	15
Ushant, Le Stiff LH	27	22
Ushant, Creac'h LH	39	20

Weather forecast area: Plymouth
Marine radio beacons: Channel West group, Round Island, Creac'h Point (Ushant).

General remarks

Falmouth to Brest is 125 miles and the distance to sail without visual navigational aids is perhaps 70 miles. These facts and the nature of the Brittany and Ushant coasts dictate that no one without considerable cruising experience on British coasts should attempt this passage. It remains challenging and interesting to a skipper who is supported by an experienced crew.

The lights on the French shores are many and generally powerful. Their spread is helpful to navigators. These qualities and the character of the coast indicate that a pre-dawn landfall is preferable. Good visibility is essential for both a landfall and the subsequent inshore passage to Brest and, if this prerequisite does not exist, a skipper must be prepared to heave to at sea until visibility improves. Although good visibility is forecast in the Plymouth sea area, it is no indication that poor visibility does not exist in the Ushant area, particularly latterly during the summer months.

Although one might sail from England in good weather, perhaps 24 hours later when a landfall is at hand, a weather change might bring foul conditions with westerlies predominating. The French coast then becomes a dangerous lee

shore and in these conditions too one must be prepared to remain at sea. The north Brittany coast may not be regarded as a true lee shore in a SW'ly gale but it must be borne in mind that typical frontal depressions are characterised by veering winds blowing themselves out from a W'ly or NW'ly direction.

Unless one is familiar with the inshore channels off the French coast, the writer would strongly advise a yachtsman to negotiate the Chenal du Four during daylight. Tidal streams in the channel reach 5 knots in places, thus a passage during the south-going stream is to be preferred, even to the extent of heaving to offshore until tidal streams are advantageous.

During a period of fine weather, some experienced yachtsmen will make for L'Abervrac'h, an easily negotiated and interesting little port to the rear of I. Vierge L.H. Spending the night there, they can then time departure so that tidal streams, daylight, good visibility and fair weather combine to make the passage to Brest an easy one.

Most cruising men avoid the passage outside Ushant for four main reasons: the distance to sail is increased considerably; tidal streams are strong within 6 miles of the western shore; shipping is profuse in the area; sea and swell can be formidable in fresh westerly winds.

Terrain: shore of departure

Lizard Point is a bold and precipitous promontory, ideal for both departures and landfalls. The lighthouse itself is a white tower 19m. in height at the eastern end of white painted buildings. These structures are on the cliff face at an altitude of about 50m.

Terrain: shore of landfall

The unfriendly lee shore of Brittany comprises moderately high cliffs punctuated with sandy beaches. Off it lie rocks, islets and shoals extending to a distance of 2 miles offshore in places. Pointe de Corsen is a sloping, steep cliff with a white hut, its lighthouse, surmounting it. Further south, Pointe St. Mathieu is equally as bold and is identifiable by its main light tower and sundry structures surrounding it. Both these headlands are readily identifiable as Chenal du Four is approached from the northward.

Ushant is relatively low, dark and craggy, a most unfriendly looking island. Its main light structures stand plainly above the skyline. One of the features of sailing in the inshore channels is the manner in which lighthouses and beacons appear to project

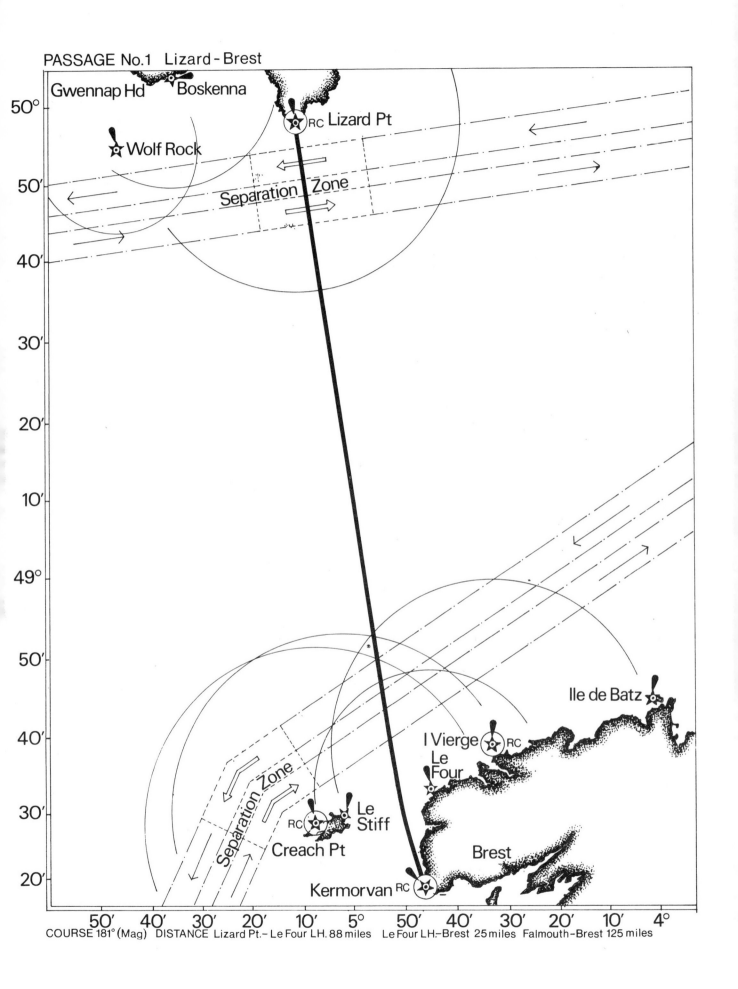

PASSAGE No.1 Lizard - Brest

Gwennap Hd   Boskenna

⊕RC Lizard Pt

☆ Wolf Rock

50°

50'

Separation Zone

40'

30'

20'

10'

49°

50'

Ile de Batz ☆

40'

I Vierge ⊕RC
Le Four

30'
RC ⊕ Le Stiff
Creach Pt

Brest

20'
Kermorvan RC ⊕

COURSE 181° (Mag)   DISTANCE Lizard Pt.– Le Four LH. 88 miles   Le Four LH.–Brest 25 miles   Falmouth–Brest 125 miles

50'   40'   30'   20'   5°   50'   40'   30'   20'   10'   4°

from the sea and shore like upheld fingers, reassuring and positive.

Tidal streams

From Lizard Point to Chenal du Four tidal streams must be assumed to be those published in the Admiralty Tidal Stream Atlas for the English Channel. The strengthening of both east- and west-going streams as the Ushant area is approached should be noted. As the land is closely approached, streams in excess of those published should be expected.

Tidal streams in the Chenal du Four are published in considerable detail on page 290 of the Channel Pilot, 1971. The streams in Chenal du Four are not in concert with the east- and west-going streams in the English Channel, an unusual feature which must be taken into consideration when planning a passage.

Soundings

A gradual increase in soundings occurs as the English coast is left behind and the passage progresses. This increase is so slow that it affords little assistance to the navigator, until the French coast is neared. A sounding of below 100m. merely indicates an approach but if one is to the eastward or westward of the course line, as a study of Admiralty chart 2643 indicates, vastly differing indications of position might be assumed. Clearly, unless position has been established by other means, such a sounding may well be a portent of danger close at hand.

Radio direction finding

Lizard, Round Island and Eddystone beacons should prove of assistance during the early stages of the passage but the ones to the southward will probably be at too great a range for clearly defined bearings. In mid-Channel a yachtsman is well served by radio beacons and, although all are at good range, reasonable fixes should be obtained in good conditions. As the French coast is neared, Ushant and I. Vierge should be heard strongly and their spread is such that good positions should be obtainable from them.

Passage advices

It is proposed that the course line is drawn from Lizard L.H. to pass Le Four L.H. to port at a range of 3 miles, thereafter to adjust course to place one's craft on the course of the leading bearings at Pte. de Kermovan and Pointe St. Mathieu, 158°(T), 167°(M). The initial course line will ensure that, in the absence of assistance from one's DF set, whether one is set to the east or west of it during passage, one is bound to make a sighting in clear weather. It is proposed that departure is so timed that one is, say, at 10 miles range from the lights on the French coast about an hour before dawn. One is then assured of initial fixes of high quality and any adjustment to course necessary can be made with assurance. Passage through the Chenal du Four will then be made in daylight, as will subsequent arrival in Brest.

On departure, regular back bearings of Lizard Point should be obtained to check one's allowances for tidal stream and leeway. They should be obtainable at perhaps 12 miles range during daylight and 20 miles at night. No indication of forward progress can be obtained from terrestial bearings and, even at this early stage, one's DF set should be brought into regular use, first to compare DF bearings of Lizard with those obtained visually and second to identify sundry other stations from which it is hoped bearings can be obtained.

Assuming progress of 5 knots, when Lizard Point is lost to view, hourly attempts should be made to fix position by DF but only if positions so obtained are absolute and conclusive should they override DR calculations made at similar intervals.

If on course, at night, Creac'h, Le Stiff and I. Vierge lights should be sighted at about the same time and position can be determined. Consideration should be given to an increase in allowance for tidal streams, and calculations may be made to determine at what time it will be possible to enter Chenal du Four at the start of the south-going stream in the Channel. Should it be found that one is widely off the course line at this time, rather than merely adjust one's course to make the position off Four L.H., it may be better to make a gross adjustment to bring one's craft back to the course line before the final approach to the channel is made.

Given clear weather, Pointe de Corsen should be sighted to the southward by the time Le Four L.H. is abeam to port, and Pointe St. Mathieu shortly afterwards. Thereafter, the passage resolves itself into an exercise in inshore pilotage in no way hazardous given good weather conditions. With the large scale Admiralty charts at hand, and the Channel Pilot, adequate information is provided to negotiate the coastal passage to Brest with relative ease.

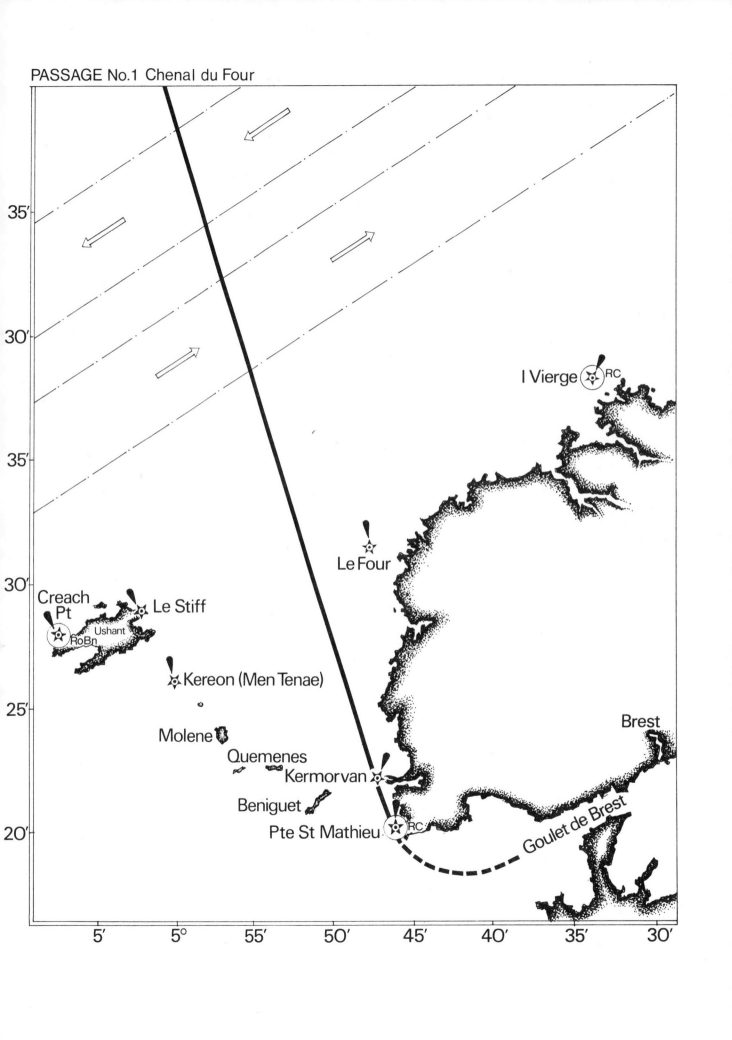

I Vierge ⊕RC

Le Four ⚝

Creach Pt ⚝
RoBn Ushant
Le Stiff ⚝

Kereon (Men Tenae) ⚝

Molene

Quemenes
Kermorvan ⚝

Beniguet
Brest

Pte St Mathieu ⚝RC

Goulet de Brest

35'
30'
35'
30'
25'
20'

5'   5°   55'   50'   45'   40'   35'   30'

PASSAGE NO.2: START POINT TO USHANT (CHENAL DU FOUR)

Wind direction and frequency in percentages.

	S	SW	W	NW	N	NE	Calm	Other
Plymouth, 0900	–	14	18	19	13	–	4	36
Plymouth, 1500	26	20	12	14	–	–	1	28
Ushant	–	16	19	17	14	12	4	22
Brest	–	19	19	14	13	13	8	24

Main visual navigational aids.

	Luminous range in miles	Visual range in miles Height of eye 2 metres
Start Point	25	19
I. Vierge LH	29	21
Le Four LH	18	14
Kermovan, front LH	23	12
St. Mathieu Ldg. Lts. (158½°)	30	18
St. Mathieu Ldg. Lts. (158½°)	28	18
Kereon (Men-Tensel) LH	17	15
Ushant, Le Stiff LH	27	22
Ushant, Creac'h LH	39	20

Weather forecast area: Plymouth
Marine radio beacons: Channel West Group, Creac'h Pt.
                                        (Ushant)

General remarks

Salcombe to Brest, the minimum to port distance, exceeds 130 miles. Minimum distance out of sight of visual navigational aids may exceed 90 miles. This is no passage for the tyro but is entirely feasible for a crew with considerable sailing experience.

The comments under this heading in Passage No.1 on page 00 should be studied as most have equal application here.

Terrain: shore of departure

From the SW, Start Point comprises five hillocks some 61m. in height, each uniform and distinct from each other. The lighthouse is on a lowering promontory which has an altitude of 34m., the structure being 28m. high and wite painted. Prawle Point some 3 miles westward is bold, sloping and craggy; Bolt Head, a similar distance further west, is dark and distinctive about 122m. high. Two radio masts close west of Start Point have a height of 263m.

Terrain: shore of landfall

See Passage No.1.

Tidal Streams

In substance, all remarks under this heading in Passage No.1 have equal application to this passage.

Soundings

A progressive increase in soundings occurs as south westing is made. It is so gradual that soundings will provide no assistance to the navigator throughout the whole channel crossing. In the latter stages of the passage it may be said that, in the absence of other information to provide indication of position, in no circumstances should soundings be allowed to fall below 100m.

Radio direction finding

Only Start Point and Eddystone will be of any assistance on departure, other beacons being a little too far away. In mid-channel, although at good ranges, sundry beacons surround a craft and bearings of three or more of them should give constant indication of position. Ushant and I. Vierge assume considerable importance south of the 49th parallel of latitude. Combined bearings should give DF positions of good quality.

Passage advices

A close study of charts, the Channel Pilot and tidal stream information is essential before sailing, so that the passage plan and tactics to be adopted in the event of unforeseen eventualities are clear in one's mind. It is suggested that course be drawn direct from Start Point to a position 300° (true), 4½ miles from Le Four L.H., with the intention of altering course in that position to the course (158° true, 167° Mag.) of the leading bearings directing one through Chenal du Four. It is proposed that a sailing time is chosen with a view to picking up the lights on the French coast perhaps an hour before daylight. The intent should be to traverse the Chenal du Four during daylight, preferably with a south-going tidal stream.

Back bearings of Start Point and later, Prawle Point, should be taken so long as they are visible and from the outset one's DF set should be in regular use. Assuming progress of 5 knots, hourly attempts should be made to fix position by DF, but only if positions so obtained are absolute and conclusive should they override DR calculations.

I. Vierge, a powerful light, should be sighted at maximum range on a clear night and so a position will be obtained but, if not, increasing allowance for tidal stream will be necessary at this time. Unless it is found that one is grossly off course, it would be sensible to continue until the lights of Ushant are sighted, and this may be 15 to 20 miles distant at this time.

With these lights in sight, position can be positively determined and course adjusted for the position off Le Four L.H. If it is found that position is markedly inshore, it would be wise to alter course grossly to bring one's vessel back to the original course line.

Assuming daylight as Le Four L.H. is approached, Ushant, Le Four L.H. and features on the French coast should combine to produce positions of sufficient quality to enable one to alter to the course of the leading bearings through Chenal du Four. Within a few miles of alteration of course both Pointe de Corsen and Pointe St. Mathieu should be sighted. Thereafter the passage is an inshore one and, presenting no marked problems to the competent and alert yachtsman, the large scale Admiralty charts and the Channel Pilot provide full information to guide the yachtsman to Brest.

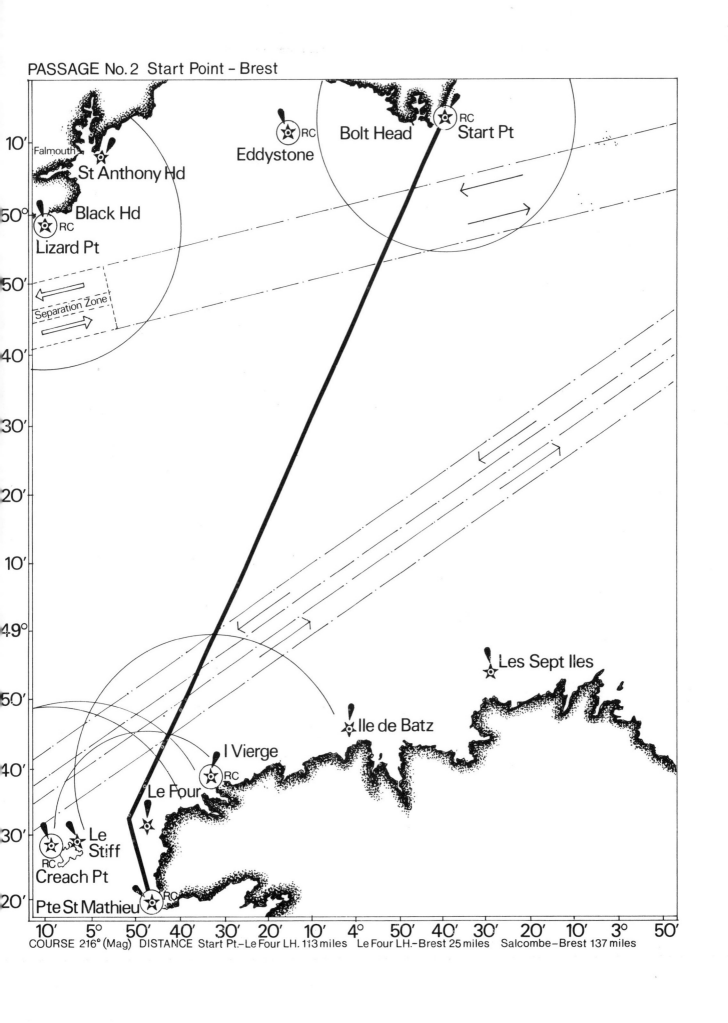

PASSAGE No. 2 Start Point – Brest

Falmouth
St Anthony Hd
Black Hd
Lizard Pt RC
Eddystone RC
Bolt Head
Start Pt RC
Separation Zone
Les Sept Iles
Ile de Batz
I Vierge RC
Le Four
Le Stiff
Creach Pt RC
Pte St Mathieu RC

COURSE 216° (Mag) DISTANCE Start Pt.–Le Four LH. 113 miles   Le Four LH.–Brest 25 miles   Salcombe–Brest 137 miles

PASSAGE NO.3: START POINT (FOR PORTS BETWEEN PENZANCE AND EXMOUTH INCLUSIVE) – CHANNEL ISLANDS

Wind direction and frequency in percentages

	S	SW	W	NW	N	E	Calm	Other
Plymouth, 0900	–	14	18	19	13	–	4	32
Plymouth, 1500	26	20	12	14	–	–	1	27
Jersey, 0900	–	14	37	–	–	–	1	48
Jersey, 1500	18	17	16	–	–	12	2	35

Main Visual navigational aids

	Luminous range in miles	Visual range in miles Height of eye 2 metres.
Berry Head LH	18	18
Start Point LH	25	19
Casquests LH	28	15
Guernsey, Platte Fougers LH	16	11
Guernsey, Les Hanois LH	23	14

Weather forecast area: Portland
Marine radio beacons: Channel West and Channel East groups.
Aero radio beacons: Berry Head, Guernsey.

General remarks

It is proposed that yachtsmen setting out from ports to the west of Start Point use that headland for departure. A night stop in Salcombe reduces strain on crew members. This similarly applies to those who sail from havens between Start Point and Exmouth.

Although the west coast of Guernsey is not an inviting one, as a study of the local chart will show, the southwest extremity has good features. They are: high land, a good lighthouse and a useful aero radio beacon. These combine to make Les Hanois preferable for a landfall in the Channel Islands when departing from Start Point.

Terrain: shore of departure

Start Point L.H. stands on a hillock 34m. high on the foreshore. The light structure is of white painted granite 28m. in height. Viewed from the SE it is below the skyline, which comprises rounded hills some 115m. in altitude. Close west of Start Point are two radio masts 263m. high.

Terrain: shore of landfall

From the west, Guernsey is wedge-shaped in appearance with high land to the south dropping in altitude towards the northern shore. The cliffs to eastward of Les Hanois L.H. are steep and craggy, with an altitude of about 76m. The lighthouse lies about 1' westward of Pleinmont Point and is a round grey granite tower 30m. high standing on Les Hanois rocks which have an elevation of about 6m. Numerous off-lying dangers exist offshore to a distance of about 2'.

Tidal streams

Complete information of tidal streams will be found in the Admiralty Tidal Stream Atlasses for the English Channel, and the Channel Islands. Other valuable information will be found on pages 455 and 456 of the Channel Pilot, 1971. It must be noted that latterly during the south west-going stream a strong inshore set occurs to the west of Les Hanois L.H.

Soundings

On this passage soundings render no assistance to the navigator until the Hurd Deep is encountered when Les Hanois L.H. is about 18 miles distant. Then soundings increase sharply from about 75m. to about 120m. for a distance of 2½ miles, and they are then restored to about their previous depths. The seabed rises precipitously to the rocks and ledges off the west coast of Guernsey and soundings alone give little warning of their presence.

Radio direction finding

The beacons at Berry Head, Start Point and Eddystone assume importance early during the passage. As the Channel Islands are approached, Roches Douvres, Guernsey aero beacon and Casquets will be of increasing value. La Corbiere, Jersey, should be used with caution if a bearing of it must be drawn over or close to Guernsey. In mid-channel all the former beacons combine to make multi-bearing fixes a possibility.

Passage advices

It is proposed that a course line be drawn from Start Point to a position 2 miles SW of Les Hanois L.H. Earlier courses may be drawn to join this line. A pre-dawn arrival off Les Hanois L.H. in clear weather is preferable and then, assuming St. Peter Port is one's first goal, a mid-morning arrival is a probability.

Start Point may be lost to view at about 6 miles in daylight. Back bearings of it should be taken as long as possible to check allowances in one's course. At this early time DF bearings should be taken of Start Point, visual and radio results being compared. Other beacons should be sought and identified. With the land lost to view one must navigate some 35 miles on DR positions only, supported where possible by, say, hourly fixes by DF. As the Hurd Deep is approached, frequent soundings must be taken to locate the charted depth contours because these, in effect, give the navigator a fairly accurate NE–SW position line. A D.F. bearing of Guernsey aero beacon which is crossed with this position line should give good indication of position. Within a few miles of crossing the Hurd Deep, Les Hanois light should be sighted. If it is not sighted at maximum range, its bearing can be combined with the information obtained from Hurd Deep to obtain a reasonable fix. D.F. bearings of Roches Douvres and Casquets should give equal support. At this time one must adjust course if necessary to pass Les Hanois L.H. at the desired distance. In the event of poor visibility preventing a sighting of Les Hanois it would be wise to stand off at least 5 miles to the southward and, using D.F. bearings for fixes, attempt a later approach on the south coast. Sounding continuously, a safe landfall should be achieved if visibility exceeds one mile. A landfall having been made, the passage resolves itself into coastal pilotage to St. Peter Port.

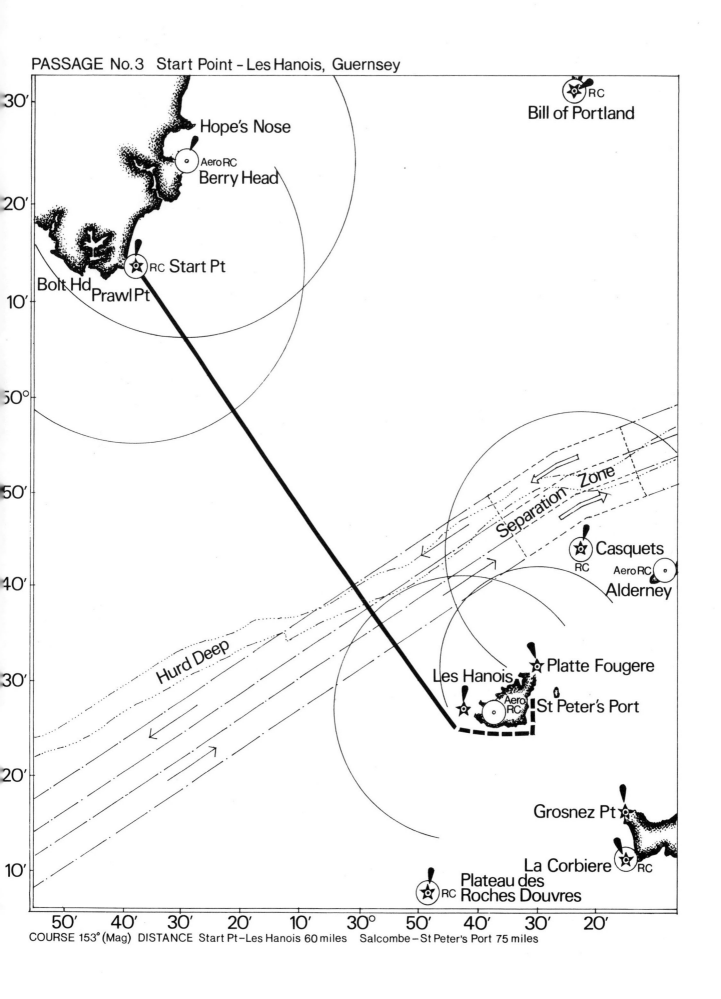

PASSAGE No.3 Start Point – Les Hanois, Guernsey

Bill of Portland RC

Hope's Nose

Aero RC

Berry Head

Bolt Hd
Prawl Pt

RC Start Pt

30°

50°

Separation Zone

Casquets
RC

Aero RC

Alderney

Hurd Deep

Les Hanois

Platte Fougere

Aero RC

St Peter's Port

Grosnez Pt

La Corbiere RC

Plateau des
RC Roches Douvres

COURSE 153° (Mag) DISTANCE Start Pt–Les Hanois 60 miles   Salcombe–St Peter's Port 75 miles

PASSAGE NO.4: POOLE HARBOUR TO CHANNEL ISLANDS

Wind direction and frequency in percentages

	S	SW	W	NW	E	NE	Calm	Other
Bill of Portland		20	22	15	–	–	2	40
Jersey 0900	–	14	37	–	–	–	1	48
Jersey 1500	18	17	16	–	12	–	2	35

Main Visual navigational aids

	Luminous range in miles	Visual range in miles Height of eye 2 metres.
Anvil Point LH	24	16
Cap de la Hague LH	24	17
Alderney LH	24	15
Casquests LH	28	15

Weather forecast area: Wight and E section of Portland
DF chains: Channel centre and Channel west.
Aero DF beacons: Hurn (Bournemouth), Alderney.

General remarks

Poole Harbour is well placed as a departure port for the Channel Islands, and for the return passage. Craft having come from the eastwards for a crossing from the Poole area should consider anchoring in Studland Bay overnight before commencing the passage. No one without local knowledge or previous experience should attempt to navigate between Alderney and the French coast, in the Alderney Race. In certain conditions of wind and tide it can be dangerous, even lethal, to small craft. The Casquests having been passed well clear on the port hand, one can choose one's courses with confidence.

Terrain: shore of departure

First Handfast Point with its bluff facade, then Anvil Point and lighthouse with identifiable high land behind it, and a little to the westward the steep-to St. Alban's Head with conspicuous radio masts northward of it, all combine to make a departure point of considerable value in clear weather.

Terrain: shore of landfall

See Passage No.5 under this heading.

Tidal streams

When local tidal stream phenomena have been cleared and Anvil Point is well abaft the beam, it must be assumed that streams on passage will be those published in the Admiralty Tidal Stream Atlasses for the English Channel and for Channel Islands, the very slightly stronger flows to the westward in the English Channel being observed. A strengthening of the tidal flow must be expected as Casquests is approached but, unless the islets are approached closely, they should not be excessive. Close westwards of the Casquests violent eddies occur at certain states of the tide. Over the Casquests S.W. bank, which extends from 2 to 6 miles SSW of the lighthouse, heavy overfalls occur.

Soundings

No valuable navigational guide will be obtained from soundings until Hurd Deep is encountered, some 8 miles north of the Casquets if on course. This sea valley is fairly steep-sided and, using the charted depth contours which define it, the mariner can obtain from his sounding equipment valuable indication of position. Thereafter, soundings reduce as land is approached.

Radio direction findings

Bill of Portland and St. Catherine's radio beacons should be heard clearly shortly after sailing. The aero beacon at Hurn Airport should have similar clarity but there will be a possibility of land effects from the Studland/Swanage coast. Bearings of Casquets and Alderney radio beacons will increase in quality and reliability as southing is made and, although Fort de l'ouest (Cherbourg) radio beacon is well outside its nominal range it too should provide useful information. Bearings of the latter should be treated as suspect when within 10 miles the Casquets, due to the possibility of land effects. Given good radio conditions, reasonable fixes may well be possible from mid-Channel onwards.

Passage advices

It is proposed that course is set when in a position 1 mile due east of Handfast point, to pass Casquets 2 miles to port, thereby keeping in soundings over 60m. and avoiding the violent eddies which occur close westward.

Adjusting course as necessary to maintain the intended track until the Dorset coast is cleared, useful back bearings and cross bearings should be obtainable from the coastline astern up to a range of perhaps 8 miles and more in clear weather. By this time St. Catherines and Bill of Portland radio beacons should be identified quite clearly. One must now listen for Casquets, Alderney and Fort de l'Ouest (Cherbourg) radio beacons; their value will increase markedly as southing is made. Given good radio conditions, useful fixes may be obtainable in mid-Channel, but no assistance will be obtained from soundings.

Greater reliance being placed upon D.F. bearings of Casquets as it is closed, bearings of Fort de l'Ouest should be regarded as suspect when they are 130° (Mag.) or less.

At night, at maximum range, Casquets light should be sighted at 15 miles. A bearing of the light or lighthouse, or indeed a good D.F. bearing in poor visibility, assumes great importance because at about 8 miles, if on course, soundings will increase markedly when Hurd Deep is encountered, to reduce sharply some 3 miles further on when it is cleared. Combined bearings and soundings at this time will give positions of good quality providing the means by which, by adjustment or alteration of course, the Casquets can be rounded with confidence.

Watching position closely for strengthening tidal streams as the Casquets are approached, constant bearings and soundings throughout will ensure that soundings are not allowed to reduce below 60m. during and after rounding the Casquets. By this means the violent eddies to the westward of Casquets are avoided and the overfalls which occur over Casquets S.W. Bank are given a reasonably wide berth. The latter bank having been cleared, one can with confidence set any desired course southward.

PASSAGE No.4 Poole Harbour - Channel Islands

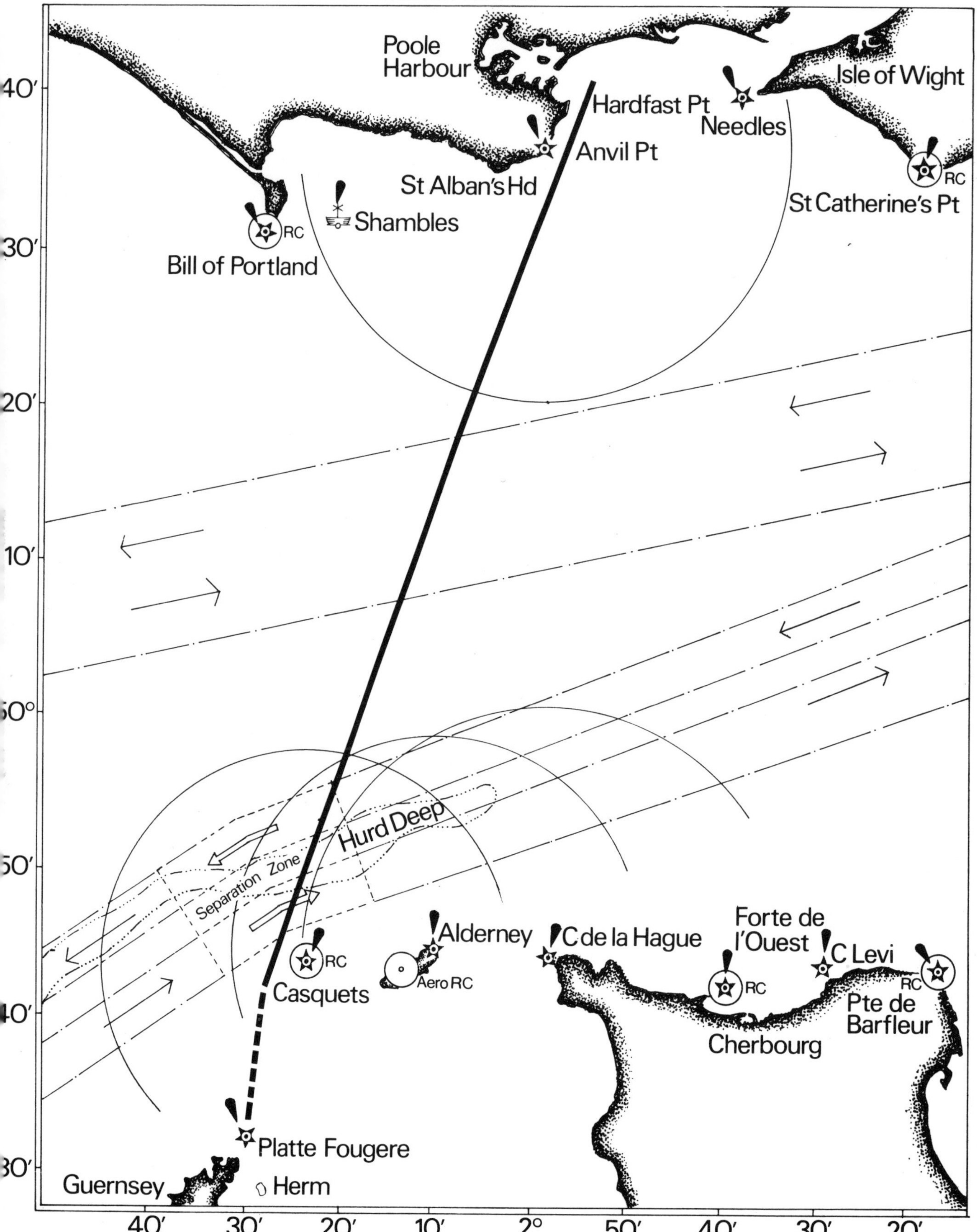

Poole Harbour

Isle of Wight

Hardfast Pt

Needles

Anvil Pt

St Alban's Hd

St Catherine's Pt

Shambles

40'

30'

20'

10'

Bill of Portland

RC

60°

50'

40'

30'

Separation Zone

Hurd Deep

Casquets

RC

Alderney

Aero RC

C de la Hague

Forte de l'Ouest

C Levi

RC

RC

RC

Pte de Barfleur

Cherbourg

Platte Fougere

Guernsey

Herm

40'   30'   20'   10'   2°   50'   40'   30'   20'

COURSE 208° (Mag) DISTANCE Start Pt-Casquets 55 miles Port to Port: Poole Harbour-CI Yacht Marina Guernsey 75 miles

PASSAGE NO.5: SOLENT AREA TO CHANNEL ISLANDS

Wind direction and frequency in percentages

	S	SW	W	NW	E	NE	Calm	Other
Portsmouth	–	18	20	20	–	–	2	40
Bill of Portland	–	20	22	15	–	13	2	28
Jersey, 0900	–	14	37	–	–	–	1	48
Jersey, 1500	18	17	16	–	12	–	2	35

Main visual navigational aids

	Luminous range in miles	Visual range in miles Height of eye 2 metres
Needles LH	17	13
St. Catherines LH	30	16
Anvil Point LH	24	16
Cap de la Hague LH	24	17
Alderney LH	24	15
Casquets LH	28	15

Weather Forecast area:	Wight.
DF chains:	Channel centre and channel west.
Aero DF beacon:	Hurn (Bournemouth), Alderney.

General remarks

The writer is of the opinion that, for all craft normally berthed anywhere on the south coast between Lymington and Newhaven, the Needles LH makes a good departure point. Should wind direction be unfavourable from a southwesterly point, there is much to be said for working to Studland Bay or Portland Harbour on a west-going stream, thereby putting the wind at a slightly kinder angle for the following day. No one without local knowledge or previous experience should attempt to navigate between Alderney and the French coast, in the Alderney Race. In certain conditions of wind and tide it can be dangerous, even lethal, to small craft. The Casquets having been passed on the port hand, one cane choose one's courses with confidnece.

Terrain: shore of departure

Although Needles LH will fairly quickly disappear, the white Needles rocks with a high white cliff behind should be retained in sight for perhaps 10 or 15 miles in good visibility. Anvil Head should show boldly to the westward during this period.

Terrain: shore of landfall

Casquets is merely a collection of low rocks. The highest of them has an elevation of 14m. and this is surmounted by the lighthouse 23m. high, together with two other stone towers. It may well be that in daytime the highest point of Alderney, some 95m., will be sighted at the same time or before Casquets L.H.

Tidal streams

Once clear of the Needles it must be assumed that tidal streams are those indicated in the Admiralty Tidal Stream Atlasses for the English Channel, the marginally stronger westward flow being noted. A strengthening of tidal flow must be expected as Casquets is approached but, if the recommended track is followed, it should not exceed the average flow

encountered in most parts of the Solent. Streams having a velocity of perhaps 7 knots exist amongst and close about Casquets islets. Immediately westward of Casquets violent eddies occur at certain states of the tide and heavy overfalls exist over the Casquets S.W. Bank, a few miles to the southward.

Soundings

Soundings are of little value until the Hurd Deep is crossed, some 12 miles NE of Casquets. This is a valuable navigational guide. Thereafter soundings decrease progressively in a helpful manner.

Radio direction finding

Although St. Catherine's will be powerful and close on the port quarter on departure, little useful information may result until some 20 miles has been traversed. From this point onwards, Bill of Portland, Hurn and St. Catherine's may give useful fixes if radio conditions are good. As the passage progresses Casquets and Alderney will increase in volume as range is decreased although, in the latter stages of the passage when Casquets is close, St. Catherine's is beyond nominal range, Bill of Portland is approaching that condition and Fort de l'Ouest (Cherbourg), having become increasingly useful as southing is made, must be regarded as suspect within about 10 miles of Casquets.

Passage advices

Course is best drawn from the Needles to pass Casquets L.H. 2 miles to port, thereby keeping in soundings over 60m. and avoiding the local strong swirls and eddies in the immediate vicinity. A pre-dawn sighting of Casquets and Alderney lights is proposed.

At the outset, fixes from the combined bearings of the Needles and Anvil Head should be possible in clear weather. By this time one should have identified St. Catherine's, Hurn and Bill of Portland radio beacons. At this early stage regular attempts to locate Casquets, Alderney and Fort de l'Ouest radio beacons should be made, although the latter is well beyond its nominal range. Albeit the value of bearings from any of these beacons will be small within 20 miles of the British coast, the possibility of reasonable DF fixes exists in mid-Channel. Greater reliance can be placed upon the bearings obtained from the three southerly beacons as southing is made.

At night, at maximum range, Casquets light will be sighted at about 15 miles range. At about this time visual cross bearings of Casquets and Alderney lights should be obtained. Notwithstanding, frequent regular soundings as Casquets is approached will locate the northern limit of Hurd Deep and this, coupled with either a visual or DF bearing of the Casquets L.H. should give the navigator a fair fix. Adjustment of course can then be made if necessary. Watching closely for strengthening tidal streams as the islets are neared, when rounding the Casquets, soundings of 60m. or more are best maintained. This gives reasonable assurance of clearing strong eddies and heavy overfalls. Remaining in 60m. or more until Casquets S.W. Bank is well clear to port, one can then with confidence set any desired course southward.

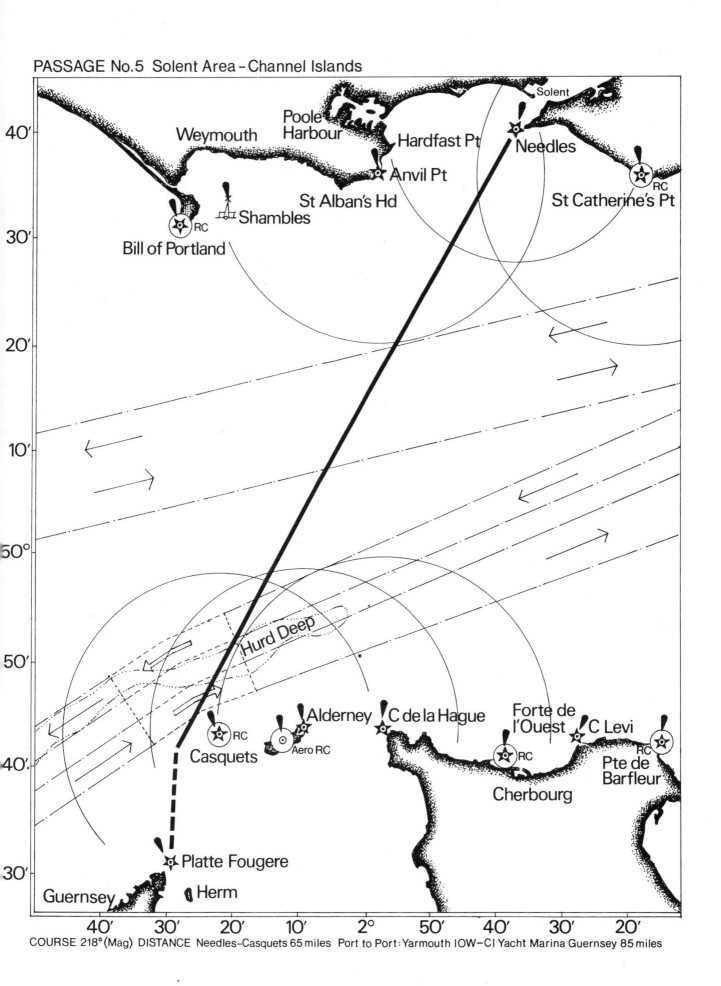

PASSAGE No.5 Solent Area – Channel Islands

40'

Weymouth
Poole Harbour
Hardfast Pt
Needles
Solent

Anvil Pt
St Catherine's Pt RC

30'
St Alban's Hd
Shambles
Bill of Portland RC

20'

10'

50°

50'

50'

Hurd Deep

Alderney
C de la Hague
Forte de l'Ouest
C Levi

Casquets RC
Aero RC
Cherbourg RC
Pte de Barfleur RC

40'

30'
Platte Fougere
Guernsey
Herm

40'   30'   20'   10'   2°   50'   40'   30'   20'

COURSE 218°(Mag) DISTANCE Needles–Casquets 65 miles Port to Port: Yarmouth IOW–CI Yacht Marina Guernsey 85 miles

PASSAGE NO.6: SOLENT AREA TO CHERBOURG

Wind direction frequency in percentages

	SW	W	NW	E	NE	Calm	Other
Portsmouth	18	20	20	–	–	2	40
Cherbourg	23	21	–	11	12	8	25

Main visual navigational aids

	Luminous range in miles	Visual range in miles Height of eye 2 metres
Needles LH	17˙	13
St. Catherines LH	30	16
Anvil Pt. LH	24	16
Cap de la Hague LH	20	17
Fort de l'quest LH	23	12
C. Levi LH	20	15
Pte. de Barfleur LH	27	20

Weather forecast area: Wight.
DF chains: Channel centre and Channel east.
Aero DF beacons: Hurn (Bournemouth), Alderney.

General remarks

Skippers of sailing craft berthed in the Solent area between Hurst Castle and Chichester harbour should consider using the Needles L.H. for a departure point. Prevailing winds in the English Channel can be put at a kinder angle on passage by so doing. A night stop in Lymington or Yarmouth, I.O.W., before sailing, reduces fatigue and time under way. Nab Tower L.H. can be considered as a departure point when easterly winds are in evidence, but as they are often short-lived one must make the decision and put it into effect forthwith. Power craft can usually select either departure point.

Terrain: shore of departure

Needles L.H. on the outermost of the white, vertical, serrated Needles rocks which are some 120m. high, is a circular granite tower 33m. in height which has a red band and a red top. The white Needles rocks and the high white cliff behind them are more readily discerned than the lighthouse and from seaward they are thrown into relief by the dark hills inland. The latter rise to an altitude of about 180m.

Terrain: shore of landfall

There are no cliffs on the northern coast of the Cherbourg peninsular. The hills inland rise to about 180m., sloping upwards from the shoreline. The rise to the uplands is more marked in the Cap de la Hague area than in that of Gatteville-Barfleur. Immediately behind and above Cherbourg are clustered while blocks of flats which show cleary particularly when the sun is shining. These and the township below should be identifiable at perhaps 6 miles in clear weather. Many off-lying dangers exist on this coast, mainly eastward of Cherbourg.

Tidal streams

The Admiralty Tidal Stream Atlas for the English Channel, supported in larger scale by that of the Channel Islands, contain all the information required by yachtsmen. Within perhaps 10 miles of the French coast both east- and west-going stream strengthen considerably. Many, like the writer, would aver that the spring rates exceed the $3\frac{1}{2}$ knots published by the Hydrographic Office. Greater velocities may be expected off Cap de la Hague.

Soundings

A gradual increase in soundings, not of marked value to a yachtsman, occurs during the first 10 miles on passage. Thereafter they level out and become wholly featureless for the major part of the passage. Shorewards from a distance of about 11 miles off Cherbourg they reduce gradually from about 75m. to the 50m. contour. Between Cap de la Hague and Gattville-Barfleur, 40m. soundings can be obtained from 2 miles offshore to a mere 2 cables, a fact which yachtsmen should mark well.

Radio direction finding

St. Catherine's, Bill of Portland and Hurn (Bournemouth) have value in the earlier stages of the passage. Quite frequently, although well beyond its nominal range, Fort de l'Ouest (Cherbourg) can be heard clearly off the Isle of Wight. In mid-Channel the yachtsman is well served by surrounding beacons and, given good conditions, multi-bearing fixes should be possible. Alderney aero beacon is of great value. Fort de l'Ouest beacon assumes increasing value as southing is made, particularly for homing, but it would be unwise to place reliance upon bearings of Casquets when within about 15 miles of the French coast.

Passage advices

Course may be drawn direct from the Needles L.H. to Cherbourg. Apart from the quality of the lights on the French coast, and Fort de l'Ouest radio beacon, it may be said that Cherbourg has the asset of being roughly in the middle of a peninsular some 26 miles in breadth. A pre-dawn arrival offshore is preferable for sailing craft but those with a speed potential in excess of 5 knots may prefer a very early start to make an afternoon arrival.

On departure frequent back bearings of the Needles and later of the high land on the Isle of Wight will assist in ensuring that course allowances are adequate. Unless visibility is very good, useful bearings of St. Catherine's L.H. and Anvil Point are not usually possible. At this early stage one must listen for surrounding radio beacons, including Fort de l'Ouest.

Thereafter one is working on DR positions in the main, supported by (say) hourly DF fixes. Great expectations should not be placed upon DF results as in mid-channel many of the beacons are at fair range; DF results often vary with the experience of the operator. The DF bearing of Fort de l'Ouest should increase in reliability as the range is closed.

If on course at night in clear weather, both Cap de la Hague and Pte. de Baffleur lights should be sighted at about 14 miles with the loom of Fort de l'Ouest light visible. At this time or a little later, given reasonable conditions, position will have been established visually and course adjusted as necessary.

Frequent bearings of Fort de l'Ouest, either visual or DF, will now be essential to ensure adequate allowance is being made for the strengthening tidal streams. Passing CH1 buoy closely will contribute towards a confident passage into the western entrance to the port of Cherbourg. There is no navigational reason why the eastern entrance should not be used, but when approaching the port from seaward, the western entrance is to be preferred.

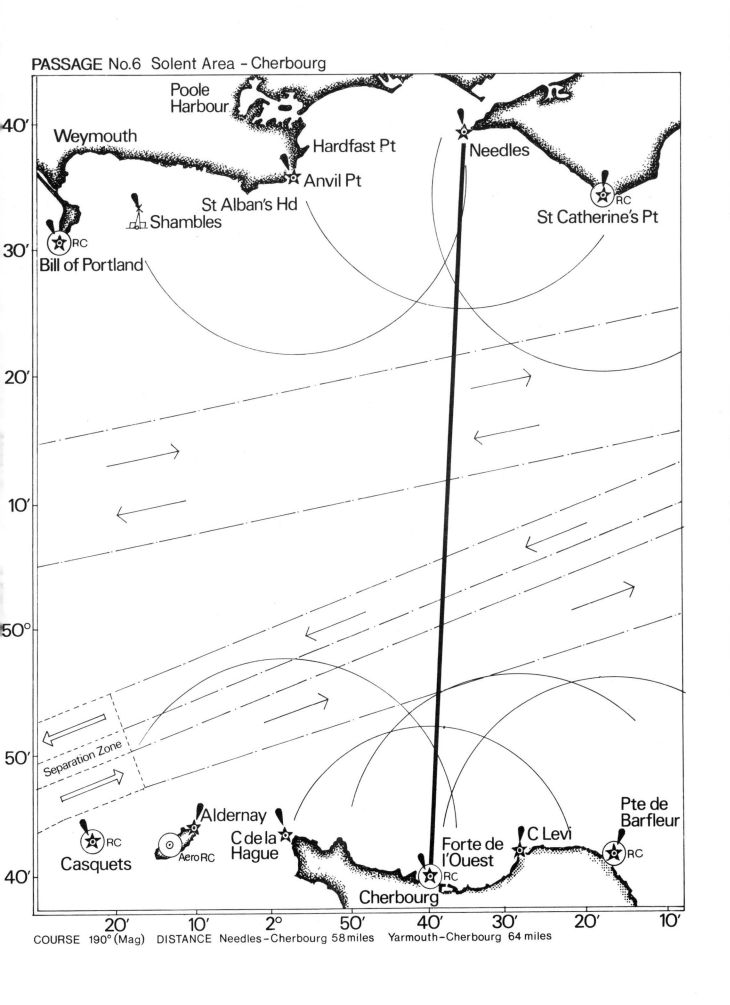

PASSAGE No.6 Solent Area - Cherbourg

COURSE 190°(Mag) DISTANCE Needles–Cherbourg 58 miles Yarmouth–Cherbourg 64 miles

PASSAGE NO.7: SOLENT/SPITHEAD AREA AND CHICHESTER TO LE HAVRE

Wind direction and frequency in percentages

	SW	W	NW	N	NE	Calm	Other
Portsmouth	18	20	20	–	–	2	40
Cap de la Heve	16	23	16	15	13	3	14

Main visual navigational aids

	Luminous range in miles	Visual range in miles Height of eye 2 metres
Nab Tower LH	20	13
St. Catherine's LH	30	16
Owers Lanby buoy	21	10
Cap d'Antifer LH	30	26
Cap de la Heve LH	26	25
Le Havre LH	20	11

Weather forecast area: Wight
DF chains: Channel centre and Channel east, Nab Tower and Fort de l'Ouest

General remarks

The high land on the Isle of Wight might appear to make that shore preferable for a departure point, but the Nab Tower is better. It is more direct and local aberrations of tidal streams close inshore are avoided. For a landfall on the French coast in summer, Cap d'Antifer has much to commend it. During these months Le Havre L.V. is usually replaced by a buoy but only Notices to Mariners give precise information about its presence or absence. Cap d'Antifer is bold, it has a good radio beacon and, as soon as position has been fixed from it, one can bear away for the entrance channel to Le Havre.

Terrain: shore of departure

In good visibility in daytime it might well be that Nab Tower is effectively lost to view astern at about 6 miles. Even before this time it is improbable that any useful promontories or landmarks on the Isle of Wight will be identifiable, although the high land could well be hazily visible at considerable range.

Terrain: shore of landfall

The whole French coastline, from eastwards of Cap d'Antifer to Le Havre itself, has the virtue of possessing steep chalk cliffs nearly 100m. in height. Valuable to seamen throughout daylight hours, in a westering sun the white faces of these cliffs are illuminated in a manner which may be imagined. Cap d'Antifer is a grey stone tower of considerable height. The water tower close southward of Cauville some 6 miles down the coast from Cap d'Antifer assists navigation. Cap de la Heve is a high white-painted tower; close to the SW of it is a disused lighthouse.

Tidal streams

Once in the English Channel, clear of the Wight area, tidal streams must be assumed to be those published in the Admiralty tidal stream Atlas for the English Channel. In no sense do the streams pose extraordinary problems for the navigator on this passage. Tidal streams set across the entrance to Le Havre, yet with no marked velocity, and diagrams opposite page 582 in the Admiralty Channel Pilot effectively portray them.

Soundings

During the main part of the crossing, soundings will be of no real assistance to the navigator until the French coast is approached. Even then, only the gradual reduction in soundings will give indication that a coastline lies ahead. A 40m. sounding can be obtained at 8 or 18 miles from Cap d'Antifer. However, once soundings decrease below this depth, the gradual clear indication that the coast is near at hand occurs.

Radio direction finding

As it is improbable that a cruising man will make the passage in foggy conditions, Nab Tower radio beacon which only operates in low visibility can be regarded as unavailable. In consequence only three radio beacons have real value on this passage: Catherine's, Barfleur and Cap d'Antifer, the latter being quite the most important. Should Le Havre L.V. be on station then its radio beacon will have equal value to that of Cap d'Antifer. It should not be overlooked that Pte. de Ver radio beacon, whose nominal range is some 10 miles short of one's course line towards Cap d'Antifer, might give a little supporting evidence of position as the French coast is approached.

Passage advices

It is proposed that the course is drawn directly from the Nab Tower to Cap d'Antifer LH so that, whether position is reasonably determined either 15 or 5 miles off the French coast, one can alter to the southward towards the buoyed channel of Le Havre with confidence.

Back bearing of Nab Tower should be frequently taken as long as possible to check allowances in one's course. Should this area be traversed in the dark hours, the light or loom of Owers Lanby buoy should be visible for perhaps 20 miles after departure from Nab Tower, hence fixes between the two will be possible for most of the period. Some 13 miles outward from the Nab, soundings increase sharply from about 30m. to about 65m.

Thereafter, one must work on DR Positions for a minimum of 35 miles when the maximum visual range of Cap d'Antifer light is encountered. During this period, although one must at, say, hourly intervals endeavour to fix position from surrounding radio beacons, it may be only the most experienced, and even then in good radio conditions, who will achieve worthwhile results. Increasing confidence may be placed upon DF bearings of Cap d'Antifer as it is closed.

If, when within range, no sighting of Cap d'Antifer light has been obtained, in view of the steady decrease in soundings as the French coast is approached, they may be put to good effect. Provided good results are being obtained from Cap d'Antifer radio beacon, one may home on the beacon and, when soundings drop to 26m., course may be altered direct for Cap de la Heve. Sounding as one proceeds because they will be the best guide to the proximity of the coast, one can gradually close it and, it is hoped, subsequently sight it. A fix from terrestrial objects having been obtained, one can square away for the entrance to the buoyed channel into Le Havre.

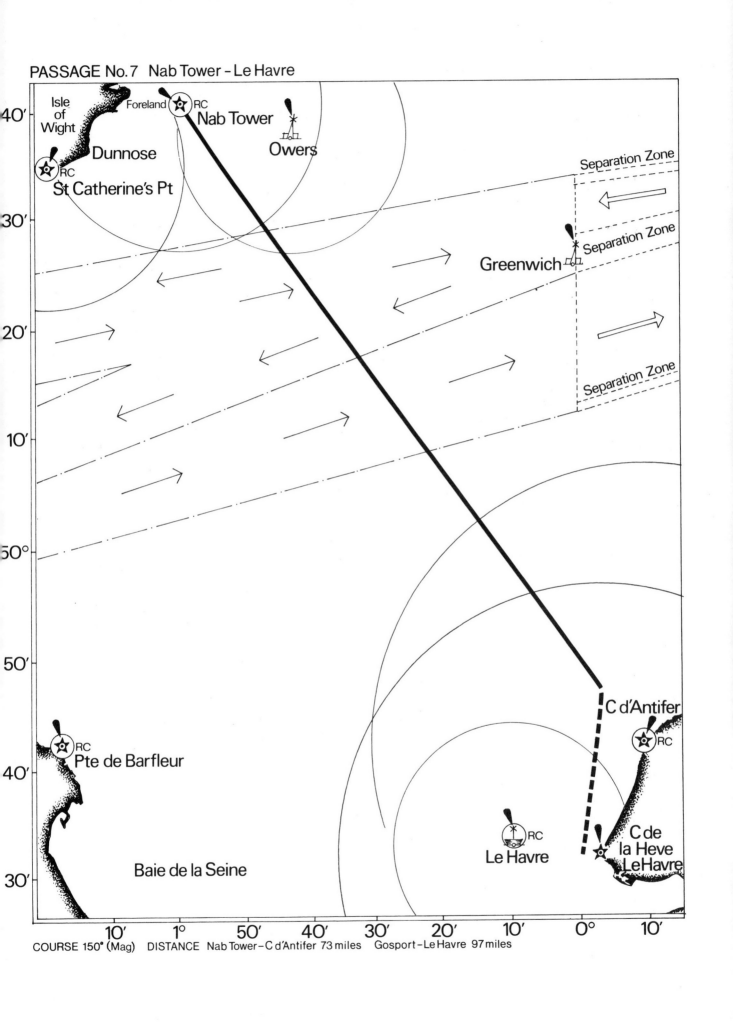

COURSE 150° (Mag)   DISTANCE Nab Tower–C d'Antifer 73 miles   Gosport–Le Havre 97 miles

PASSAGE NO.8: LITTLEHAMPTON/SHOREHAM/BRIGHTON/NEWHAVEN TO DIEPPE

Wind direction and frequency in percentages

	SW	W	NW	E	Calm	Other
Dungeness 0900	26	15	16	13	1	29
Dungeness 1500	16	33	13	11	+	27

Main visual navigational aids

	Luminous range in miles	Visual range in miles Height of eye 2 metres
Newhaven Breakwater LH	12	11
Beachy Head LH	24	14
Royal Sovereign Lt. Tower	28	14
Greenwich Lanby buoy	21	10
Pte. d'Ailly LH	30	23
Dieppe — Jetee Ouest Hd. LH	12	10

Weather forecast area: Wight, bordering on Dover.
DF chain: Channel East.
Aero radio beacon: Dieppe.

General remarks

Advantages exist in using Newhaven as the departure port for craft setting sail from ports on the coast between Littlehampton eastwards to Newhaven. They are: improvement of terrestial aids on the departure shore, enhanced DF facilities, reduction of distance on passage and the crossing of sea lanes nearly at right angles. Pte. d'Ailly is useful for a landfall and in general the passage is uncomplicated.

Terrain: shore of departure

In most respects Newhaven is featureless from seaward. The breakwater light tower may be still identifiable 4 to 5 miles after departure. The coast from Seaford Head eastwards to Beachy Head is distinctive, with its steep-to, chalk-faced cliffs and the latter headland rising to some 160m. Beachy Head L.H. is round and grey, with a red band in the middle and a red top. Detached from the headland as it is and located at sea level, its height of 43m. does not make it readily identifiable in daytime from seaward if its background is a section of the cliffs.

Terrain: shore of landfall

Pte. d'Ailly L.H. is located on a distinctive, vertical, white faced promontory at an altitude of about 80m. The white-painted light tower is 21m. high and should be identifiable at 8 miles or more in clear weather. Dieppe possesses no particular feature from seaward, although its profusion of buildings flanked as they are by white cliffs should leave the yachtsman at sea in no doubt as to its location.

Tidal streams

Adequate tidal stream information is published in the Admiralty Tidal Stream Atlas for the English Channel. There are no inconsistencies of note except for one and that is of small consequence: close inshore between Pte. d'Ailly and Dieppe a reverse stream, an eddy, runs during the first 3 hours of the east-going stream.

Soundings

Newhaven having been cleared, a helpful and uniform increase in soundings occurs until the 50m. contour is encountered some 12 miles after departure.

Thereafter, soundings on passage have small value until the 50m. line is recrossed some 24 miles from Pte. d'Ailly. This contour is well defined and, like the former one, is of value to the navigator. Again, a helpful uniformity occurs in the reduction in soundings as the coast is approached but the irregularity of both the 50m. and the 20m. lines should be noted.

Radio direction findings

Although generally audible, Pte d'Antifer radio beacon is best ignored. Of the sundry beacons at one's disposal Royal Sovereign, Basurelle LV, Pte. d'Ailly and Dieppe aero beacon assume considerable importance. The two former ones, when coupled with the latter, are well placed for 2- and 4-bearing fixes in mid-Channel. The latter one has considerable value for homing as the French coast is approached.

Passage advices

There is much to commend a course line drawn direct from Newhaven to Pte. d'Ailly, it being a feature on the French coast: Dieppe is not. The intention should be to alter course for Dieppe as soon as position has been determined off Pte. d'Ailly, a distance off which will vary according to visibility and quality of information.

After departure, cross bearings between Newhaven breakwater light tower and Beachy Head should provide positions for the first 3 or 4 miles. Thereafter, one must work on single bearings of Beachy Head until adequate recognition ceases perhaps 8 miles distant. Regular soundings should locate the 50m. contour and this, coupled with transference of the last bearing of Beachy Head, may give useful indication of position.

By this time both Royal Sovereign and Basurelle L.V. radio beacons should be clearly audible but the range of Pte. d'Ailly at this stage may make it less easy to identify. Hourly attempts to determine position by this means should be worthwhile, if only for the practice, and Basurelle having been brought abaft the port beam, 3-bearing fixes become possible. The quality and reliability of DF bearings of Pte. d'Ailly should steadily improve as southing is made.

Some 23 miles from the French coast, if on course, the 50m. line will be re-crossed. A study of the chart will indicate that one has only to be a few miles to the east or west of the course line and inconsistencies in the 50m. contour will produce widely differing indications of position.

However, homing on Pte. d'Ailly radio beacon, coupled with the steady reduction in soundings as the land is approached, should produce valuable indication of position in the latter stages. With soundings indicating, say, 25m. at about 7 miles offshore, with Pte. d'Ailly in sight in clear weather, one can with confidence alter course for Dieppe. DF1 pillar buoy some 2½ miles WNW of the harbour entrance is best closed, so that the harbour entrance is approached directly from seaward.

The cross channel ferries plying regularly between Newhaven and Dieppe progressing as they do on well established tramlines, often give support for one's calculations during passage.

PASSAGE No.8 Newhaven–Dieppe

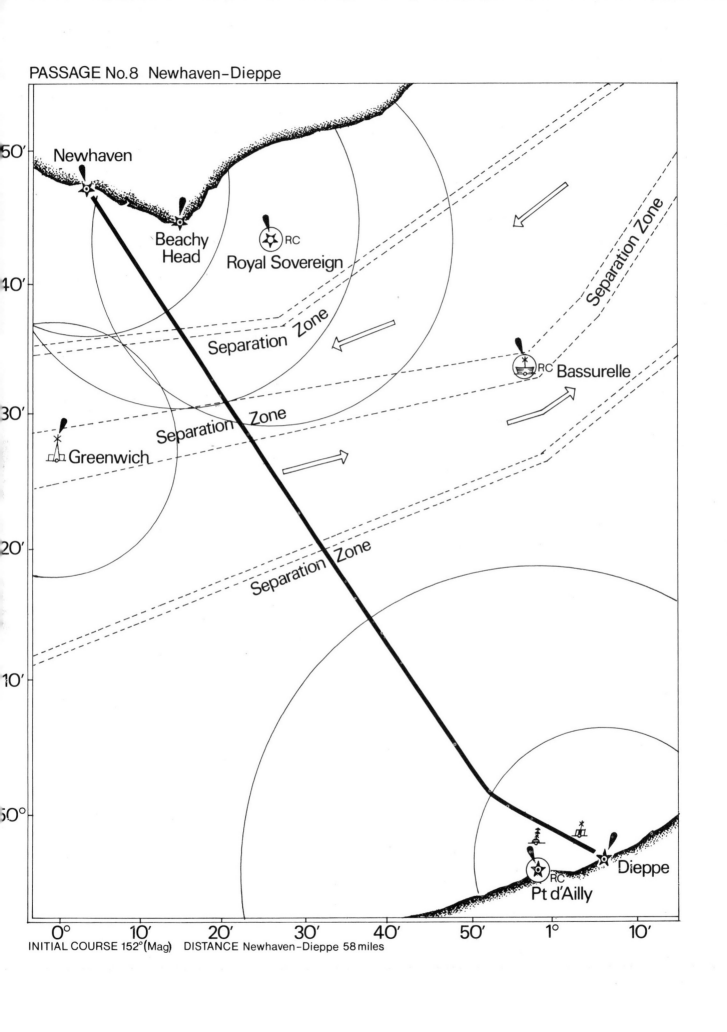

INITIAL COURSE 152°(Mag)   DISTANCE Newhaven–Dieppe 58 miles

PASSAGE NO.9: LITTLEHAMPTON/SHOREHAM/BRIGHTON/NEWHAVEN TO BOULOGNE

Wind direction and frequency in percentages

	SW	W	NW	N	E	Calm	Other
Dungeness 0900	26	15	16	–	13	1	29
Dungeness 1500	16	33	13	–	11	–	27
Calais	45	–	–	–	14	4	37

Main visual navigational aids

	Luminous range in miles	Visual range in miles Height of eye 2 metres
Newhaven Breakwater LH	12	11
Beachy Head LH	24	14
Royal Sovereign Lt. Tower	28	14
Dungeness LH	23	16
Cap d'Alprech LH	23	19
Digue Carnot Sud LH (Boulogne, Sthn. breakwater LH.)	13	13

Weather forecast areas: Wight and Dover
DF chain: Channel East.

General remarks

Skippers of craft berthed to the west of Newhaven should consider making a night stop in that port. The route Newhaven/Boulogne is dictated by offshore traffic lanes which are wide and busy. Taking the proposed route, the distance to Boulogne is 62 miles. A favourable tidal stream will be experienced when it has the greatest influence upon forward progress and a dawn departure is proposed. Good visibility is highly desirable, both from the point of view of position fixing and of the concentrated sea traffic in the Dover Strait area.

Terrain: shore of departure

Features in the Newhaven area from seaward are negligable but at night the breakwater light is usually visible to a range of 4 or 5 miles. The coast from Seaford Head eastwards to Beachy Head is distinctive, with its sheer, chalk-faced cliffs. Beachy Head rises steeply from the sea to an altitude of about 162m. Located on the foreshore, Beachy Head LH is round and grey, with a red band circling its middle and a red top. Royal Sovereign LH is a vertical, round white tower, surmounted by a helicopter platfordm. The light structure is offset on this platform. Dungeness is a flat, wide spit with a pebbly beach. The lighthouse on it is painted black and has white bands: it is floodlit at night. A large water tower inland from the lighthouse can occasionally be mistaken for the lighthouse.

Terrain: shore of landfall

2½ miles south of Boulogne harbour entrance is the headland, Cap d'Alprech. On the cliff face at approximately 47m. altitude, the light tower is 15m. high and is painted white with a black top. Boulogne is not difficult to recognise from seaward and within 5 miles its charted features should be identifiable. They are: the cathedral tower; the belfry to the right and slightly lower; further to the right and lower still, yet bold, a group of four blocks of flats with a white appearance. All these features are below the skyline.

Tidal streams

— Assuming one takes full advantage of the east-going stream which will be astern in the first stages, one should be able to traverse the 32 miles to Dungeness durings it flow. Thereafter, the streams having reversed and the yachtsman altered course broadly to starboard, it will be near athwart one's course. The streams are consistent and uncomplicated, as defined in the Admiralty Tidal Stream Atlas for the English Channel, and for the Dover Strait.

Soundings

Soundings taken at, say, 30 minute intervals will be of assistance throughout. Between Royal Sovereign and Dungeness they provide valuable information as to whether one is inside or outside one's course line. Over Les Ridens Bank soundings fall to about 20m., giving indication of progress and position. Later, having increased to 60m., a gradual, informative reduction in soundings occurs as land is approached.

Radio direction finding

Until Royal Sovereign is a few miles astern, radio beacons will probably be of small value. Thereafter, the following Channel East beacons combine to make 3- and 4-bearing fixes feasible until Boulogne is close at hand: Royal Sovereign, Basurelle LV, Dungeness, Cap Gris Nez and Boulogne. A directional beacon is located at Bouloge with a published range of 5 miles, but a greater range may be expected. Details of it will be found in the Admiralty List of Radio Signals, Volume 2 and in Stanford's Sailing Companion. This gives 'homing' information with marked simplicity and high precision.

Passage advices

The following route is suggested: Newhaven – 1' off Seaford Head – 1' off Beachy Head LH – ¼' south of Royal Sovereign – 2' off Dungeness on a bearing of 240° – Le Colbart buoy – Boulogne. No comment is necessary here until Royal Sovereign is reached. Thereafter, one lays course for Dungeness LH *direct*, so remaining inside the shipping lanes with the shore clearly visible. With the Royal Sovereign astern, D/F bearings and fixes should not be neglected, nor the evidence of sounding apparatus. Dungeness having been located and closed, one alters course for Boulogne, and Le Colbart buoy – a big one – is on this track. The buoy is then 14 miles distant and, by hourly correction of course for the effect of tidal streams, in good visibility it should be located. But mark well: even large buoys can seldom be seen at ranges in excess of 3 miles. It is wiser to pass to the south of Le Colbart buoy rather than the north, where shoal water is not far away. If soundings of 20m. occur without sighting, one must re-assess position and adjust course for Boulogne some 12 miles distant, homing if necessary on Boulogne marine radio beacon which should then be heard loudly and clearly. The directional beacon has great value in all states of visibility. Sighting of Cap d'Alprech should occur at about 8 miles in clear weather and soundings will give constant information about distance off as the port is approached.

PASSAGE No.9 Newhaven–Boulogne

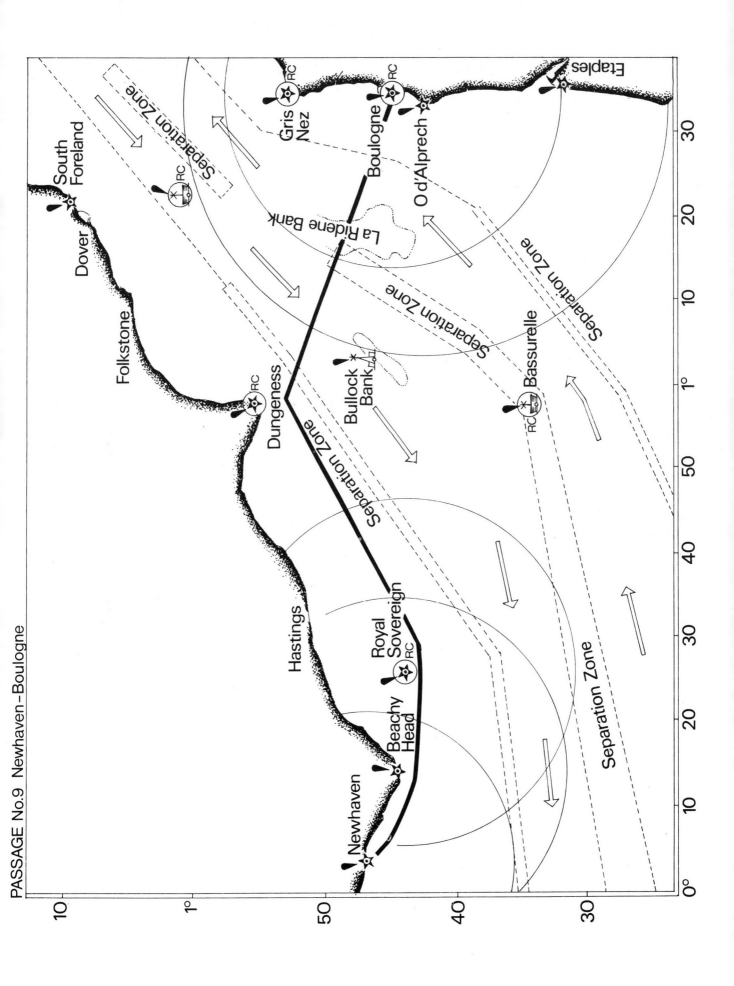

PASSAGE NO.10: DUNGENESS (FOR PORTS NORTHWARDS) TO LE HAVRE

Wind direction and frequency

	SW	W	NW	N	NE	E	Calm	Other
Dungeness 0900	26	15	16	–	–	13	1	29
Dungeness 1500	16	33	13	–	–	11	–	27
Cap de la Heve	16	23	16	15	13	–	3	14

Main visual navigational aids

	Luminous range in miles	Visual range in miles Height of eye 2 metres
Dungeness LH	23	16
Royal Sovereign LH	28	14
Beachy Head LH	24	14
Greenwich Lanby buoy	21	10
Cap d'Antifer LH	30	26
Fecamp, Jetee Nord LH	16	11
Cap de la Heve LH	26	25
Le Havre LH	20	11

Weather forecast areas:	Dover Wight
DF groups:	Channel east and Channel centre
Aero radio beacon:	Lympne

General remarks

Craft sailing from ports northwards of Dungeness should, in fine weather, consider anchoring in the lee of that headland for sleep; the passage, Dungeness – Le Havre is a long haul. Rye is an alternative for craft which comfortably take the ground but the port imposes tidal restrictions for departure. From every navigational point of view, Royal Sovereign as the final departure point is to be preferred.

Terrain: shore of departure

Dungeness is a low promontory with a steep sandy beanch on its eastern face. On the foreshore is the main lighthouse, a round stone tower painted white with two broad black bands. Its elevation is 43m. The nuclear power station close to the site of the old lighthouse is conspicuous. Reference to terrain in the Royal Sovereign area is given in Passage No. 9 under this heading. Useful bearings of features in both the Dungeness and Royal Sovereign areas are unlikely at ranges in excess of 6 miles except in conditions of excellent visibility.

Terrain: shore of landfall

In fine weather the proposed approach to Cap d'Antifer has good qualities. White or grey vertical chalk cliffs nearly 100m. high, angled usefully to the approach course, have value by day. At night, given clear conditions, Cap d'Antifer light will be sighted at good range and Fecamp light will give warning if one is too far to the eastward as the coast is approached. It must be emphasised that in bad weather, when the wind blows from the south west through north to northeast, this section of coast is a dangerous lee shore.

Tidal streams

Adequate tidal stream information will be found in the Admiralty Tidal Stream Atlas of the English Channel. Between Dungeness and the Royal Sovereign the tidal flow will be either dead ahead or right astern. This fact should be taken into account when deciding at what time one should sail. Streams off the French coast have no vagaries of consequence.

Soundings

During this passage there are three areas where soundings give a guide to the navigator: firstly, between Dungeness and Royal Sovereign where lessening depth contours run parallel with the course line: second, some 5 miles south of Royal Sovereign where the 30m. and 50m. lines are clearly defined; and third, as the French coast is approached, gradually reducing soundings give warning of an impending landfall.

Radio direction finding

Radio beacons which assume importance during passage are Royal Sovereign, Basurelle L.V., Pte. d'Ailly and Cap d'Antifer. Assuming a summer passage, it is improbable that Le Havre L.V. will be on station.

With Royal Sovereign astern, some reliance may be placed upon back bearings of it up to a range of, say, 20 miles. Later, bearings of Basurelle L.V. should give indications of forward progress. About midway across the Channel distinct possibilities exist for 3- and 4-bearing fixes from the listed beacons. Latterly Cap d'Antifer assumes increasing importance for homing as the coast is approached but, at this time, bearings of Pte. d'Ailly will be increasingly suspect due to coastal refraction.

Passage advices

If Dungeness is passed at ½' range and course is laid direct for Royal Sovereign, the bulk of coastal shipping will be outside one's track. Soundings and DF bearings of Dungeness and Royal Sovereign will give indication if one is inside or outside the course line. In clear weather, the townships of Hastings and Bexhill will give rough indication of progress.

For the Channel crossing, from Royal Sovereign course may be laid off to pass Cap d'Antifer 2' to port. At the outset, all listed radio beacons should be identified and one should plan to use one's set at regular intervals throughout. Some 5 miles south of Royal Sovereign, visual back bearings of that lighthouse should combine with 30m. and 50m. depth contours to fix position.

Perhaps 15 miles from Royal Sovereign the loom of Greenwich Lanby buoy should be sighted at night but it will be out of range by day. Thereafter, regular 3, perhaps 4-bearing DF fixes should be obtainable until the French coast is some 20 miles distant and soundings start decreasing. No useful depth contour will be found but decreasing depths coupled with either visual or DF bearings of Cap d'Antifer should give satisfactory positions. With this cape abeam one may confidently square away for Cap de Heve and the entrance to Le Havre.

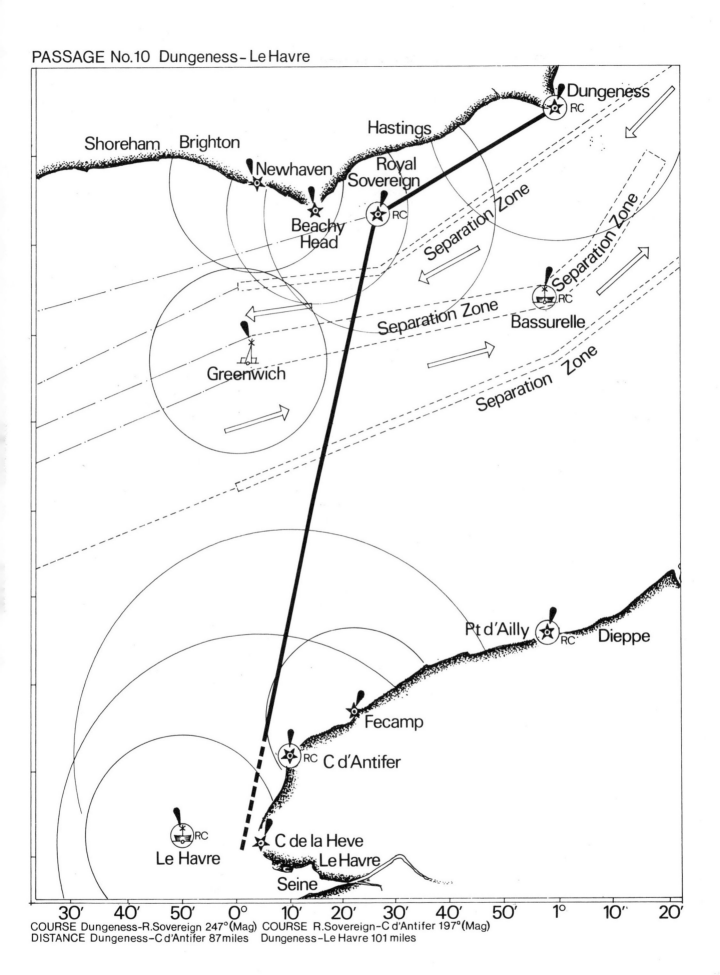

COURSE Dungeness–R.Sovereign 247°(Mag) COURSE R.Sovereign–C d'Antifer 197°(Mag)
DISTANCE Dungeness–C d'Antifer 87 miles   Dungeness–Le Havre 101 miles

PASSAGE NO.11: DOVER TO BOULOGNE

Wind direction and frequency in percentages

	S	SW	W	NW	N	Calm	Other
Dover	11	32	15	10	–	2	30
Calais	–	45	–	–	14	4	37

Main visual navigational aids

	Luminous range in miles	Visual range in miles Height of eye 2 metres
South Foreland LH	25	24
Dover, Pier extension LH	20	12
Folkestone breakwater LH	22	10
Dungeness LH	23	16
Varne LV	22	10
Calais LH	23	19
Cap Gris Nez LH	27	20
Cap d'Alprech LH	23	19
Boulogne, Digue Sud LH	19	13

Weather forecast area: Dover
Marine radio beacons: Channel East and Dover Strait groups.
Aero radio beacons: Lympne

General remarks

The comments relating to the concentration of shipping in the Dover Strait under this heading in Passage No.12 have equal substance here. For this and other reasons it is, therefore, good seamanship to head direct from Dover to Cap Gris Nez, then to alter course southward until a direct approach can be made towards Boulogne harbour and thereafter to head portwards.

Once south of Cap Gris Nez, a yacht may with safety pass inside Bassure de Baas, the narrow shoal which reaches from southwards roughly parallel with the shore to a position some 7 miles north of Cap d'Alprech and about 1½ miles offshore. For sundry reasons the writer would propose the track described, and make the passage in daylight when visibility is good.

Terrain: shore of departure

Remarks made under this heading in Passage No.12 are equally applicable to this passage.

Terrain: shore of landfall

Cap Gris Nez has much to commend it for a landfall. The promontory being dark and jutting with an elevation of about 45m., it is surmounted by lighthouse, a white tower 27m. high. Between this cape and Boulogne some 10 miles southwards the coast comprises dark red cliffs with grassy summits. It is probable that Cap d'Alprech and its lighthouse 2½ miles southward of Boulogne will be recognised somewhat earlier than the town itself. Within 5 miles of Boulogne, charted features within the town should be recognisable. They are detailed in Passage No.9.

Tidal streams

Using the Admiralty Tidal Stream Atlas for the Dover Strait, it will be noted that the main direction of the south west flowing stream is so angled to one's course throughout that there is considerable advantage in making this passage during the period when it is running.

The admonitory remarks under this heading in Passage No.12 should be noted.

Soundings

Remarks under this heading in Passage No.12 have equal substance here.

As Cap Gris Nez is approached, soundings reduce helpfully. Thereafter, when on the second leg of the passage, it should be noted that the sea bed rises steeply to the shoal, Bassure de Baas. The Varne and Le Colbart shoals, which are southwards of the Varne L.V., are to be avoided. Although soundings over them are such that any small craft may pass over them, heavy overfalls in many conditions of sea render their crossing extremely uncomfortable.

Radio direction finding

All advices contained under this heading in Passage No.12 apply to this passage also. In conditions of low visibility, the directional beacon at Boulogne has infinite value during the latter stages of approach. Details of it are contained in the Admiralty List of Radio Signals, Vol.2, and Stanford's Sailing Companion.

Passage advices

It is proposed that the course line is drawn from Dover harbour direct to Cap Gris Nez. When that headland is 3 miles distant and the sounding is about 50m., course may be altered southward to pass Bassure de Baas shoal to port and to close the Occ R. large pillar buoy 2.2 miles to the westward of Boulogne harbour entrance, thence to alter course for the port itself.

It is suggested that an a.m. daylight departure is made 4 to 5 hours after H.W. Dover, thereby ensuring a favourable tidal stream and daylight throughout the passage. Either entrance to Dover harbour may be used but perhaps the eastern one is to be preferred. Traffic signals are in operation for both. Attention is drawn to Passage No.12 and to the comments made under this heading of the importance of terrestial, and particularly back bearings, very shortly after sailing.

If on course, the Varne L.V. will be passed 1.3 miles to starboard. It is navigationally undesirable to pass southward of it. Given good visibility, Cap Gris Nez will shortly afterwards become visible and, using shore bearings and soundings, course should be altered southward when it is 3' distant. This distance should not be reduced. One will then pass Gris Nez at a range of 1½'.

Shore bearings and soundings should give considerable assistance at this time and the buoy marking the northern extremity of Bassure de Baas shoal will give added assurance. The buoy (Occ. R) off Boulogne being closed, and making adequate allowance for the southerly set, it remains to enter the harbour some 2' distant.

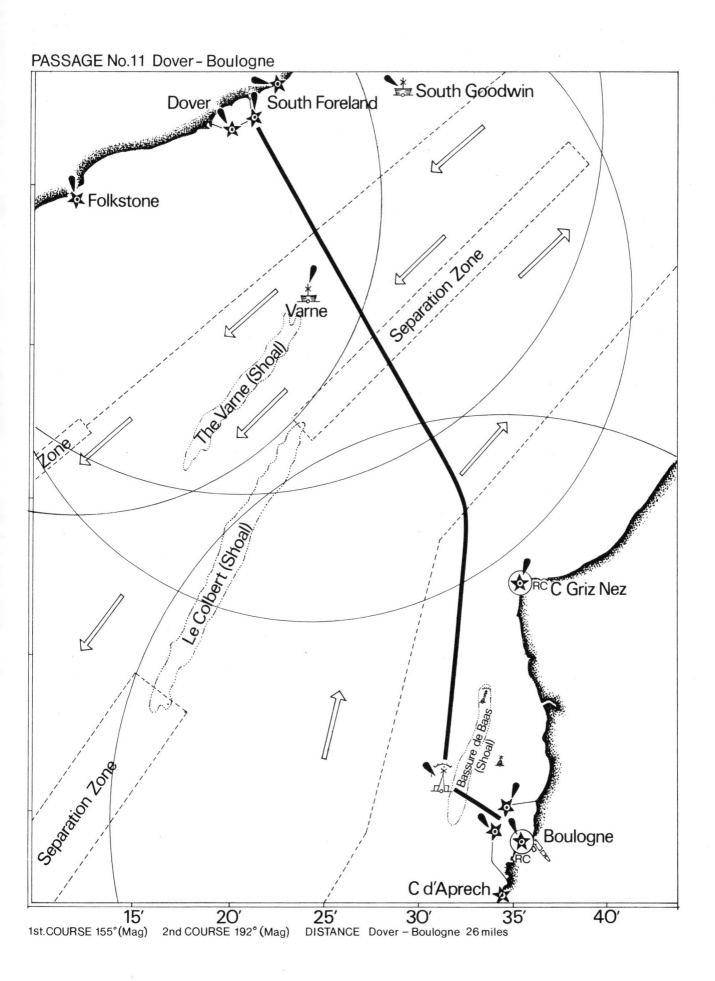

1st. COURSE 155° (Mag)   2nd COURSE 192° (Mag)   DISTANCE Dover – Boulogne 26 miles

PASSAGE NO.12: DOVER TO CALAIS

Wind direction and frequency in percentages

	S	SW	W	NW	N	Calm	Other
Dover	11	32	15	10	–	2	30
Calais	–	45	–	–	14	4	37

Main visual navigational aids

	Luminous range in miles	Visual range in miles Height of eye 2 metres
North Foreland LH	21	18
South Foreland LH	25	24
Dover, Pier extension LH	20	12
Folkestone breakwater LH	22	10
Dungeness LH	23	16
Varne LV	22	10
South Goodwin LV	25	10
East Goodwin LV	26	10
C. Gris Nez LH	27	20
Calais LH	23	19
Calais, Jetee Est. Head LH	19	9

Weather forecast area: Dover
Marine radio beacons: Channel East and Dover Strait groups.
Aero radio beacon: Lympne.

General remarks

Those who have yet to make a sea crossing might well regard the Dover – Calais passage as the easiest of them all. The distance is short, the navigational aids are numerous and one is almost making a landfall before the departure point dips below the horizon. However, the funnelling of all shipping bound to and from the east coast of England and the whole of the North Sea continental coast makes the crossing hazardous to the inexperienced and the unwary. On a clear day, assuming alertness and good seamanship, the run is in fact relatively simple due to the advantages listed above. Ample reason nevertheless exists for yachtsmen to make the passage in daylight and to delay sailing if visibility is anything but good.

Terrain: shore of departure

The long breakwaters of Dover harbour, the gaps in them which denote entrances and their integral stubby lighthouses make them distinctive to yachtsmen at a range up to about 5 miles. Behind Dover harbour is a vertical chalk cliff some 65m. high surmounted by Dover Castle of which bearings should be possible up to 8 or 10 miles. South Foreland lighthouse, 21m. high, even more bold, lies 1½ miles northwards. It is a short, white tower at an elevation of 93m. with chalk cliffs beneath.

Terrain: shore of landfall

Cap Blanc Nez with a marked white face and an elevation of about 154m. some 5 miles southwest of Calais is more readily seen as the coast is approached. It is surmounted by a conspicuous monument and a radar tower. The relatively low lying land behind Calais itself tends to throw the township into relief, hence faulty identification is unlikely. Conspicuous structures above the skyline are the main lighthouse and the tower of Hotel de Ville.

Tidal Streams

The best guide is the Admiralty Tidal Stream Atlas for the

Dover Strait. However, it must be emphasised that only average rates are published. Variations from those advertised are no reason for dismay, particularly after strong south westerly or northerly winds. One must be prepared for the full force of any stream flowing in the Strait immediately Dover breakwaters are cleared.

Soundings

Until the French coast is nearly approached soundings will afford the yachtsman minimal guidance. The 20m. line being a mere 2 miles from the French coast in the approach region, it would be imprudent to proceed beyond that contour if position has not been definitely ascertained.

Radio direction finding

Assuming the yachtsman selects a clear day for this passage, he does not really need DF bearings. It remains an ideal opportunity for the cruising yachtsman to obtain practice with his DF set.

Should visibility be reduced during passage, one is virtually surrounded by radio beacons and DF fixes should be obtainable throughout. Calais beacon will be the most important to him as he can use it for homing, the advantages of the others being clearly apparent to him by inspection of the Admiralty Chart No.1895.

Passage advices

Either entrance to Dover harbour can be used but perhaps the eastern one is to be preferred. Traffic signals are in operation for both. Although yachts can leave and enter Dover at any state of the tide, the Admiralty advise a time which is between two hours before and one hour after H.W. Dover. Clearly this is more applicable to large vessels but it is to be preferred for this passage, it being the period of slack water before the commencement of the northeast flowing stream in the Strait. A yachtsman can, therefore, carry this stream throughout the passage.

Back bearings of Dover harbour, and later Dover Castle, should be taken frequently so long as these features are visible. They are the means by which the mariner may be constantly aware whether the allowance he is making for the tidal stream is adequate. These bearings can be supplemented by ones of the South Goodwin and Varne light vessels, and terrestial features also, to perhaps half way across the Strait, and so position need not be in doubt.

During the latter half of the passage, features on the French coast will assume increasing importance. Prominent amongst these will be Cap Gris Nez some 10 miles to the southward and Cap Blanc Nez fine on the starboard bow. The buildings of Calais should become apparent at perhaps 6 or 7 miles distant and, when position has been positively ascertained, course should be adjusted to close CA4 buoy 2 miles north north west of the port entrance. Thereafter the channel buoys, as illustrated on Admiralty Chart No.3152 should be followed to the entrance. During strong winds from west south west, through north, to east north east, seas can be heavy off the entrance, rendering approach and entry impossible.

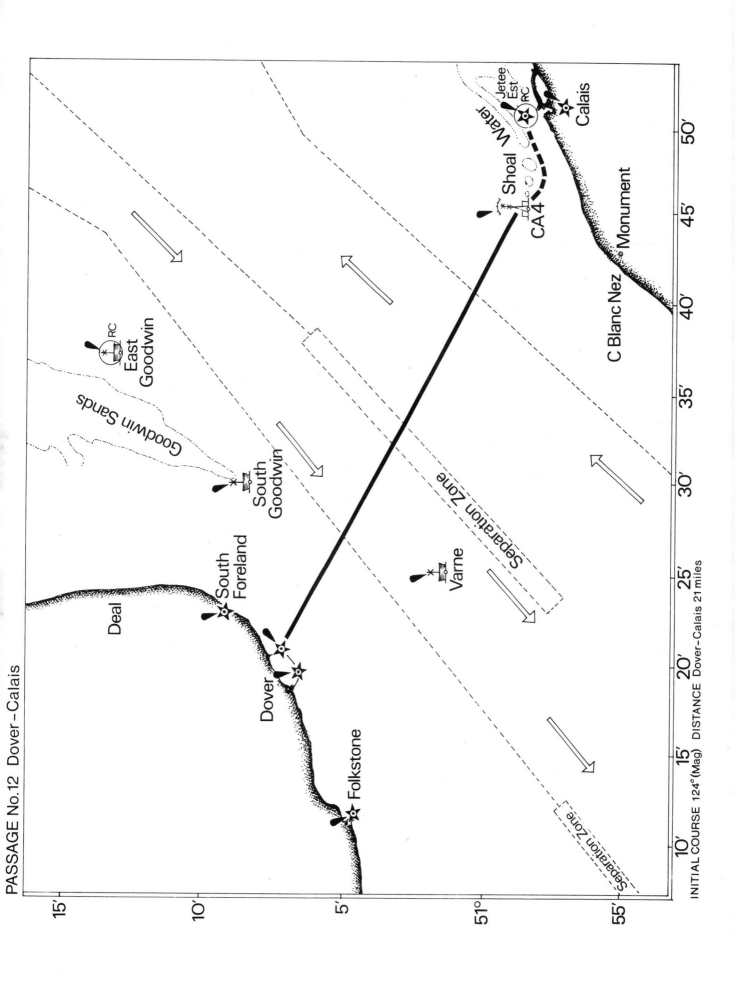

PASSAGE No.12 Dover–Calais

INITIAL COURSE 124°(Mag)   DISTANCE Dover–Calais 21 miles

PASSAGE NO.13: NORTH FORELAND (FOR THAMES AND KENTISH NORTH COAST PORTS) TO CALAIS

Wind direction and frequency in percentages

	S	SW	W	NW	N	Calm	Other
Margate	12	20	17	17	–	2	32
Dover	11	32	15	–	–	2	40
Calais	–	45	–	–	14	4	37

Main visual navigational aids

	Luminous range in miles	Visual range in miles Height of eye 2 metres
North Foreland LH	21	18
South Foreland LH	25	24
Dover, Pier extension LH	20	12
Folkestone breakwater LH	22	10
Dungeness LH	23	16
North Goodwin LV	26	10
East Goodwin LV	26	10
South Goodwin LV	25	10
Cap Gris Nez LH	27	20
Calais LH	23	19
Calais, Jetee Est. Head LH	19	9

Weather forecast area: Thames, Dover.
Marine radio beacons: Channel East and Dover Strait groups.

General remarks

Although at first glance it would seem sensible to proceed from North Foreland to North Goodwin L.V. and thence to Calais direct, the writer would propose that the Gull Stream channel to the west of the Goodwins is used, thereafter to make one's departure from the South Goodwin L.V. Distance is increased by roughly 4 miles. To pass eastward of the Goodwin Sands entails passing through the Sandettie L.V. area which the writer likens to Piccadilly Circus during rush hour.

All remarks made under this heading in Passage No.12 have equal substance here and therefore it is wise to make the passage in daylight when visibility is good.

Terrain: shore of departure

Between North Foreland and Ramsgate the coast is distinctive, the sheer chalk cliffs varying in elevation between 18m. and 36m. North Foreland L.H. is set back from the cliff edge somewhat but is bold. South of Ramsgate the coast recedes into Pegwell Bay and becomes characterless, apart from conspicuous charted features, until the South Foreland area is reached. South Foreland itself is chalk-faced and bold, some 90m. in height. The lighthouse upon it is white and 21m. in height. Somewhat lower and to the eastward of the main lighthouse is a disused one, also painted white.

Terrain: shore of landfall

The remarks under this heading in Passage No.12 have equal application on this passage.

Tidal Streams

The Admiralty Tidal Stream Atlases for the Thames Estuary and the Dover Strait give the yachtsman the most informative guidance. Remarks under this heading in Passage No.12 should be noted.

Soundings

During the early stages of the passage, due to the proximity of the Goodwin Sands to the eastward and the gradually shelving seabed to the west, it is prudent to be watchful of soundings throughout. Thereafter, with South Goodwin L.V. astern, remarks under this heading in Passage No.12 should be noted.

Radio direction finding

The comments under this heading in Passage No.12 relate equally to this passage.

Passage advices

The writer proposes the following basic passage plan: selection of a time of departure from North Foreland at the commencement of the south-going tidal stream during daylight which will yet ensure that the whole passage is made in daylight with some time in hand. If arrival in the North Foreland area does not coincide with these conditions one might consider anchoring in Margate Road or in the Ramsgate area. Taking the south-going stream, one is on a rising tide and one's craft is carried through the Gull Stream by it; the southwest-going stream will be carried during the crossing and near high water conditions will prevail in the vicinity of Calais.

Having left the North Foreland area one should close the Can buoy (Gr.Fl.(4)R) which is 112°, distant 1.8' from Broadstairs (F.R.) and then proceed direct to the can buoy (Qk.Fl.R.) which is 118°, 3.3' from Ramsgate breakwater light. Shore bearings will give ample reassurance during the run between these buoys. Thereafter, the buoys in the Gull Stream channel are roughly 1' apart. The channel being cleared, no difficulties present themselves in making South Goodwin L.V.

On the course S. Goodwin L.V. – Calais, back bearings of the light vessel and South Foreland L.H. should be taken, by which means one is constantly aware whether the allowance being made for the south-west-going set is adequate.

These features being lost, one is half way across the Dover Strait, and the yachtsman must commence searching for Cap Blanc Nez fine on the starboard bow.

The buildings of Calais should become apparent at perhaps 6 or 7 miles distant and, when position has been positively ascertained, course should be adjusted to close CA4 buoy 2' NNE of the port entrance. During strong winds from WSW, through N, to ENE, seas can be heavy off the entrance, rendering approach and entry impossible.

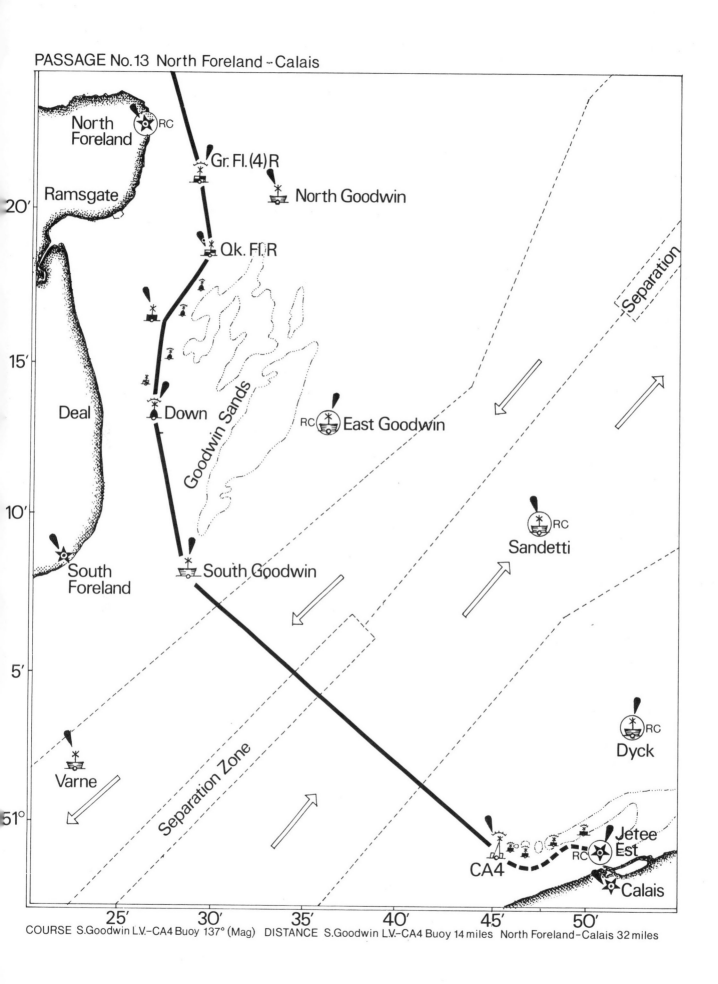

PASSAGE No.13 North Foreland – Calais

North Foreland ⊕RC

Ramsgate

20'

Gr. Fl.(4) R

North Goodwin

Qk. Fl.R

15'

Goodwin Sands

Deal

Down

East Goodwin RC⊕

Sandetti RC⊕

10'

South Foreland

South Goodwin

Separation

Separation Zone

5'

Dyck RC⊕

Varne

51°

CA4 RC⊕ Jetee Est

Calais

25'   30'   35'   40'   45'   50'

COURSE S.Goodwin L.V.–CA4 Buoy 137° (Mag)   DISTANCE S.Goodwin L.V.–CA4 Buoy 14 miles   North Foreland–Calais 32 miles

PASSAGE NO.14: NORTH FORELAND (FOR THAMES AND KENTISH NORTH COAST PORTS) TO OOSTENDE

Wind direction and frequency in percentages

	S	SW	W	NW	N	NE	Calm	Other
Margate	12	20	17	17	–	–	2	32
Dover	11	32	15	–	–	–	2	40
Dunkerque	–	22	22	13	–	12	3	28
Oostende	14	23	19	–	11	–	4	29

Main visual navigational aids	Luminous range in miles	Visual range in miles Height of eye 2 metres
North Foreland LH	21	18
South Foreland LH	25	24
Dover, pier extension LH	20	12
North Goodwin LV	26	10
East Goodwin LV	26	10
South Goodwin LV	25	10
Falls LV	24	10
Sandettie LV	25	10
Dunkerque LH	31	18
Nieuwpoort LH	21	13
Oostende LH	27	19

Weather forecast area:	Thames, Dover
Marine radio beacons:	Dover Strait group.
Aero radio beacon:	Wulpen (near Nieupoort, Belgium)

General remarks

Bearing in mind that a yachtsman has probably sailed from a point eastward of North Foreland, the total passage will be a long one; North Foreland – Oostende alone is 58 miles. An early morning arrival should be considered. Ample navigation aids exist throughout but, as the Sandettie area must be traversed with its concentration of shipping, a period of good visibility should be chosen. The course indicated is proposed so that shipping lanes are cleared with maximum despatch. Assuming a speed of 5 knots, no marked advantage will be obtained from tides by departing at a particular time from North Foreland.

Terrain: shore of departure

Between North Foreland and Ramsgate the coast is distinctive, the sheer chalk cliffs varying in elevation between 18m. and 36m. North Foreland L.H. is set back from the cliff edge but is bold.

Terrain: shore of landfall

The whole of the Belgium coast is low-lying and characterless, comprising in the main of sandhills of varying height, yet none being of assistance to the navigator. The coastal resorts and sundry charted conspicuous objects provide the means by which position may be ascertained in daylight, yet even those may well be unrecognisable at ranges beyond 5 or 6 miles.

In daylight in clear weather the concentration of buildings in Oostende should be visible at greater range. A tower block some 115m. in height lies close SW of the port. Other features are St. Joseph's church which has the highest pointed steeple and the cathedral with its twin spires.

Tidal streams

On this passage the Admiralty Tidal Stream Atlasses for the Thames Estuary, Dover Strait and North Sea, Southern portion, combine to provide tidal stream information. If these are supplemented by the information given on Admiralty charts, ample information is obtained. For planning purposes it is helpful to note that in the North Foreland area tidal streams run roughly north and south; in the Sandettie region they are NE and SW and on the Belgium coast they run roughly parallel to the shore.

Soundings

Whilst soundings remain of considerable importance throughout this passage, the profusion of visual navigational aids available until Sandettie bank is crossed render soundings merely of supplementary value to the navigator. This remark would be invalid if visibility was less than good.

The almost bewildering changes in soundings as the tongue-like shoals off the Belgian coast are crossed are valuable in the sense that they support or refute positions obtained by visual means. Some shoals which have soundings of 2m. and less should be noted: they could be hazardous to a yacht except in a flat calm. And there is the ominous fact that soundings of 8m. can be obtained both 10 miles and 4 cables offshore.

Radio direction finding

On this passage one is surrounded by fairly close range radio beacons, almost always so angled to one's course that multi-bearing fixes of good quality should be obtainable throughout. A study of Admiralty Chart No. 1406 will confirm this. The value of the continuous transmissions from Wulpen aero beacon is considerable latterly.

Passage advices

With a dawn arrival and clear weather in mind, the writer proposes the following courses, to cross traffic lanes quickly and so that the 2m. patches on the shoals off Belgium are avoided: North Foreland – Falls L.V. – Sandettie E. light buoy – continuation of course until the traffic lane is cleared, thence Bergues buoy – Oostendebank West buoy – Buitenstroombank buoy – Oostende entrance. No mention is made here of D.F. facilities: they are valuable and numerous and may be used throughout to assist navigation.

Passage of Falls L.V. presents no problems. Back bearings of North Foreland and North Goodwin L.V. will combine to guide one to it. Course can then be altered for Sandettie E. light buoy. Continuous back bearings of Falls L.V. will ensure that proper allowance is being made for the tidal stream and one is in effect guided to the buoy. It is a red flashing buoy and therefore sighting should not be expected beyond 2 to 3 miles. The loom and light of Sandetti L.V. light will give indication of forward progress. The green flashing wreck buoy 2′ SE of Sandettie E. buoy will later give further assistance and one should continue 2′ beyond it on the same course.

This distance being completed, one is outside the main traffic lane and course should be altered for Bergues buoy, some 6½′ to the ENE. Dunkerque main light should be clearly visible by this time.

Bearings of the loom and later the light of W. Hinder L.V., combined with those of Dunkerque light, should ensure that one can locate the buoy. Thereafter course can be altered for Oostendebank buoy and so, via Buitenstroombank buoy to Oostende. During this latter stage the lights of Dunkerque, Nieuwpoort, Oostende, W. Hinder L.V. and latterly Blankenberge will combine to assist accurate navigation.

The banks off the Belgium coast produce a nasty, even a dangerous sea during heavy weather and are to be avoided by small craft.

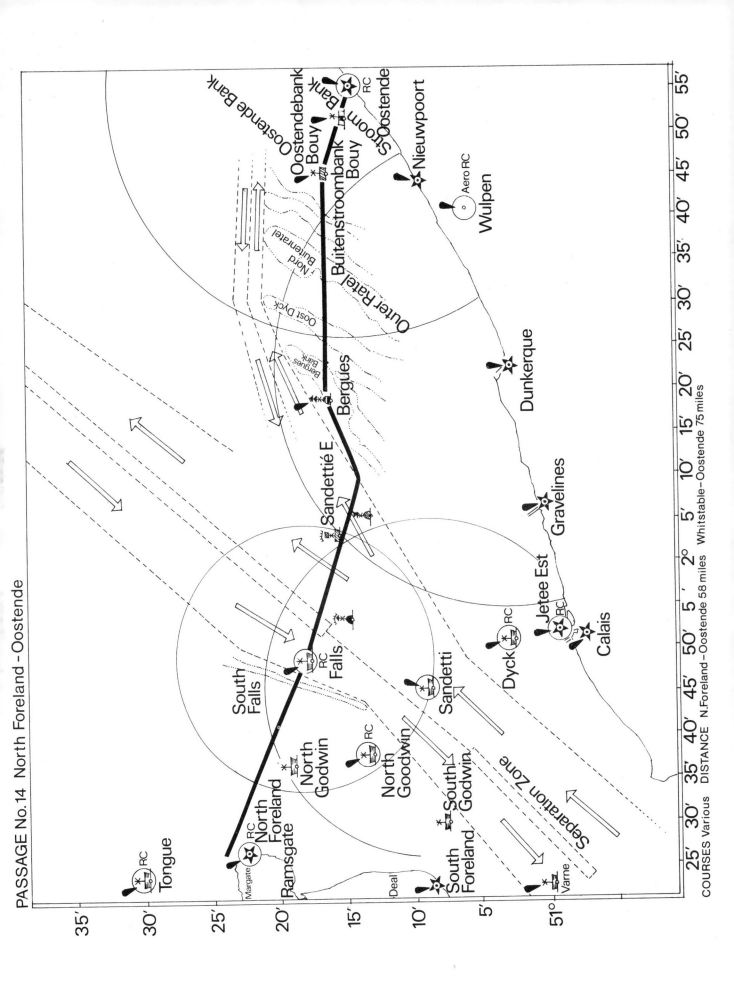

PASSAGE No.14 North Foreland – Oostende

COURSES Various   DISTANCE N.Foreland–Oostende 58 miles Whitstable–Oostende 75 miles

Oostende Bank

Oostendebank
Bouy

Buitenstroombank
Bouy

Oostendebank

Nord
Buitenratel

Buitenratel

Oost Dyck

Outer Ratel

Bergues
Bank

Bergues

Sandettié E

Oostende

Nieuwpoort

Wulpen

Aero RC

Dunkerque

Gravelines

Jetee Est

Calais

Dyck   RC

Sandetti

North Goodwin

South Goodwin

Separation Zone

South Falls

North Godwin   RC

North Godwin

South Falls   Falls   RC

North Foreland   RC

Ramsgate

Margate

Deal

South Foreland

Varne

Tongue   RC

35'
30'
25'
20'
15'
10'
5'
51°

25' 30' 35' 40' 45' 50' 55' 2° 5' 10' 15' 20' 25' 30' 35' 40' 45' 50' 55'

PASSAGE NO.15: SUNK LV (FOR ESSEX COAST PORTS) TO OOSTENDE

Wind direction and frequency in percentages

	SE	S	SW	W	NW	N	NE	Calm	Other
Gt. Yarmouth (noon)	13	15	13	15	—	14	12	4	14
Margate	—	12	20	17	17	—	—	2	32
Oostende	—	14	23	19	—	11	—	4	29

Main visual navigational aids

	Luminous range in miles	Visual range in miles Height of eye 2 metres
Sunk LV	24	10
Galloper LV	27	10
Kentish Knock LV	26	10
W. Hinder LV	17	10
Nieuwpoort LH	21	13
Oostende LH	27	19
Blankenberge LH	20	14

Weather forecast area: Thames and northern limit of Dover

Marine radio beacons: Sunk LV, Outer Gabbard LV, N. Hinder LV, N. Foreland LH and beacons of the Dover Strait group.

Aero radio beacon: Wulpen (near Nieuwpoort, Belgium)

General remarks

Skippers of craft normally berthed in ports or havens to the SW of Harwich should consider making a night stop in this port. Even then, the total passage distance will be some 75 miles: a long haul. The writer would commend a night passage and a pre-dawn arrival off the Belgian coast. An attempt at a daylight passage could commit one to a night arrival if unforeseen delays are encountered.

The passage is uncomplicated and, although10 or 20 miles may have to be traversed during dark hours with no visual navigational aid, considerable assistance may be obtained from marine radio beacons during this period.

Terrain: shore of departure

This heading has no application here as, when Sunk L.V. is neared, the Essex/Suffolk coasts will be below the horizon.

Terrain: shore of landfalls

The remarks under this heading in Passage No.14 have equal application here.

Tidal Streams

The Admiralty Tidal Stream Atlasses for the North Sea, Southern Portion, and the Thames Estuary, coupled with the information given on Admiralty charts, give complete information. It will be noted that, for all practical purposes, tidal streams are at right angles to one's course throughout. They give neither advantage nor disadvantage at any point.

Soundings

In certain sections of this passage, soundings provide valuable information. North Falls bank, south of Galloper L.V., provides near precise indication to the three shoal areas running athwart one's course which comprise the Fairy Bank to the NW of N. Hinder L.V. With this light vessel astern the fairly rapid changes in soundings as the tongue-like shoals off the Belgian coast are crossed have value in that the soundings they produce will assist navigation. In no circumstances should this coast be closed on soundings alone. Variations are such that, when position is seriously in doubt in thick weather, one could be 10 miles or 2 cables offshore.

Radio direction finding

From Sunk L.V. to N. Hinder L.V., one is literally surrounded by marine radio beacons which are at relatively short range. The Admiralty Chart No.1405 proves this point. Nulls should be sharp and bearings easy to obtain. Multi-bearing fixes should be obtainable throughout and, at worst, one can home on to W. Hinder L.V.

Thereafter, one's set will assume lesser importance unless visibility has deteriorated when one may consider homing on Oostende beacon.

Passage advices

The writer proposes the following track: Sunk LV — W. Hinder LV — Oost-Dyck buoy — Middelkerke buoy — Buitenstroombank buoy — Oostende.

Assuming a passage speed of 5 knots and departure from Sunk L.V. in daylight, back bearings of the L.V. should be possible up to a range of about 5 miles. These are essential to check allowances in one's course. This check will be supported by Sunk, Trinity and Long Sand Head buoys being passed in succession wide to starboard.

Some 15 miles after leaving Sunk, assuming daylight remains, Galloper L.V. should be sighted as it approaches the port beam at a range of perhaps 5 miles. DF bearings will indicate the arc of the horizon to be searched as the area is approached. During dark hours, two-bearing fixes between Galloper and Kentish Knock L.V's should be possible at this time. Continuous soundings should locate North Falls bank, giving additional information.

With North Falls bank astern, hourly multi-bearing DF fixes should produce indication of position throughout. Latterly one must constantly sound for the three tongues of shoal ground which comprise Fairy Bank. Being located, when coupled with DF bearings of W. Hinder L.V., these informative soundings will assist in determining position.

W. Hinder L.V. being passed, the passage becomes one of proceeding from buoy to buoy. Oost-Dyck buoy, 3½' SE of W. Hinder, should easily be located yet from this buoy to the next, Middelkerke, is a distance of some 6½'. If it is borne in mind that radio beacons are located both at W. Hinder and Oostende, one right astern and the other dead ahead, it will be seen that one's DF set should ensure that a good course is made. At Middelkerke buoy Oostende should be visible and so, via Buitenstroombank buoy, the harbour entrance can be made.

PASSAGE No.15 Sunk Lt.V.–Oostende

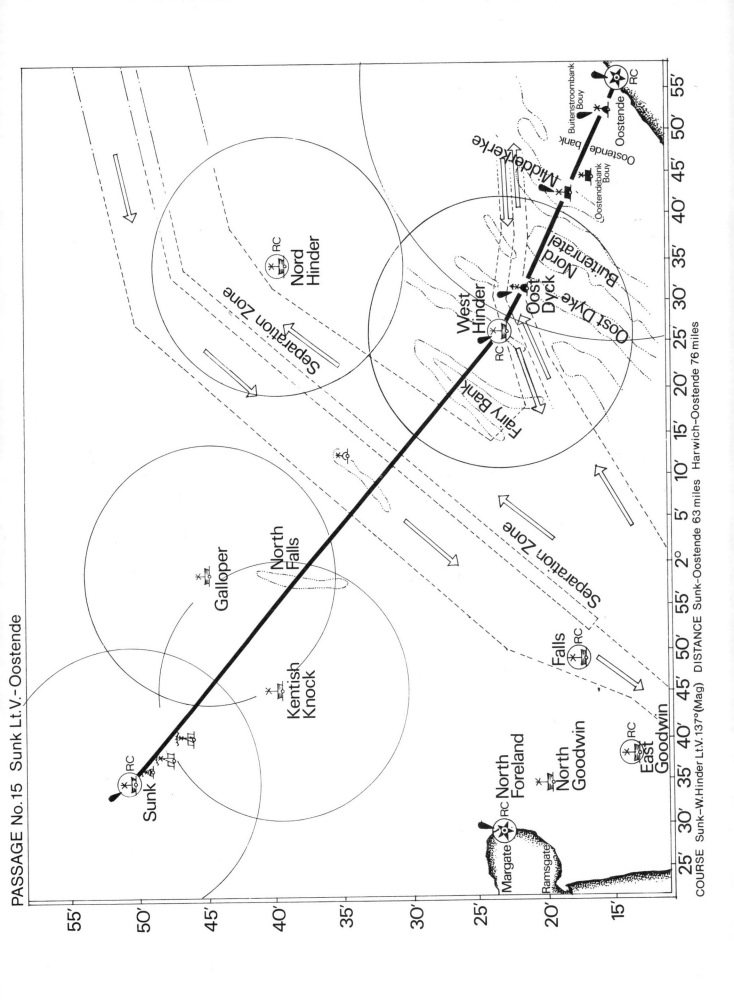

COURSE Sunk–W.Hinder Lt.V. 137°(Mag) DISTANCE Sunk–Oostende 63 miles Harwich–Oostende 76 miles

PASSAGE NO.16: SUNK LV (FOR ESSEX COAST PORTS) TO HOOK OF HOLLAND

Wind direction and frequency in percentages

	SE	S	SW	W	NW	N	NE	Calm	Other
Gt. Yarmouth (noon)	13	15	13	15	–	14	12	4	14
Amsterdam	–	–	18	21	16	11	–	.	34

Main visual navigational aids

	Luminous range in miles	Visual range in miles Height of eye 2 metres
Lunk LV	24	10
Galloper LV	27	10
Noord Hinder LV	27	10
Westkapelle LH	28	17
Goeree Light Tower	28	14
Hook of Holland LH	28	14

Weather forecast area:	Thames
Marine radio beacons:	Sunk, Outer Gabbard LV, Galloper LV, N. Hinder LV, W. Hinder LV, Oostende, Goeree LV, Hook of Holland.
Aero radio beacons:	Costa (near Zeebrugge) Haamstede (Schouwen)

General remarks

Skippers of craft whose home port is to the SW of Harwich should consider making a night stop in this port. The passage still remains a long haul of some 111 miles. Tidal stream considerations tend to outweigh the advantages of making a dawn arrival; if the two go hand in hand, so much the better. The proposed course is not a direct one; it is from light vessel to light vessel each having their inherent advantages to the navigator, and one crosses the main sea lane nearly at right angles. Off the Dutch coast an abundance of shipping is invariably found and a period of clear weather for the passage is highly desirable. Many yachtsmen prefer Haringvliet as an alternative entrance to the Dutch canal systems, it being free of heavy traffic.

Terrain: shore of departure

This heading has no application here as, when Sunk L.V. is neared, the Essex/Suffolk coasts are below the horizon.

Terrain: shore of landfall

Low sand dunes are virtually unbroken along most sections of the Dutch coast and the navigator must depend upon charted conspicuous objects by day to fix position by terrestial bearings. Hook of Holland is a township in itself and Europoort, the new docks complex on the south bank of the Nieuwe Waterweg, combine to produce features on the skyline which are charted.

Tidal Streams

The Admiralty Tidal Stream Atlas for the North Sea, Southern portion, provides the best guide. It should be noted that on passage before reaching N. Hinder L.V. tidal streams are near athwart the course. Thereafter, streams will assist or hinder progress to a considerable degree. Tidal streams set strongly across the entrance to the Nieuwe Waterweg.

Soundings

The first real assistance from soundings will be from the swatch of deep water south of Inner Gabbard Bank. Galloper L.V. should be sighted before Galloper Bank is located with sounding equipment. Some 10 miles beyond Galloper L.V. the sharp reduction in sounding from 50m. to 30m. should be sought. Other than the crossing of North Hinder Bank, soundings thereafter will be of small assistance to the navigator.

Radio direction finding

Homing by DF on to each light vessel in turn is of considerable value on this passage and bearings for this purpose should be taken at regular intervals throughout. Outer Gabbard L.V. in the early stages, and the sundry beacons southward may well provide DF positions of fair quality during the whole passage but unless 3- or more bearing fixes are obtained, results of this nature should be regarded with marked suspicion.

Passage advices

The writer proposes the following track: Sunk L.V. – Galloper L.V. – N. Hinder L.V. – Goeree L.V. – Hook of Holland. If Haringvliet is preferred for entry into Holland, one proceeds from Goeree L.V. to SG buoy (R.W.Fl.) some 14' ESE and so to the buoyed channel leading towards the locks.

As the distance to be traversed may well take 20 hours or more, the writer will not presume to propose a departure time at Sunk L.V. He will, however, propose that departure is so calculated that the whole of one NE-flowing tidal stream is encountered during the leg, N. Hinder – Goeree, which is one of 45 miles. At 5 knots, in theory at least, this leg could almost be completed in a 6-hour tidal flow.

Back bearings as a means of checking course allowances should be possible up to a range of about 5 miles from Sunk L.V. during daylight, and greater than this in darkness. The DF set should be used for homing bearings of Galloper L.V., and back bearings of Sunk L.V., this ahead and astern technique being adopted from start to finish during the voyage.

Galloper L.V. being closed and passed, indication of forward progress should be obtained from the marked reduction in soundings midway between Galloper and N. Hinder L.V.'s. N. Hinder L.V. being located and passed, one is faced with the 45 mile passage to Goeree L.V. Course being altered, visual back bearings will give a check on allowance for tidal stream being made, a navigational process which assumes great importance at this time. Soundings will give small help and so DF fixes will of necessity loom large in calculations. Oostende, Costa and Haamstede beacons will have value.

Having homed on to Goeree L.V., passage to the Hook becomes an uncomplicated process of sailing from buoy to buoy. Features in the Hook of Holland area should become recognisable at about 6 miles on a clear day. Should Haringvliet be one's goal, one is guided to SG buoy by DF back bearings of Goeree L.V., with Westhoofd L.H. visible latterly on the starboard bow.

PASSAGE No.16 Sunk Lt.V.- Hook of Holland

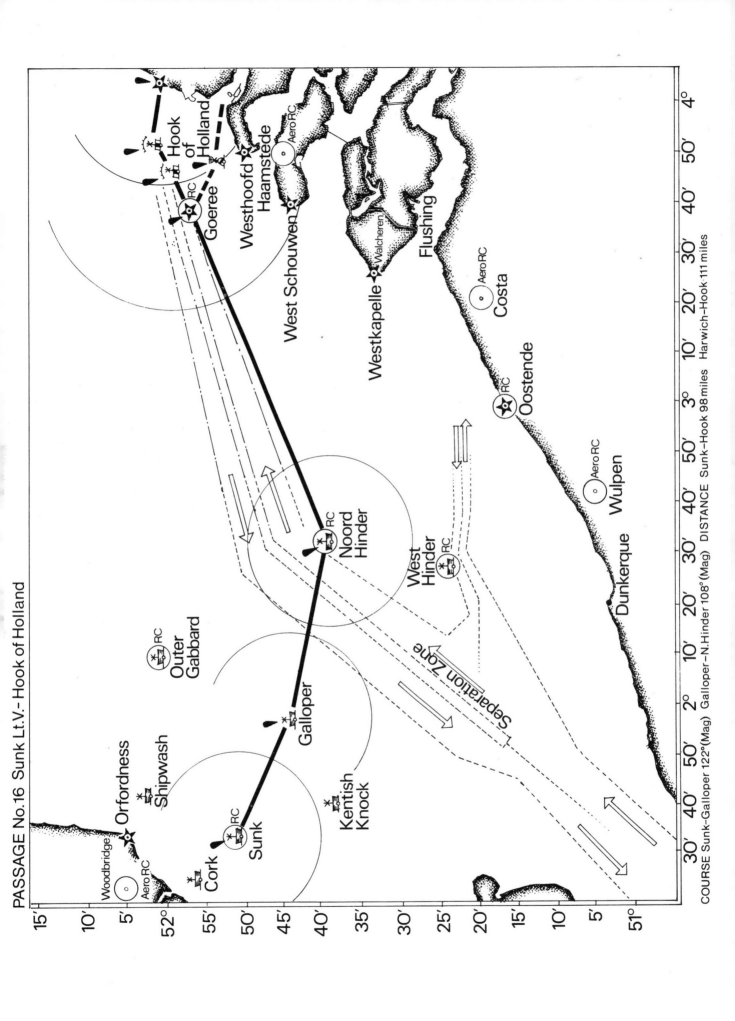

COURSE Sunk–Galloper 122°(Mag) Galloper–N.Hinder 108°(Mag) DISTANCE Sunk–Hook 98miles Harwich–Hook·111 miles

PASSAGE NO.17: GREAT YARMOUTH (FOR PORTS NORTH AND SOUTH) TO ZEEGAT VAN TEXEL, HOLLAND

Wind direction and frequency in percentages

	SW	SW	W	NW	N	Calm	Other
Great Yarmouth, 0700	–	21	25	15	–	7	32
Great Yarmouth, 1300	13	15	13	15	–	4	40
Den Helder (Texel)	–	23	19	17	11	3	27

Main visual navigational aids

	Luminous range in miles	Visual range in miles Height of eye 2 metres
Lowestoft LH	28	15
Cross Sand LV	24	10
Smith's Knoll LV	24	10
Texel LV	26	11
Kijkduin, rear, LH	30	18

Weather forecast area:	Thames and Humber
Marine DF beacons:	Smith's Knoll LV, Outer Gabbard LV, Texel LV, Terschellingerbank LV, Ijmuiden, Eierland LH.
Aero DF beacons:	Great Yarmouth/North Denes, Amsterdam/Spijkerboor, Valkenburg.

General remarks

Although for many the 77 miles between Smith's Knoll and Texel L.V. may be regarded as a formidable distance to sail with only DR positions and DF bearings to give real assistance, such a venture should not be dismissed out of hand. It provides a quicker means by which craft berthed in the Thames area can visit the Ijsselmeer, the Fresian Islands and beyond. It brings the continent within the orbit of Yorkshire-based yachtsmen who have yet to make a sea crossing when a direct run from, say, Bridlington is wisely left to the man with vast experience.

Terrain: shore of departure

The low sandy coast of Norfolk is featureless in the Great Yarmouth area; the buildings of the town cluster to make a feature in themselves. The diminutive piers which form the entrance to Great Yarmouth haven are at the southern extremity of the town. Sundry conspicuous objects are listed in the North Sea Pilot, Vol. 111 on page 206 but, from the yachtsman's point of view, it would be unrealistic to expect to identify them in ranges in excess of 6 miles and the entrance to the haven at more than 4 miles.

Terrain: shore of landfall

The island of Texel is separated from the mainland, on which northern extremity is the township of Den Helder, by the passage, Zeegat van Helder; this provides access to Waddenzee and Ijselmeer, the two combined being the former Zuiderzee. The low coast northward of Zeegat van Helder comprises sand dunes; that to the south is of similar character. Admiralty charts and the North Sea Pilot, Vol. IV adequately feature every conspicuous object but, from a practical point of view it tends to be the Texel L.V. which guides one into waters in which they are identifiable.

Tidal streams

Excellent working diagrams of tidal streams which will be experienced on this passage are contained in the Admiralty Tidal Stream Atlas for the North Sea, southern portion. It will be noted that streams are generally stronger on the English coast than the Dutch. Local vagaries, familiar to any yachtsman, are to be expected at both departure and lanfall points.

Soundings

Apart from the necessary regular soundings, it is improbable that soundings will give indication of position until some 19 miles after Smith's Knoll L.V. has been left astern. Thereafter, for some 22 miles a series of swatches are encountered, with soundings varying about the 30m. contour. As Texel L.V. is approached a similar swatch occurs and, the contour having been located, indication of the distance off the Texel L.V. is obtained.

Radio direction finding

On this passage one must harbour no doubts about the efficiency of one's DF equipment; the information it will give assumes great importance. In effect one sails away from Smith's Knoll on a DF bearing and later homes on to the Texel L.V. Early in the passage bearings of North Denes aero beacon will serve to support those of Smith's Knoll. Latterly, when bearings of Texel L.V. assume greater importance fixes become feasible from bearings of both aero and marine beacons on and about the coast ahead, and those well to the southward in the latitude of the Hook of Holland.

Passage advices

It is proposed that the yachtsman makes his way from Great Yarmouth haven to Smith's Knoll L.V.; he then shapes course for Texel L.V. and, this having been made, he alters course for ZH buoy, to SG buoy and so through Schulpengat and Breewijd buoyed channels to Den Helder. Channels and shaosl shifting from time to time in this area, modern Dutch charts of Zeegat van Texel are desirable but not essential if Admiralty charts are corrected to date. There is advantage in sailing from Great Yarmouth at the Start of the N-flowing stream and planning a pre-dawn arrival off the Texel L.V.

From Great Yarmouth haven one passes S. Scroby buoy, 4′ distant, close to starboard and then shapes course for Cross Sand L.V. 6′ to the NE. This having been made, Smith's Knoll L.V. lies 13′ further to the NE and it must be closed. DF bearings of Smith's Knoll and East Denes should be distinct and reliable and bearings of the former will guide one to it.

Course having been set for Texel L.V., back bearings of Smith's Knoll L.V., visual at first and by DF later, will give a check on course being made good. One must search for and locate by constant soundings the 30m. depth contours: they will give indication of progress. Texel DF beacon should now be clearly audible: this and other Dutch DF beacons should be located. As forward progress is made, increasing value may be placed upon bearings of all these beacons and DF fixes become possible. Deliberately homing on to Texel L.V., the loom of it should be visible at 15 miles and more at night in clear weather. As it is neared Kijkduin L.H. comes within range. Texel L.V. having been made, assuming dawn by this time, course may be altered to the SE to pass ZH buoy 1′ to port. Features on shore become visible during this leg. As soon as Zanddijk leading beacons come into line, course may be altered towards them and one is guided to SG buoy. This lies at the southern extremity of the buoyed channel to Den Helder.

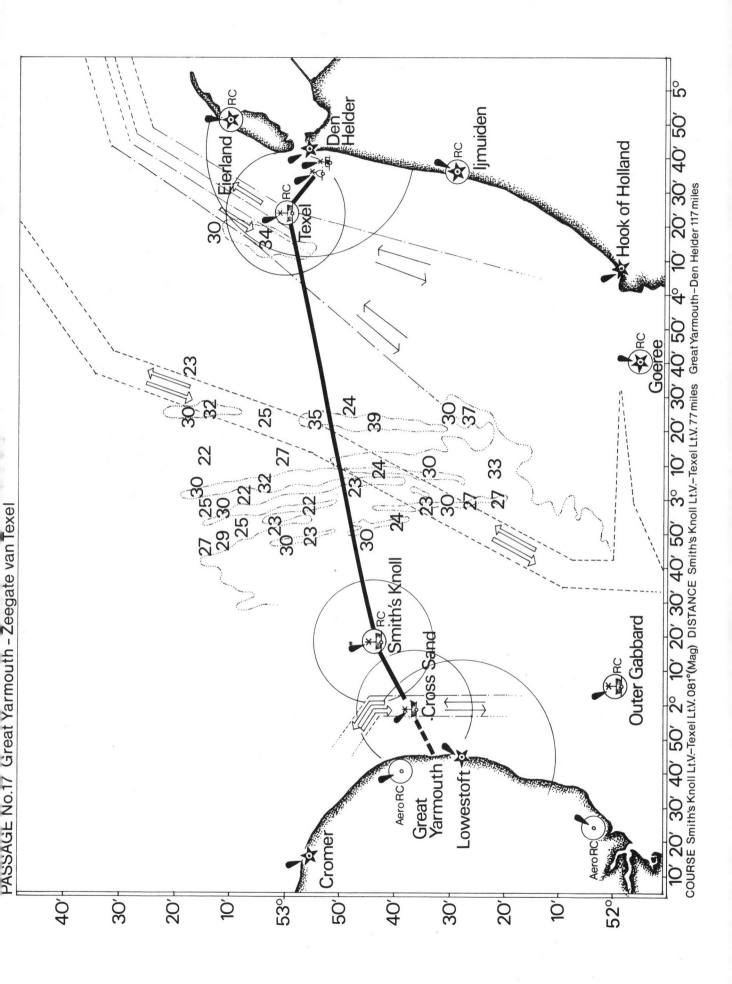

COURSE Smith's Knoll Lt.V.–Texel Lt.V. 081°(Mag) DISTANCE Smith's Knoll Lt.V.–Texel Lt.V. 77 miles Great Yarmouth–Den Helder 117 miles

PASSAGE NO.18: LAND'S END TO CORK HARBOUR

Wind direction and frequency in percentages

	SE	S	SW	W	NW	N	Calm	Other
Scilly Isles, 0700	–	–	17	19	20	14	3	27
Scilly Isles, 1300	–	–	16	24	19	15	2	24
Cork Harbour, 0600	–	–	15	18	24	16	9	18
Cork Harbour, 1200	12	21	15	13	23	–	5	11

Main visual navigational aids

	Luminous range in miles	Visual range in miles Height of eye 2 metres
Round Island LH	24	18
Seven Stones LV	25	10
Wolf Rock LH	23	15
Longships LH	19	15
Pendeen LH	27	18
Old Head of Kinsale LH	25	20
Daunt LV	22	10
Ballycotton LH	22	18

Weather forecast areas:	Fastnet and East Lundy
Marine radio beacons:	Round Island, Daunt LV.
Aero beacon:	St. Mawgan.

General remarks

This passage, although a long one at 141 miles, cannot be called difficult. A craft is subject to the sea and swell of the western ocean but tidal streams are relatively gentle and for a landfall few coasts are better than those of southern Ireland. Arrival on this shore opens up excellent but little frequented cruising grounds.

Terrain: shore of departure

Longships is a cluster of rocks 6m. to 13m. high. Upon them is the round granite tower of Longships L.H. The coast of Cornwall northward of Lands End, and then north eastwards towards St. Ives, is rugged. Cliffs 15m. to 30m. high are much idented and the hills behind them rise to over 200m. In clear weather the land itself may be visible at 15 to 20 miles from a yacht, yet the sundry promontories are unlikely to be identifiable at ranges in excess of 8 miles. At night useful visual fixes from the listed lights should be obtainable to ranges of near 18 miles after leaving the Longships.

Terrain: shore of landfall

The coast on each side of Cork Harbour is generally bleak, high and precipitous. Hills on the coastline commonly have a height of 60m. to 90m. It may well be Knockmealdown mountains many miles inland north of Youghal township, the highest peak of which is near 800m., is the first sighting in clear weather. Disregarding this range, in good visibility sighting should occur at 15 or 20 miles: and at 10 miles range the marked break in the craggy cliffs, the entrance to Cork Harbour, should be easily identified, together with other features on the coast.

Soundings

With Land's End well astern there is a dreary similarity in soundings almost to the Irish coast. And then their character abruptly changes. Along almost the whole coastline ample warning is given of an impending landfall. Generally a sounding of 70m. indicates a distance off of about 5 miles, although it could be as little as 2 miles. Clearly, soundings of less than 70m. must be unacceptable to yachtsmen unless position has been established.

Tidal streams

The Admiralty Tidal Stream Atlasses of the Irish Sea, and the English and Bristol Channels, give tidal stream information in part. That contained on Admiralty Chart No.1123 provides the best guide for yachtsmen on passage in the open sea. On this passage tidal currents are regular and seldom exceed a $\frac{1}{2}$ knot, a pleasant change for the average British yachtsman. Mild increases in strength and vagaries must be expected off Land's End and in the region of Cork Harbour.

Radio direction finding

On departure one has Round Island and St. Mawgan, and all know that fixes from only two bearings of radio beacons must be regarded with extreme caution. Nevertheless, the crosses which these bearings will produce cannot be wholly negative. In the latter stages of the passage the yachtsman has Daunt L.V. upon which to home, a valuable navigational asset. It would be unwise to place excessive credance upon results obtained from other beacons which are outside their nominal ranges.

Passage advices

It is proposed that course be set direct for the Daunt L.V. when Longships is bearing east (say) 1' distant. Given a period of settled weather, it is perhaps only motor yacht skippers who can plan with a reasonable degree of certainty their estimated time of arrival at Cork Harbour. A morning arrival, either before or after dawn, should be the broad plan of any skipper. Weather changes during passage may intercede to set at nought the most practical calculation of this nature. Assuming Penzance is the port of departure, certainly it will be advantageous to plan to be off the Longships at HW Dover so that, for the following 3 hours, one is borne by tidal currents more rapidly through the area where streams are at their strongest.

In clear weather in daytime, useful visual fixes from terrestial features may well become unobtainable by the time the Longships are 8' astern: yet this distance could be 14 to 18 miles at night. Before visual contact is lost one should identify Round Island and St. Mawgan DF beacons. Thereafter, unless the quality of DF bearings is high and there is a consistency of cross bearings so obtained, it will be more seamanlike to place a greater degree of reliance upon one's own DR calculations. So follows the long passage towards Cork Harbour.

Daunt L.V. marine radio beacon is given a nominal range of 30 miles, yet one should commence listening for it at double that distance and more. At about 40 miles, if located, it will be sensible to commence homing on the bearing of it. Assuming Daunt L.V. beacon is located, a practical assumption, in clear weather at 10 miles or more in daytime, Robert's Head, Cork Head and Roche's Point should be clearly apparent, with the entrance to Cork Harbour equally as evident. At night, some 16 miles from the Daunt L.V., when it is still below the horizon, fixes by cross bearings of Old Head of Kinsale L.H. and Ballycotton L.H. should be obtainable. In thick weather, keeping the DF bearing at NNW and homing on to it, soundings will efficiently guide one to the Daunt and then, depending upon the degree of visibility, one may proceed into port.

PASSAGE No.18 Lands End - Cork Harbour

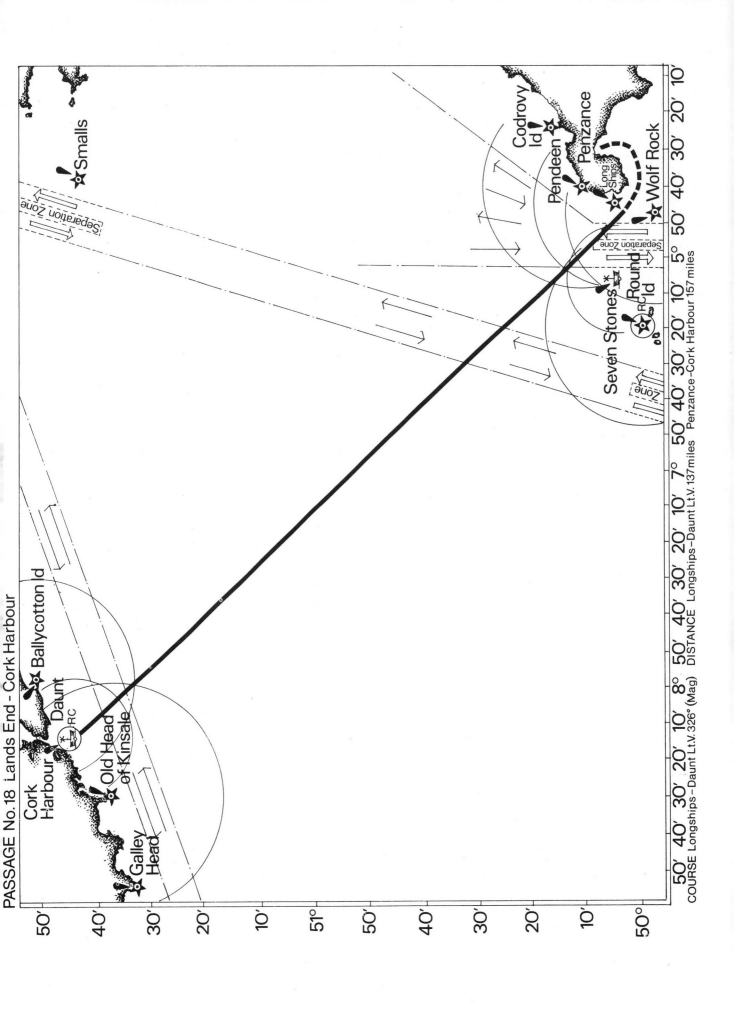

Smalls

Separation Zone

Ballycotton Id

Cork
Harbour

Daunt
RC

Old Head
of Kinsale

Galley
Head

Codrovy
Id

Pendeen

Penzance

Long
Ships

Separation Zone

Round
Id

RC

Seven Stones

Zone

Wolf Rock

50' 40' 30' 20' 10' 8° 50' 40' 30' 20' 10' 7° 50' 40' 30' 20' 10' 6° 50' 40' 30' 20' 10'

50'
40'
30'
20'
10'
51°
50'
40'
30'
20'
10'
50°

COURSE Longships–Daunt Lt.V. 326° (Mag)   DISTANCE Longships–Daunt Lt.V. 137 miles   Penzance–Cork Harbour 157 miles

PASSAGE NO.19: LAND'S END – SMALLS (FOR MILFORD HAVEN AND POINTS NORTH)

Wind direction and frequency in percentages.

	S	SW	W	NW	N	Calm	Other
Scilly Isles, 0700	–	17	19	20	14	3	27
Scilly Isles, 1300	–	16	24	19	15	2	24
St. Ann's Head, 0700	)	20	19	14	11	8	28
St. Ann's Head, 1300	12	25	26	16	–	1	20

Main visual navigational aids.

	Luminous range in miles	Visual range in miles Height of eye 2 metres
Round Island LH	24	18
Seven Stones LV	25	10
Wolf Rock LH	23	15
Longships LH	19	15
Pendeen LH	27	18
St. Ann's Head LH	23	17
Skokholm Island LH	20	18
Smalls LH	26	15
South Bishop LH	24	14

Weather forecast area: Lundy
Marine radio beacons: Round Island, South Bishop LH, Tusker Rock, Lundy.
Aero radio beacons: St Mawgan, Strumble.

General remarks

Craft bound north from the Land's End area should find this an uncomplicated passage, although fairly long at 98 miles. If remaining at sea to continue northwards it will be best to pass to the west of the Smalls, so avoiding the strong tidal currents and sundry races inshore. When this is not the intention it is proposed that one makes for Milford Haven directly. The writer would make three points: the first haven northward of the Smalls is Fishguard which can be made in any weather at any time; the Welsh coast is a dangerous lee shore during gales from a westerly point; when northward of the Smalls during strong westerlies it must be adjudged preferable to make one's northing on the Irish coast.

Terrain: shore of departure

Remarks under this heading in Passage No. 18 have equal substance here.

Terrain: shore of landfall

The Smalls are a cluster of rocks, all except two of which are awash as high water, and these lie to the eastward of the lighthouse. Located on the largest and westernmost rock is the lighthouse. It is a circular tower which has red and white horizontal bands and has an elevation of 43m. With the Smalls close at hand it is probable that Skomer Island (70.4m.) will be visible low on the horizon to the eastward.

Tidal streams

The Admiralty Tidal Stream Atlasses for the English and Bristol Channels and for the Irish Sea give the best information. A changing pattern of streams throughout this passage occurs, although rates well offshore should not exceed 1 knot. Rates increase markedly as the Smalls are approached, being as much as 5 knots close to them, yet only about 3 knots at 2 or 3 miles distant. Reference should be made to the West Coast of England Pilot, particularly if one determines to enter Milford Haven.

Soundings

Although soundings contribute little to navigation in the early stages of the passage, northward of the 51st parallel of latitude their character changes perceptibility. The seabed shelving in a fairly regular pattern from west to east, soundings are greater to the westward of the course line than they are to the east. As the Smalls are closed the inclination of the seabed is more marked and, if one keeps in soundings of 100m. and more, the Smalls can be safely rounded in thick weather.

Radio direction finding

Although Round Island and St. Mawgan should prove of limited assistance at the outset, some 40 miles after departure, bearings of Lundy Island may be crossed with those of the two former stations to give useful positions. When 40 miles off the Smalls one is within nominal range of South Bishop radio beacon: the distance off one's target being reduced to 15 miles, bearings of Tusker Rock may be taken with confidence. These sundry beacons will, in good conditions, provide adequate coverage throughout the passage. It would be unwise to use bearings of Strumble aero beacon until north of South Bishop.

Passage advices

It is suggested that when Longships L.H. bears east (say) 1′ distant, course is altered to pass no less than 3′ westward of the Smalls L.H., thereby avoiding strong tidal currents inshore. The writer considers it of small consequence when one arrives off the Smalls as one will be on passage. In addition, between visual sighting, soundings and DF bearings the mariner is well served: any two of these facilities are sufficient to enable him to round the Smalls with confidence. Assuming Penzance is the port of departure, it will be advantageous to plan to be off the Longships at HW Dover so that, for the following 3 hours, one is borne northwards through an area where tidal currents are fairly brisk.

During daylight in clear weather visual fixes from terrestial features should be possible until Pendeen L.H. is some 8 miles on the starboard quarter. Although high land may be visible for many miles thereafter, bearings of it may well prove increasingly indeterminate. At night, Pendeen Lt. having been dropped astern, back bearings first of Longships Lt. and later of Pendeen Lt. will give clear indication of course being made good.

By this time Round Island, Mawgan and Lundy radio beacons should have been identified but, until Lundy closes to its nominal range of 50 miles, bearings of it should be regarded as suspect. Thereafter, 3-bearing fixes should be possible throughout, utilising the beacons northward as they are closed. North of latitude 51°N. soundings should be watched with increasing vigilance as they by themselves will indicate whether one is holding to the course line. If the Smalls area is approached when visibility is less than good, and DF results are indeterminate, it would be wise to head NW until a sounding of 100m. or more is obtained. Remaining in these depths, one can then head about 025°(Mag.) until the Smalls are cleared.

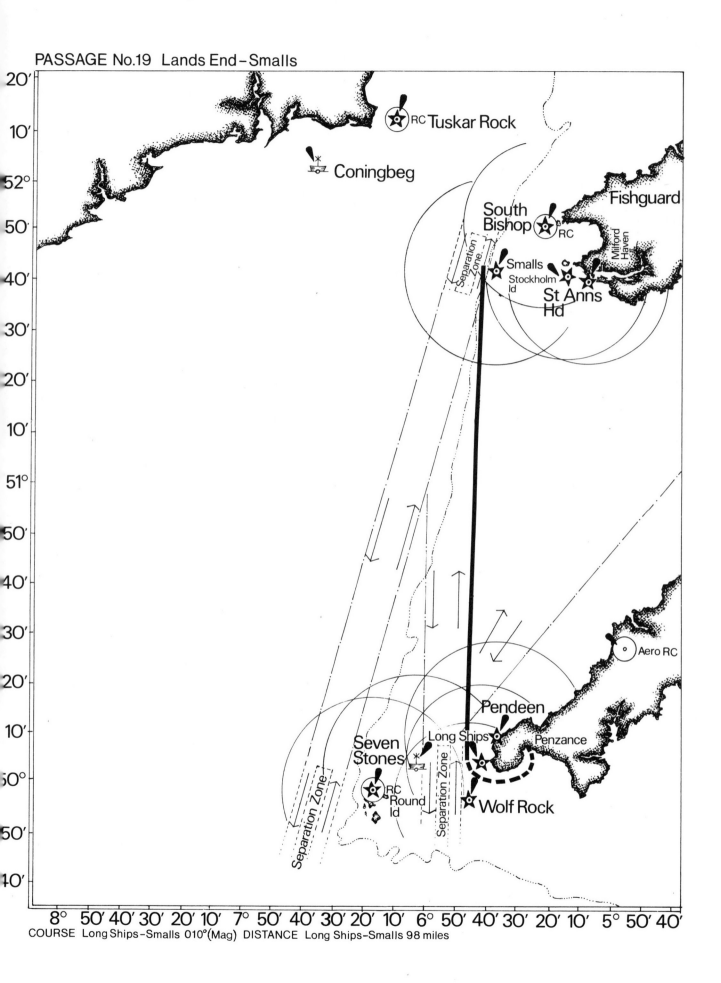

COURSE Long Ships–Smalls 010°(Mag) DISTANCE Long Ships–Smalls 98 miles

PASSAGE NO.20: BAR LV, LIVERPOOL, VIA MENAI STRAIT TO DUN LAOGHAIRE, DUBLIN BAY

Wind direction and frequency in percentages.

	SE	S	SW	W	NW	N	Calm	Other
Birkenhead, 0700	14	—	14	30	13	—	3	26
Birkenhead, 1300	—	—	11	30	30	—	2	27
Holyhead, 0700	—	19	22	15	13	14	7	10
Holyhead, 1300	—	23	22	14	20	15	1	5
Dublin, 0600	—	—	21	41	—	—	7	31
Dublin, 1200	—	—	17	38	12	—	1	32

Main visual navigational aids

	Luminous range in miles	Visual range in miles Height of eye 2 metres
Llanddwyn Island LH	7	10
South Stack LH	28	19
Baily LH	27	16
Kish Bank light tower LH	28	14
Dun Laoghaire, east breakwater LH	22	11
Poolbeg LH	15	12

Weather forecast area:	Irish Sea
Marine radio beacons:	Skerries, Kish Bank Ltd, Cregneish, I.O.M.
Aero radio beacon:	Dublin/Rush

General remarks

At first appraisal the route northward of Anglesey, perhaps breaking the passage at Holyhead, is the obvious one to take. The writer considers that the one via the Menai Strait has more to commend it. During daylight one can make one's way to the SW end of the Menai Strait, there to spend the night. Next morning, again during daylight, one makes the fairly simple passage to Dublin Bay with prevailing wind perhaps at a kinder angle. The passage to and within the Menai Strait is not discussed here, it being coastal navigation within the competence of the average yachtsman.

Terrain: shore of departure

The shores to the north and south of the SW entrance to the Menai Strait are best described as characterless, albeit they are backed by lofty green Welsh mountains, particularly to the southward. The dull uniformity of the low coast to the south is broken by a small hill, Dinas Dinlleu, about 3 miles south of the low promontory, Belan, which defines the southern entrance to the strait. The northern Boundary of the entrance, Abermenai Point, appears at high water as a narrow strip of sand connected to Anglesey. Llanddwyn Island L.H. is a round tower some 9m. in height. Both north and south of the entrance at low water extensive sandbanks are visible.

Terrain: shore of landfall

Kish Bank lighthouse projects from the sea. It is a white concrete tower with a red band and an elevation of 30m. In clear weather, in daylight, it should be sighted at about the same time as the mountains of Ireland. With the light tower abeam, the land to the north and south of Dublin Bay should be distinctive with features recognisable. On the coastal range behind Dalkey Island on the port bow, charted outlines and marks should prove of value but at this time the piers of Dun Laoghaire harbour will be unrecognisable. To the north on the starboard bow will be the

Hill of Howarth, striking and conspicuous, with Baily L.H. on its foreshore. With Kish Bank L.H. astern perhaps 2 or 3 miles, the outline of Dun Leoghaire breakwater should become apparent.

Tidal streams

On this passage tidal streams are uncomplicated and their spring rates do not exceed 2 knots. The Admiralty Tidal Stream Atlas for the Irish Sea provides essential information but, because a strengthening of streams occurs in the Dublin Bay area, reference should be made to the Irish Coast Pilot where full details are given.

Soundings

Soundings are of considerable value between Caernarvon Bar and Kish Bank L.H. From the outermost channel buoy a steady increase in sounding occurs to the 50m. contour, some 9 miles distant. For the next 15 miles soundings remain at about 60m. and then they sharply increase to varying depths of between 120m. and 150m. About 15 miles from Kish a sudden decrease occurs to about 90m. and they then decrease fairly uniformly to Kish Bank. Chart No. 1824a best portrays these features, and the helpful depth contours.

Radio direction finding

From the outset one can home on Kish radio beacon and homing bearings will be supported by bearings of Rush aero beacon. It would be unwise to use bearings of Skerries until some 20 miles after departure; land effect errors may occur prior to that time. Cregneish can be used almost throughout and these four beacons should provide useful positions, particularly when well offshore.

Passage advices

Departure from the Bar light vessel should, it is suggested, be timed so that passage through the Menai Strait occurs during a HW period in daylight, the intention being to anchor off Caernarvon for the night. The Cruising Association Handbook perhaps best describes navigation for yachtsmen in the whole Menai Strait area.

Sailing outwards, departure must be timed so that one can pick one's way across Caernarvon Bay from buoy to buoy at HW during daylight. Thereafter a straight forward passage of 55 miles remains to Kish L.H. DF facilities should be used from the outset, for homing on to Kish L.H. and, particularly in mid-Irish Sea, for obtaining fixes at, say, 1 hour intervals. The depth contours earlier described will give valuable information about forward progress. Kish L.H. being passed at about 1 mile range, either north or south, Dun Laoghaire is some 6 miles distant. At this time during both daylight and darkness ample visual navigational aids exist. One proceeds north of No.1 buoy, thence to South Burford buoy and so to Dun Laoghaire entrance. It will be noted that Caernarvon Bar HW dictates the time of departure and thus arrival in Dublin Bay is not necessarily a time one prefers.

The return passage to Bar L.V. should be both easier and speedier by passing northward of Anglesey.

PASSAGE No.20 Bar Lt.V - Dublin Bay

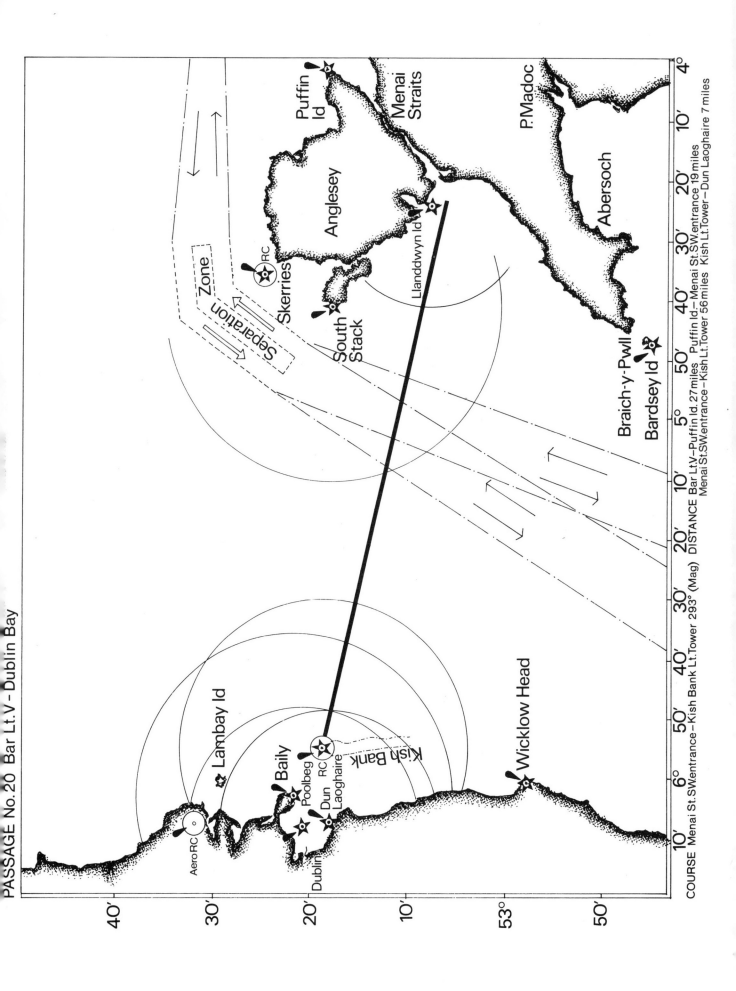

COURSE Menai St.SWentrance–Kish Bank Lt.Tower 293° (Mag)

DISTANCE Bar Lt.V–Puffin Id. 27miles Puffin Id.–Menai St.SWentrance 19miles
Menai St.SWentrance–Kish Lt.Tower 56miles Kish Lt.Tower–Dun Laoghaire 7 miles

PASSAGE NO 21: BAR LV, LIVERPOOL TO STRANGFORD LOUGH, IRELAND, VIA ISLE OF MAN

Wind direction and frequency in percentages

	SE	SW	W	NW	Calm	Other
Birkenhead, 0700	14	14	30	13	5	24 24
Birkenhead, 1300	–	11	30	30	2	27
Douglas, 0900	–	15	18	24	5	38

Main visual navigational aids

	Luminous range in miles	Visual range in miles Height of eye 2 metres
Bar Lt. F.	12	10
North West Lt. F.	8	10
Maughold Head LH	22	19
Douglas Head LH	20	14
Langness LH	21	12
Chicken Rock LH.	13	15
Calf of Man LH	28	22
St. John's Point LH	23	15
South Rock LV	24	10

Weather forecast area:	Irish Sea.
Marine radio beacons:	Skerries, Walney Island, Point of Ayre, Cregneish, South Rock LV.
Aero radio beacons:	Wallasey, Blackpool, Ronaldsway.

General remarks

The practical way of sailing from Liverpool area to Strangford Lough is to make two separate passages of the voyage: Bar L.V. – Isle of Man, and Isle of Man – Strangford Lough. One plans with a view to conducting both passages in daylight. Although for the purposes of this voyage, Douglas is given as the port for an over-night stop, in fact it is often overcrowded and adjacent ports are possible alternatives. In addition, ports on the south east coast of the Isle of Man are uncomfortable to yachtsmen in south-easterly winds and one may have to consider sailing on to the north-western shore in these conditions.

Terrain: shore of departure

Bar light float is a red-hulled vessel with a metal framework tower surmounting it. From its position, as yachtsmen in this area will well know, the shore is usually a vague outline even with a fairly clearly defined horizon.

Terrain: shore of landfall   1.   Isle of Man

Although the Isle of Man has as its maximum elevation Snaefell range (620m.), its aspect from seaward is neither marked nor characterful. Steep cliffs, ending abruptly at Douglas Head, define the south-western aspect of the Douglas Bay area. Douglas Head L.H. is a white tower 20m. in height, located some 12m. above the sea. At greater altitude (71m.) is Douglas Head Hotel, a large building with a tower. The coast which demarcates Douglas Bay comprises steep slopes on which houses are studded everywhere. The coast north-eastward is bold, high and steeply sloping to the sea.

2.   Strangford Lough

The promontories which define the entrance lack the boldness common around the Isle of Man but, as the distance between the two is relatively short, recognition presents no problem in clear weather. Angus Tower, a white stone structure 13m. high, stands on Angus Rocks and these divide the entrance into two channels.

Tidal streams

The Admiralty Tidal Stream Atlas for the Irish Sea gives adequate information for the passage from Bar L.V. to Douglas and this is supported by that to be found on Admiralty Chart No. 1824a. However, when on passage from Isle of Man to Strangford Lough, offshore stream directions are given but not their rates. They should not exceed 1½ knots, even during spring tides. Rates inshore around the Isle of Man increase slightly above offshore rates and the ebb in the entrance to Strangford reaches an impressive 7 knots on the ebb during spring tides.

Soundings

Should visibility be lost, it may be said that soundings offer only a coarse guide to position between Bar L.V. and Douglas, as a study of Admiralty Chart No. 1824a will indicate. Soundings of 30m. off the south-eastern shores of the Isle of Man may indicate that one is dangerously close to grounding. Between Chickens Rock and Strangford Lough the 100m. contours are helpful in that they give indication of forward progress and a gradual reduction in depth occurs as Strangford Lough entrance is approached.

Radio direction finding

On the Isle of Man there are three marine radio beacons and one aero radio beacon. These offer homing facilities of extraordinary quality on passage. If one adds to these Wallasey astern and Blackpool and Walney Island to starboard, the yachtsman may agree that he is well served indeed.

Between the Isle of Man and Strangford Lough entrance only Cregneish astern will be of positive value, although South Rock L.V. should be loud and clear on the starboard bow.

Passage advices

Course may be drawn direct to Douglas and departure made early so that a daylight arrival is assured with many hours of daylight remaining. Negligable advantage is to be gained from tides by sailing at a particular time from the Bar Lt.F. So long as Bar Lt.F. remains visible back bearings should be taken of it to check allowances in one's course. At this early time identification of all radio beacons should be attempted, bearings laid off on the chart and soundings taken to support the evidence of the bearings. Assuming clear weather, Bar Lt.F. may well be lost to view at 5 miles and the high land of the Isle of Man picked up at about 15 miles, leaving a mere 25 miles to sail without tangible evidence of position. Course should be held until the evidence of one's eyes, the DF set and soundings combine to assure a confident approach and entry into Douglas Harbour.

The nature of the later passage from Douglas to Strangford Lough needs little comment here. It would be well to set course to the westward to pass outside at (say) 2′ range from Chickens Rock L.H., thence to alter course to Strangford Fairway pillar light and whistle buoy and so to pass through the eastern channel. Ebb streams of up to 7 knots being experienced in the Narrows, one should either time one's arrival to arrive on the flood, or stand off until the flood is making, or slack water exists.

PASSAGE No. 21 Bar Lt.V. – Strangford Lough

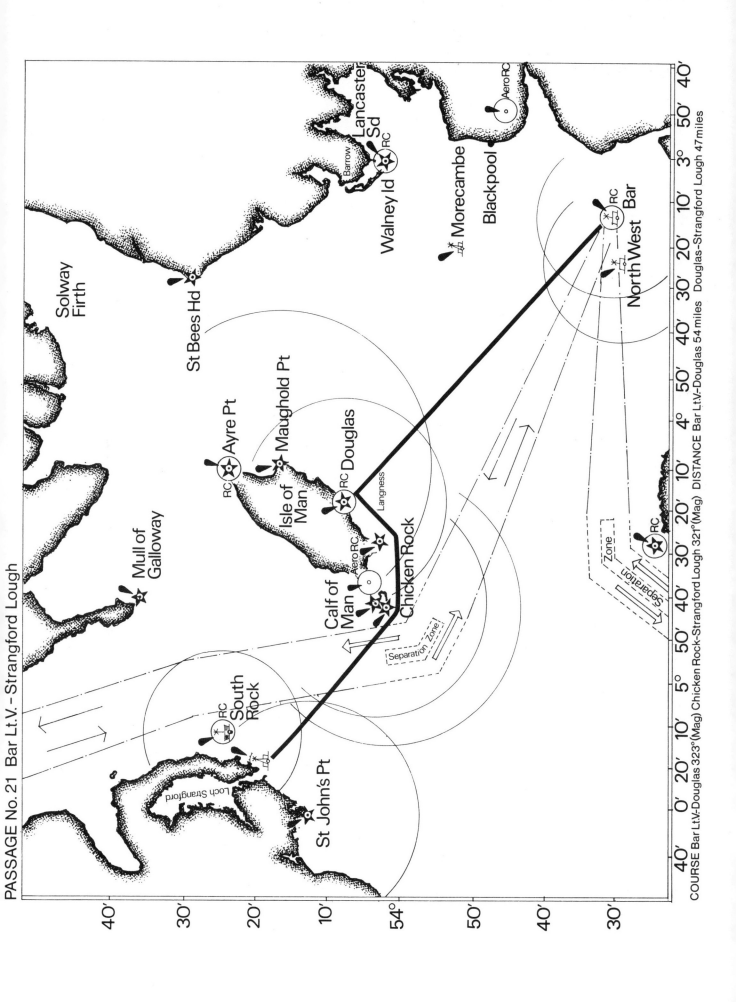

Solway Firth

Mull of Galloway

Loch Strangford

St John's Pt

RC South Rock

Separation Zone

RC Ayre Pt

Maughold Pt

Isle of Man

Calf of Man

AeroRC

Chicken Rock

Langness

RC Douglas

Separation Zone

St Bees Hd

Barrow

RC Walney Id

Lancaster Sd

Morecambe

Blackpool

AeroRC

Separation Zone

RC North West Bar

RC

40' O' 20' 10' 40' 50' 3°

40' 30' 20' 10' 54° 50' 40' 30'

COURSE Bar Lt.V.-Douglas 323°(Mag) Chicken Rock-Strangford Lough 321°(Mag) DISTANCE Bar Lt.V.-Douglas 54miles Douglas-Strangford Lough 47miles

PASSAGE NO.22: MORECAMBE BAY LANBY BUOY TO BELFAST LOUGH VIA ISLE OF MAN

Wind direction and frequency in percentages

	S	SW	W	MW	N	Calm	Other
Belfast, 0600	12	19	23	14	12	8	12
Belfast, 1200	–	17	27	17	13	3	23
Douglas, 0900	–	15	18	24	–	5	38

Main visual navigational aids

	Luminous range in miles	Visual range in miles Height of eye 2 metres
Morecambe Bay Lanby buoy	21	10
Chicken Rock LH	13	15
Calf of Man LH	28	22
Langness LH	21	12
Maughold Head LH	22	19
Point of Ayre LH	19	14
Mull of Galloway LH	28	23
Crammag Head LH	18	15
Mew Island LH	30	15

Weatherforecast area: Irish Sea.
Marine radio beacons: Point of Ayre, Douglas, Cregneish, South Rock LV, Mew Island, Walney Island.
Aero radio beacons: Wallasey, Blackpool, Ronaldsway.

General remarks

It is proposed that two distinct passages are made of this voyage. Both may be conducted in daylight, with a night stop in the Isle of Man. Although distances are such that it would seem unnecessary to deviate to Morecambe Bay Lanby Buoy, for the yachtsman who has done little long distance sailing, there is much to commend it. Other comments under this heading in Passage No.21 have equal application.

Terrain: shore of departure

This heading has no application here as no land will be in sight in the vicinity of Morecambe Bay Lanby Buoy and, from whichever yacht haven it is approached on this section of the coast of Lancashire, the relatively short passage should present no problem.

Terrain: shore of landfall

1. **Isle of Man**
   See Passage No.21 under this heading.
2. **Mull of Kintyre and Coast of N. Ireland**
   In clear weather long before Point of Ayre fades astern the precipitous cliffs of the Mull of Kintyre will be bold on the starboard bow. This coast, with its clearly defined headlands and lighthouses, is ideal for fixes by terrestial bearings. The slopes of the land which comprises the peninsular between the North Channel and Strangford Lough on the Irish coast are gentle and it is probable that Mew Island L.H. will be sighted at about the same time as features on shore are recognised. Mew Island is the northernmost and lowest of three islands, Copeland Island, Old Lighthouse Island and Mew Island. The latter is about 6m. high. The lighthouse has an elevation of 37m. and is black tower with a white band.

Tidal streams

The Admiralty Tidal Stream Atlas for the Irish Sea, although adequate for tidal stream information between Morecambe Bay and the Isle of Man is of insufficient assistance for the run from the Isle of Man to Belfast Lough. Admiralty Chart No.45 includes tidal stream information with sufficient detail to enable a yachtsman to set courses with confidence. It should be noted that streams off the Point of Ayre and in the North Channel are frequently strong, and they flow southwards for a longer period than they do northwards. Ram Race off Mew Island, which is clearly shown on Admiralty Chart No.45, is more awe-inspiring and uncomfortable to yachtsmen than it is dangerous, but it is well to give it a reasonable berth.

Soundings

This is a passage which, although in theory soundings will give assistance, in practice they may well prove superfluous to yachtsmen on passage. They will be of value when making a landfall on the Isle of Man where they reduce sharply as land is approached, and rounding the island inshore towards the past the Point of Ayre and, if required, in the North Channel where the seabed undulates sharply.

Radio direction finding

The spread of the combination of aero and marine radio beacons on this passage, both before and after the Isle of Man, is such that position need never be in serious doubt should visibility diminish.

Passage advices

The following route is proposed: Morecambe Bay Lanby buoy – Douglas – inshore to Point of Ayre – position 2′ NE of Mew Island – destination. Making a night stop in the Isle of Man, both parts of the passage are of such length that they can be conducted in daylight.

As soon as one clears the land, attempts should be made to identify the following aero beacons: Wallasey, Blackpool, Walney Island, Point of Ayre, Douglas and Cregneish. Having passed Morecambe Bay Lanby buoy closely, course may be set direct for Douglas some 34′ distant. Assuming that the buoy is effectively lost to view at 4′ and Douglas Head is sighted at 10 miles, a mere 20 miles remains to traverse out of sight of land. This is no reason for not endeavouring to obtain at (say) hourly intervals both DF and DR positions. Course should be held until position by terrestial bearings is established and one can approach Douglas Bay with confidence.

Departing from Douglas, it will be advantageous to sail on the north-going stream. No off-lying dangers exist offshore until the Point of Ayre is reached and, provided one steers direct from Maughold Point to the narrow strait defined by Point of Ayre and Whitestone Bank buoy close eastward, the passage is uncomplicated. Having rounded Point of Ayre, one may set course for the position off Mew Island. Very shortly after Point of Ayre is lost to view, Mull of Kintyre should be sighted and thereafter position should never be in doubt in clear weather. As Crammag Head is lost to view astern, Mew Island and the coast of Ireland should be sighted. With Ram Race off Mew Island cleared well to port, one can alter course into Belfast Lough.

PASSAGE No.22 Morecambe Bay Lanby Buoy – Belfast Lough

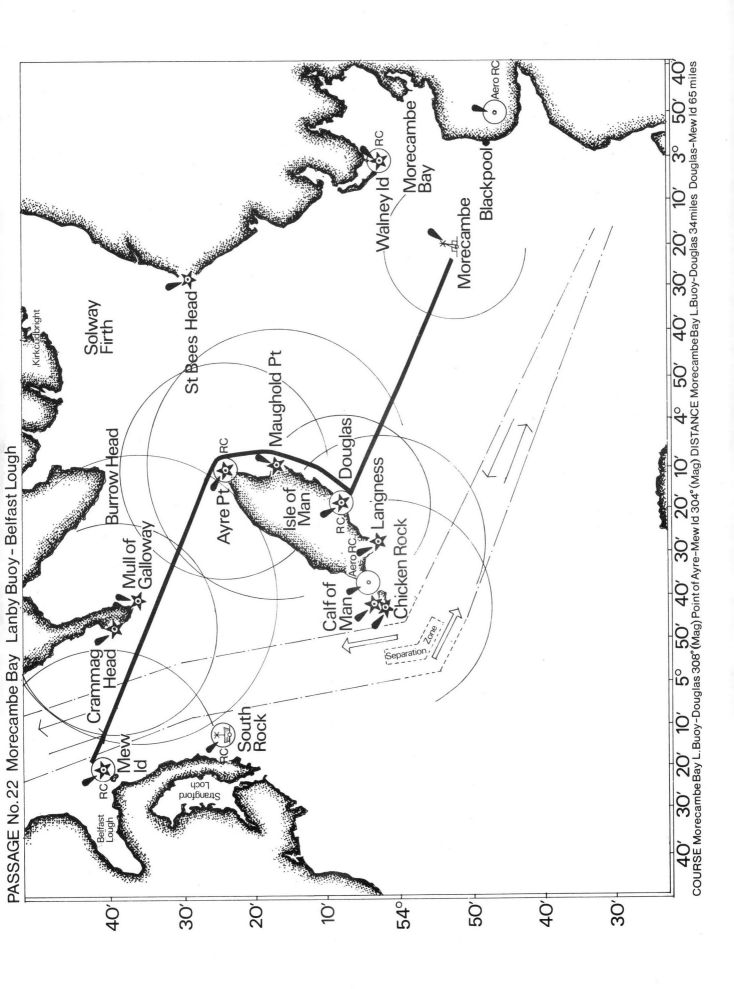

COURSE Morecambe Bay L.Buoy–Douglas 308°(Mag) Point of Ayre–Mew Id 304°(Mag) DISTANCE Morecambe Bay L.Buoy–Douglas 34miles Douglas–Mew Id 65 miles

CHAPTER 9

Return Passages

The humorist who suggested that this chapter is unnecessary because one has merely to advise a yachtsman to read backwards the passage advices contained in the preceding chapter was not being quite as waggish as he sounded. Like most generalisations, his had a little truth in it. After all, on a return journey a point of departure can be read as a point of landfall; a useful change in soundings remains just as useful when sailing in the opposite direction. This is a theme upon which one can enlarge considerably. When, however, this dictum of reversal is applied to the needs of particular passages, flaws in the mode of reasoning rapidly become apparent.

In most cases a lighthouse, a radio beacon, a sounding assumes a *change of importance* to the mariner when he is sailing in the reverse direction. It really depends whether a yachtsman is searching ahead for a navigational aid, or whether he is leaving it behind. To enlarge, sailing in one direction he may readily be guided to it by other aids, yet in the other a period of anxiety may be experienced while he wonders whether it will be located at all. On a somewhat different theme, it is not always wise to return along the same track as one chose for the outward passage. For example, the point of departure on the outward passage may be quite unsuitable as a point of landfall on the return passage. Dominating weather expectancies and other factors may also indicate that another track must be used.

From a less technical point of view, a yachtsman does not always wish to sail to a single foreign port and, having visited it, retrace his course homewards. The Solent – Cherbourg – Solent run has much to commend it as an exercise, but if one seeks a further reason for completing this round voyage it may be rather hard to find. A foreign venture is generally more enjoyable when one plans to visit more places than one. With the English Channel particularly in mind, it is generally better to work *westward* along the French coast. Although winds might be foul in the process, one can utilise west-going tidal streams, sailing craft motoring to their next destination if that seems to be the sensible thing to do. In the opinion of the writer, the overriding factor is that on a return passage one loads the dice in one's favour by putting prevailing winds at such an angle that a sailing craft can in many cases return to England on a single course, and a power craft is relieved of the buffeting the wind and sea, on an ahead bearing, may give him.

In the following advices – which remain the opinions of one yachtsman, one seaman, supported by the opinions of some yachtsmen friends – much information has not been included because it would be to repeat that which is already published in the former chapter. It is, therefore, essential to read the appropriate outward passage advices in conjunction with those of return passages which follow.

PASSAGE NO 1: Brest to Lizard Point

The outward track may be used for the return course. A pre-dawn landfall off the Lizard has lesser importance than carrying the north-going stream in Chenal du Four during daylight. Departure from Brest, therefore, should be timed to achieve the latter object. The Chenal du Four having been cleared, regular bearings of the sundry promontories, lighthouses and cliffs will be essential for as long as they remain recognisable to ensure that adequate allowance is being made for the prevailing tidal stream offshore.

At this early stage one must endeavour to identify Lizard radio beacon, the intention being to home on it throughout. Round Island and Eddystone beacons assume lesser importance, but they provide the means of obtaining D/F fixes during the latter stages of the passage. Decreasing soundings should be of assistance as the English coast is neared. On this return passage, as in the case of so many others, one is returning to familiar haunts. An impending landfall, even though anxieties about position and forward progress may be present, is less daunting than one which is entirely new. Assuming good visibility, whether by day or by night, few headlands exceed the value of Lizard Point for a landfall. This being located and position having been established, then, and only then, one can square away for one's destination.

PASSAGE NO 2: Brest to Start Point

The opening paragraph of Passage No 1 has similar substance in connection with this return passage.

The main course line for a return across the English Channel may be drawn from a position (say) 1′ to seaward of the Gr. Occ. buoy off Roches de Portsall direct to Start Point. If this line is extended into Chenal du Four, it will be clear that the point at which to alter course is that where the leading marks in the channel meet this course, near Le Four L.H.

I. Vierge having been passed, the French coast will gradually be lost and a long dead reckoning haul follows. At this time only I. Vierge and Ile d'Oussant radio beacons will be in range. Roches Douvres and Guernsey aero beacon will be some 60 miles eastward, too far distant to be really useful. In mid-Channel one must commence listening for Start Point and Eddystone radio beacons. These two, and later that of Lizard Point will assume increasing importance as land is approached.

One will of course home on to Start Point beacon. It will be noted that the constant transmissions of Berry Head aero beacon to the north will be almost on the same bearing as that of Start Point. With reservations, this is most useful but if there is difference between these two bearings, reliance must be placed upon those of Start Point. Land effects may give Berry Head false readings.

It will be noted that soundings give little indication of a close approach to the English Coast. In reduced visibility and with indeterminate D/F information, the utmost caution is essential. For this and other reasons, regular application to the calculation of DR positions is of considerable importance.

PASSAGE NO 3: Guernsey to Start Point

If one ignores the fact that, on a course of about NW, one may well be butting the elements, from the point of view of navigation, this return run is relatively simple.

A pre-dawn landfall off Start Point must be adjudged preferable and therefore time of departure from one's final port in the Channel Islands will be dictated by this fact.

It will be seamanlike to draw a course line from a position from (say) 2′ SE of Les Hanois LH, direct to Start Point. With the former lighthouse well abaft the beam to starboard, and with supporting D/F evidence from Guernsey aero beacon, it should be possible to obtain from soundings almost precise evidence of position as one crosses the Hurd Deep. The bearings of Guernsey can be crossed with the depth contours of it. This swatch having been cleared, Start Point is a mere 40-odd miles away.

D/F bearings of Start Point, Berry Head aero beacon and Eddystone should by this time have been obtained and homing on to Start Point is uncomplicated. As one closes Start Point, bearings of these three beacons broaden, and combine to make D/F fixes of good quality possible. They may well be supported by bearings of both Bill of Portland and Lizard Point during the latter stages. For this reason, although soundings will give the yachtsman no comfort with a landfall impending, ample indication of position should be obtained and reassurance remains in the knowledge that Start Point light has both good power and good range.

PASSAGE NO 4: Channel Islands to Poole Harbour

Having visited and decided to sail direct homewards from the Channel Islands, for the relative stranger a departure from the Casquets is considered best. This being adopted, it follows that with a Channel crossing to make, one's final port might well be one on Guernsey. Guernsey to Anvil Point being a distance of 80-odd miles, this is reason in itself for not planning a departure from some more distant port.

It should prove relatively easy to navigate northwards from Guernsey to a position (say) 3′ west of the Casquets, giving Casquets S.W. Bank, a wide berth in the process. From this position one can draw a course direct for Anvil Point. Between regular soundings and both visual and D/F bearings of Casquets, Hurd Deep will be located. This combination giving a fix of good quality, only 46 miles remain to Anvil Point itself and, provided visual and D/F conditions are good, a less distance to a fix off the English coast.

During the Channel crossing, one is literally surrounded by radio beacons and, with reasonable fortune and skill, D/F fixes should be possible throughout. The value of Bournemouth/Hurn aero beacon should not be overlooked. With certain reservations about the possibility of coastal refraction, one can more or less home on to it, and Anvil Point in the process.

Fixes from surrounding beacons should give indication whether bearings of Hurn are suspect. Approaching the English coast, regular soundings will locate the 50m. depth contour

which is some 10 miles offshore. In the absence of reliable D/F information, having taken care with one's DR positions throughout, it will be from this contour that one must feel one's way shorewards.

PASSAGE NO 5: Casquests to the Needles

Although in no way could it be considered unseamanlike to head direct for the Needles, for the yachtsman with few or no sea crossings to give him the confidence he admires in others, there is much to be said for heading for Anvil Point, as described in the preceding passage. Position having been fixed perhaps 4 or 5 miles south of Anvil Point in clear weather, and course altered towards the Needles, from this point onwards no doubts and fears about a final landfall will remain. Distance is increased only minimally by adopting this tactic.

PASSAGE NO 6: Cherbourg to Solent area

(a)   *To pass westward of Isle of Wight*

It is proposed that a course be drawn from Cherbourg to Bournemouth/Hurn aero beacon, with the intention of homing onto its continuous signals until position is established SW of the Needles. Although it is fair to say that D/F beacons on this run are of assistance throughout, homing on to Hurn gives a near perfect spread between Bill of Portland/Hurn/St Catherine's Point at a time when soundings are falling below the 50m. contour. In daylight in clear weather, with Anvil Point abeam some 9 miles to the westward, the Needles with the high land behind should be clearly in evidence and one may alter course for the Needles Channel.

In daylight in reduced visibility, provided one is on course, as indicated by Hurn aero beacon, it is practicable to continue shorewards towards Hengistbury Head, sounding continuously. One can approach this coast fairly closely and, provided visibility is 1 or 2 miles, once landfall has been made one can head eastwards, closing the land in Christchurch Bay to about 2 cables and maintaining this distance through North Channel, later rounding Hurst Point to enter the Solent. At night in clear weather, Needles light should be sighted at maximum range and at that point one can alter course towards it. Anvil Point light will then be in sight and, shortly afterwards, St Catherine's Point light.

(b)   *To pass eastward of the Isle of Wight*

For this passage, course should be drawn to St Catherine's Point, this being dictated by its boldness, its powerful light and its radio beacon. Soundings will give some assistance from a range of about 12 miles off when the 50m. contour is crossed. Whether by day or night in clear weather, it will be wise to close the point to a range no greater than 5 miles and then adjust course to pass Dunnose Head and later, Foreland. In reduced visibility one can depend upon the homing bearing and soundings. The two swatches of deeper water within 6 miles of the coast may prove unsettling but deep water for yachts exists close inshore and, provided some visibility exists and sounding equipment is functioning, grounding is highly unlikely. The typhon foghorn of St Catherine's will give added information, and Nab Tower D/F beacon will be transmitting.

General Remarks

Whether track (a) or (b) is used, constant visual and D/F

back bearings for as long as they may be taken are important after departure from Cherbourg, due to the strong tidal streams off the Cherbourg peninsular up to a range of perhaps 10 or 15 miles. With a good D/F set in experienced hands, position need never be in doubt on either of these tracks, due to the number of relatively close range radio beacons angled beneficially to them.

PASSAGE NO 7: Le Havre to Spithead, Solent and Chichester area

Whilst the fact will be of little consequence to the owner of a motor yacht, the sailing man will immediately note that his course homeward is about northwest. He will have to hope prevailing westerlies, if they are blowing, remain somewhere between south and west if he is not to beat homewards, or even to motor back.

Having sailed to the Le Havre lightvessel, a course drawn from that point to St Catherine's Point is proposed. A landfall having been made in the Dunnose Head area, an excellent one from the yachtsman's point of view, one may alter course northwards to pass between Nab Tower and Foreland. Some 80 miles having to be traversed, a pre-dawn arrival off the Isle of Wight is desirable. Homing on to the D/F bearing of St Catherine's Point latterly, the 50m. sounding contour used in conjunction with the bearing should give a position of fair quality. As is indicated in the comments on the outward passage, the degree of assistance obtained from radio beacons in mid-channel is not great, therefore great care is necessary with DR positions, but the homing quality of St Catherine's Point is reassuring.

PASSAGE NO 8: Dieppe to Newhaven

A course line drawn direct from Dieppe to Beachy Head is proposed. When position has been established off that promontory, the line of the coast may be followed to Newhaven. The reader should reflect that, using this tactic, if in the latter stages of the passage visibility is reduced and one happens to be too far to the eastward, Royal Sovereign lies ahead: if too far to the westward, then the only result can be that direct progress is made towards Newhaven which is one's ultimate goal.

For further passage advices those given for the outward passage should be found adequate.

PASSAGE NO 9: Boulogne to Newhaven and points westward

Apart from drawing a yachtsman's attention to the prevalence of southwesterly winds in this area, the author will not add to the observations made for the outward passage.

PASSAGE NO 10: Le Havre to Dover Strait and northwards

There are two routes a yachtsman should consider:

(a) Retracing the track described for the outward passage, adequate information for which will be found in the appropriate section. It is uncomplicated but a fairly long haul.

(b) Coasting from Le Havre to Dieppe, a distance of about 57 miles, there to spend an adequate period for sleep and relaxation. From Dieppe heading for a

position (say) 2′ westward of Cap Gris Nez, thereby keeping to the SE of the traffic lanes; that position being made, heading direct for Dover. If one's destination is further north, course can be altered when on the Kent coast, clear of the shipping lanes, with the intention of passing through the Downs, westward of the Goodwin Sands. This route gives fair assurance that position will not be in doubt at any time.

In this passage plan an indeterminate distance to be traversed from Dieppe is being considered. One may decide to break the passage at Boulogne or Dover. It is well to note that if one sails from Dieppe at 6 hours before HW Dover, either slack water or favourable tidal stream will be experienced for some 10 hours, and 10 hours may be a reasonable allowance for the 60 mile passage to Boulogne. Obviously daylight, clear weather and a NE-flowing tidal current will contribute considerably to a quick and safe passage across the shipping lanes in the Dover Strait.

PASSAGE NO 11: Boulogne to Dover

It is proposed that one returns to Dover along the track described for the outward passage, taking full note of the sundry comments contained therein. To ensure that one takes advantage of a favourable tidal stream throughout, the yachtsman should consider sailing at about 2 hours before HW Dover. A morning departure in clear weather is most desirable.

PASSAGE NO 12: Calais to Dover

For this passage, for all practical purposes, a yachtsman merely retraces the track he followed outward, hence the reader may reverse the procedural comments made in the previous chapter. 4 to 5 hours after HW Dover is indicated as being a slightly more favourable time to sail from Calais although the SW-flowing tidal stream will be athwart one's course, which is to say that it will give neither advantage nor disadvantage, for the greater part of the distance to be sailed.

PASSAGE NO 13: Calais to North Foreland

Again it may be said that the lines drawn upon the chart for the outward passage, with accompanying advices, may be redrawn for the return passage. That is, with certain reservations.

Sailing from Calais at 2 hours before HW Dover one can be assured of 7 hours tidal flow to the NE. A little assistance will be gained shortly after sailing, no material advantage will be present on the passage to South Goodwin Lightvessel but, for the passage northward throughout the Gull Stream, considerable advantage will be felt. 7 hours having elapsed, the commencement of the tidal flow outward from the Thames Estuary will occur. This could well be a good reason in a low powered motor craft or in a sailing craft for entering Ramsgate for a few hours to await the commencement of the flood stream off North Foreland. The thoughtful yachtsman will appreciate that here is no simple problem. Depending upon the speed he expects to make through the water, he may well elect to cross the Dover Strait during the SW-flowing stream to ensure a favourable tidal current on entry into the Thames Estuary. These comments, inconclusive as they must necessarily be, are made with the desire to draw to the attention of the reader that boat speed, tidal stream, prevailing weather and the distance to one's destination will combine to dictate departure time from Calais.

Finally, if a yachtsman decides to sail when the tidal flow is north eastward, then he should draw his course line direct to the S. Foreland lighthouse. Given good visibility, he will sight it at perhaps 6 or 7 miles and, keeping it on a steady bearing, he is assured of not being swept northward of the S. Goodwin lightvessel and so on to the sands.

PASSAGE NO 14: Oostende to North Foreland

This is a passage which, given the option – and all of us have options – the writer would not make. He would so plan his cruise that his final departure point from this continental coast was Calais. With thought, care and study of charts, coasting off Belgium is well within the competence of yachtsmen addressed. The passage homeward from Calais is described above. Perhaps the writer was unfortunate but in his occasional sorties in the Sandettie region, with its ceaseless profusion of ships seemingly proceeding in all directions, and with its apparently common moderate visibility, he sees no point in proving to himself in the future that his earlier impressions were wrong.

PASSAGE NO 15: OOstende to Sunk Lt. V

One may safely return along the track used outward, planning to arrive off the Sunk Lightvessel a little before dawn. General advices in connection with the use of navigational aids for the outward passage may be followed.

As the chart indicates, the final leg between West Hinder and Sunk is one of 44 miles. A closer study reveals that, when Fairy Bank is cleared, before one has progressed 25 miles, both Galloper and Kentish Knock lightvessels should be in sight at night in clear weather. With fixes obtained from these, a mariner is guided to Sunk Lt.V. and, long before they dip below the horizon, the Sunk light will have been sighted. It will remain wise to take regular D/F bearings of Sunk from the time it is first located, which may well be long before any of these lights are sighted. The writer is aware that, with visual bearings, a homing bearing is rendered superfluous. This is no reason for ignoring the D/F bearing of Sunk, because it cannot be known if visibility may be reduced. If the tidal stream is flowing towards the SW during this leg, it will be essential to ensure that a craft is not carried downstream, particularly latterly. Long Sand spit which dries at low water is not far away to port.

PASSAGE NO 16: Hook of Holland to Sunk Lt.V.

Before sailing outward from England to the Dutch coast it is well to reflect that, in the absence of adequate propulsive power, and with the wind on an ahead bearing when wishing to head homeward from the Hook of Holland, alternatives may have to be considered. They may be to wait for the wind to shift, to take another route home, or even to leave one's craft in a safe haven on the continent. These are gloomy possibilities and they cannot be shrugged aside as extraordinary or unlikely occurrences.

Given suitable weather conditions, the writer proposes no change in the lightvessel to lightvessel technique recommended for the outward passage. Planning to be off the Goeree at the start of the SW-going stream will reduce navigational uncertainties during the long haul to North Hinder.

PASSAGE NO 17: Zeegat Van Texel to Great Yarmouth

If a yachtsman commences his summer cruise from a point to the north or south of Great Yarmouth and departs from that port to cruise in the Texel area, time will be a factor which will constantly enter his thoughts. The common two-weeks' summer cruise is scarcely adequate provision for the venture, not least because he must eventually return to his home port. With limited time, it will be preferable to cruise southward from Texel, even to the Belgian coast from which the return run to Great Yarmouth becomes a relatively easy undertaking, probably with southwesterly winds broad on the port side. Where time is not a controlling factor, one can cruise north and eastward to the Fresian Islands, returning to a suitable departure port at one's leisure.

For the return passage to Great Yarmouth from Zeegat Van Texel, a reversal of the procedure outlined for the passage outward will be seamanlike. It being possible to pinpoint a lightvessel at considerable range during dark hours, a night arrival off Smith's Knoll should be planned.

PASSAGE NO 18: Cork Harbour to Land's End

It is proposed that a yachtsman returns from Cork along the track recommended for the outward passage. Some night consider that to head for Round Island radio beacon initially and at a later stage when the Scillies are sighted, to bear away towards the Longships is preferable. The writer considers that potential hazards are increased by adopting this latter tactic. Should visibility decrease during passage, soundings will give little warning that the Scillies are close ahead. These islands, comforting and friendly in clear weather, are best given wide berth in reduced visibility.

On the track recommended and when westerlies are in evidence, a fairly fast run towards Land's End is likely, and so DR positions of good quality should be obtained. At about 10 miles off Land's End, assuming either lights by night or high land by day have not been sighted, the 100m. depth contour will be crossed, soundings thereafter giving slow but increasing warning of a landfall. Should strong westerlies then be blowing, it will be wise to err on the side of over-estimation for leeway, perhaps re-drawing one's course line towards Wolf Rock. The Land's End coast can be a worrying lee shore in these conditions and to find oneself well to the northeast of the course line is something to be avoided.

PASSAGE NO 19: The Smalls to Land's End

One may be guided by advices given for the northward passage, but prudence dictates that the course line be drawn from the Smalls to a position 3' westward of the Longships, to hold away from Land's End until it is known that the coast may safely be closed. Comments made about the character of Land's End latterly in the previous section have even greater substance on this run, due to the different angle of approach. Running south on this particular track in half a gale, the writer recalls a nerve-wracking experience while he wondered whether he could weather Land's End at all. He afterwards reflected that it would have been wiser to heave to well off shore until better weather conditions prevailed.

PASSAGE NO 20: Dublin Bay to Liverpool

At the outset it may be said that, given normal prevailing weather, this should be an easy and pleasurable return run totally different from the outward one. The writer would make this passage in two stages. Firstly, he would head direct for South Stack lighthouse and, as soon as the shipping lanes off the

Skerries were cleared, he would work round the coast to spend a night in Holyhead. Provided a dawn departure is made from Ireland and winds are helpful, the distance of about 55 miles should comfortably be traversed with the daylight available, with time in hand.

The second leg, Holyhead to Liverpool, might well cross waters already familiar to the Liverpool area based yachtsman. The writer would pass outside the Skerries, yet inside the shipping lanes, thereafter sailing direct for North West and Bar light floats. The distance considered being under 60 miles, one might elect to make a pre-dawn start with a reasonable expectancy of making Liverpool before dark or, with the intention of making a night passage, plan to navigate the Anglesey area before dark. This being achieved, the dark hours would be spent running down one's easting between Point Lynas and North East light float, holding south somewhat to keep clear of shipping.

PASSAGE NO 21: Strangford Lough to Bar Lt.V. Via Isle of Man

If the tracks and the techniques advised for the outward passage are used for a return to Liverpool Bay, they should prove uncomplicated and adequate.

Strangford Lough to Douglas is a relatively short leg which demands no further comment here. During the latter stages of the final leg from Douglas to Bar light float, anxieties as to whether the float will be located may occur. Neither Bar nor Northwest light floats provide facilities capable of being utilised by the ordinary D/F set. However, with the course line drawn for this complete leg, the chart indicates that Wallasey areo beacon lies almost precisely ahead, on an extension of the course line. Clearly, valuable homing facilities are provided by it. Using this technique and keeping a constant check upon the warning signs of reducing soundings, even in poor visibility one or other of the light floats should be located.

PASSAGE NO 22: Belfast Lough to Morecambe Bay Lanby Buoy Via Isle of Man

Whether one chooses to sail from the Mew Island area to Douglas via Point of Ayr on the northern tip of the Isle of Man, or round the Chickens at the southern extremity will be dictated by winds and tidal currents prevailing at the time. Either route may be used with safety.

Morecambe Bay Lanby buoy has no marine radio beacon although it is massive, has a good light and is surrounded by radio beacons. Of these, Blackpool aero beacon lies nearly ahead when on course between Douglas and the Lanby buoy. This beacon in particular, and others in general, should enable the yachtsman to locate the buoy. In the event it is not sighted, soundings shoreward of the buoy provide the mariner with adequate warning that he is approaching the coast long before real danger exists.

Charts For Passages

Local Charts as appropriate in all cases.

PASSAGE NO.1

Admiralty	154	Approaches to Falmouth
	777	St. Ives to Dodman Point
	2565	Trevose Head to Dodman Point and the Scilly Isles
	2649	English Channel – Western portion.
	2644	Ile d'Ouessant (Ushant) to Les Sept Iles.
	2643	Raz de Sein to Goulven including Brest and Ushant.
	2694	The channels between Ushant and the mainland.
Stanford	2	The English Channel – Western Section.

PASSAGE NO.2.

Admiralty	1613	Prawle Point to Straight Point.
	442	Lizard Point to Straight Point.
	2649	English Channel – Western portion.
	2644	Ile d'Ouessant (Ushant) to Les Sept Iles.
	2643	Raz de Sein to Goulven including Brest and Ushant.
	2694	The channels between Ushant and the mainland.
	3345	Chenal du Four.
Stanford	2	The English Channel – Western Section.

PASSAGE NO.3.

Admiralty	1267	Dodman Point to Start Point.
	2454	Prawle Point to Hengistbury Head.
	2649	English Channel – Western portion.
	2668	Lannion Erquy, including Guernsey, Sark and the Casquets.
	2669	Channel Islands and adjacent coasts of France.
	60	Alderney and the Casquets.
Stanford	2	The English Channel – Western Section.
	12	The English Channel – The Needles to Start Point.
	16	The Channel Islands.

PASSAGE NO.4.

Admiralty	2175	Poole Harbour
	2219	Western Approaches to Solent.
	2615	Portland to Christchurch.
	2675	English Channel – Eastern portion.
	2669	Channel Islands and adjacent coasts of France.

	60	Alderney and the Casquets.
Stanford	2	The English Channel – Western Section.
	7	The English Channel – mid section.
	12	The English Channel – The Needles to Start Point.
	16	The Channel Islands.

PASSAGE NO.5.

Admiralty	2219	Western Approaches to Solent
	2615	Portland to Christchurch.
	2045	Christchurch to Owers.
	2675	English Channel – Eastern Portion.
	2669	Channel Islands and adjacent coasts of France.
	60	Alderney and the Casquets.
Stanford	2	The English Channel – Western Section.
	7	The English Channel – mid section.
	16	The Channel Islands.

PASSAGE NO.6.

Admiralty	2219	Western Approaches to Solent.
	2045	Christchurch to Owers.
	2450	Anvil Point to Beachy Head.
	2675	English Channel – Eastern Portion.
	2669	Channel Islands and adjacent coasts of France.
	1106	Cap de Flamanville to Iles de St. Marcouf.
	2602	Rade de Cherbourg.
Stanford	2	The English Channel – Western Section.
	7	The English Channel – mid section.

PASSAGE NO.7.

Admiralty	2050	East Approaches to Solent – Nab Tower to Spithead.
	2045	Christchurch to Owers.
	2450	Anvil Point to Beachy Head.
	2675	English Channel – Eastern Portion.
	2613	Cherbourg to Cap d'Antifer.
	2146	Approaches to Le Havre, Dives to Cap d'Antifer.
	2990	Le Havre and Approaches to La Seine.
Stanford	1	The English Channel – Eastern Section.

PASSAGE NO.8.

Admiralty	1652	Owers to Beachy Head.
	2451	Newhaven to Calais.
	2675	English Channel – Eastern Portion.
	2612	Cap d'Antifer to Pte. Haut Banc.

	2147	River Durdent to Cayeux.
	2147	Dieppe
Stanford	9	The English Channel – The Goodwins to Selsey Bill.
	1	The English Channel – Eastern Section.

PASSAGE NO.9.
Admiralty	1652	Owers to Beachy Head.
	536	Beachy Head to Dungeness.
	2675	English Channel – Eastern Portion.
	2451	Newhaven to Calais.
	1895	Dover Strait.
	438	Boulogne.
Stanford	1	The English Channel – Eastern Section.
	9	The English Channel – The Goodwins to Selsey Bill.

PASSAGE NO.10.
Admiralty	1895	Dover Strait.
	536	Beachy Head to Dungeness.
	2451	Newhaven to Calais.
	2675	English Channel – Eastern Portion.
	1431	Approaches to Dover Strait – Fecamp to North Foreland.
	2146	Approaches to Le Havre – Dives to Cap d'Antifer.
	2990	Le Havre and Approaches to La Seine.
Stanford	1	English Channel – Eastern Section.
	9	English Channel – The Goodwins to Selsey Bill.

PASSAGE NO.11.
Admiralty	1698	Dover Harbour.
	1895	Dover Strait.
	2451	Newhaven to Calais.
	438	Boulogne.
Stanford	1	The English Channel – Eastern Section.
	9	The English Channel – The Goodwins to Selsey Bill.

PASSAGE NO.12.
Admiralty	1698	Dover Harbour.
	1895	Dover Strait.
	323	Calais to Dunkerque.
	1352	Calais Road: Dunkerque Road.
Stanford	1	The English Channel – Eastern Section.
	19	Southern North Sea.

PASSAGE NO.13.
Admiralty	1828	The Downs.
	1698	Dover Strait.
	323	Calais to Dunkerque.
	1352	Calais Road: Dunkerque Road.
Stanford	1	The English Channel – Eastern Section.
	19	The Southern North Sea.

PASSAGE NO.14.
| *Admiralty* | 1828 | The Downs. |
| | 1698 | Dover Strait. |

	1406	Dover and Calais to Orfordness and Scheveningen.
	323	Calais to Dunkerque.
	1872	Dunkerque to Flushing.
	125	Approaches to Oostende, including inset of port.
Stanford	19	The Southern North Sea.

PASSAGE NO.15.
Admiralty	1975	Thames Estuary – Northern Part.
	1406	Dover and Calais to Orfordness and Scheveningen.
	1872	Dunkerque to Flushing.
	125	Approaches to Oostende, including inset of port.
Stanford	19	The Southern North Sea.

PASSAGE NO.16.
Admiralty	1975	Thames Estuary – Northern Part.
	1406	Dover and Calais to Orfordness to Scheveningen.
	3371	Gabbard and Galloper Banks to Hook of Holland.
	110	Approaches to Ooster Schelde – Hook of Schouwen.
	122	Mouths of the Maas – Hook of Holland to Goeree.
	132	Entrance to the Maas, including Hook of Holland, Europoort and Botlek.
Stanford	19	The Southern North Sea.

PASSAGE NO.17.
Admiralty	1536	Approaches to Great Yarmouth and Lowestoft.
	1543	Haisborough to Orford Ness.
	1504	Cromer to Harwich.
	1408	Harwich to Terchelling, Cromer to Rotterdam.
	2182a	North Sea – Southern Sheet.
	2322	Goeree to Texel.
	191	Zeegat van Texel.
Stanford	19	Southern North Sea.

PASSAGE NO.18.
Admiralty	777	St. Ives to Dodman Point.
	2565	Trevose Head to Dodman Point, including the Scilly Isles.
	1598	English Channel and Western Approaches.
	1123	South Coast of Ireland to Land's End.
	2049	Kinsale to Wexford.
	2424	Valencia to Cork.
	1765	Cork Harbour and approaches.
	1777	Port of Cork. Lower harbour and approaches.

PASSAGE NO.19.
Admiralty	777	St. Ives to Dodman Point.
	2565	Trevose Head to Dodman Point, including the Scilly Isles.
	1123	South Coast of Ireland to Land's End.
	1178	Approaches to the Bristol Channel.

1478 St. Gowans Head to St. David's Head.
1482 Plans on the coast of Wales.

PASSAGE NO.20.

Admiralty
1951 Approaches to Liverpool.
1978 Great Ormes Head to Liverpool.
1977 Holyhead to Great Ormes Head.
1826 Burrow Head to Liverpool.
1464 Menai Strait – The Swellies.
1971 Cardigan Bay – Northern Sheet.
1411 Braich-y-Pwll to Clogher Point.
1468 Wicklow to Skerries Islands with Dublin Bay.
1415 Dublin Bay.
1471 Dun Laoghaire.

Stanford
17 Liverpool Bay.

PASSAGE NO.21.

Admiralty
1951 Approaches to Liverpool.
1978 Great Ormes Head to Liverpool.
1826 Burrows Head to Liverpool.

2094 Isle of Man – Calf Sound, Port St. Mary, Peel, Erin and Ramsey Bay. Castletown Bay.
2696 Douglas Bay.
45 Clogher Head to Burrow Head.
2156 Stranford Lough.
1824a East Coast of Ireland with the Irish Sea and St. George's and North Channels.

Stanford
17 Liverpool Bay.

PASSAGE NO.22.

Admiralty
2010 Morecambe Bay.
1981 Approaches to Preston.
1826 Burrows Head to Liverpool.
2094 Isle of Man – Calf Sound, Port St. Mary, Peel, Erin and Ramsey Bay. Castletown Bay.
45 Clogher Head to Burrow Head.
2198 North Channel – Southern Part.
1753 Belfast Lough, Belfast Docks, Bangor Bay.
1824a East Coast of Ireland with the Irish Sea and St. George's and North Channels.

Stanford
17 Liverpool Bay.

Weather forecasts and reports obtainable by use of a radio receiver

Listed below are sundry sources from which, by use of a radio receiver, a yachtsman may receive weather forecasts and reports. It must not be overlooked that by telephone, before sailing and even before leaving home, one can obtain forecasts, reports and advices from various authoritative bodies. These are listed in Appendix 3.

The writer is aware that many yachtsmen use any domestic transistor radio receiver of convenient size which is handy at home. It is well that they are aware of weather information most deny themselves by so doing. Using loose designations, the writer would summarise portable radio receivers used aboard small craft as follows:

(a) *Radio receivers with medium wave and VHF bands only.*
These sets are quite inadequate to meet the needs of a cruising yachtsman. They will receive:
Radio 4 coastal weather forecasts.
BBC local radio stations which broadcast local coastal forecasts.

(b) *Radio receivers with medium and long wave bands.*
Although it is possible to manage with one of these sets when cruising, their coverage is not quite adequate. They will receive:
Radio 2 shipping weather forecasts and gale warnings.
Radio 4 coastal weather forecasts.
BBC local radio stations which broadcast local coastal forecasts.

(c) *Radio receivers with medium, long and marine wave bands.*
The marine waveband is roughly between 1800 and 2900 kHz and is not usually included in sets which are intended wholly for domestic use. However, sets which include it are readily available in radio shops in coastal towns. One might reflect that many people in sea ports other than yachtsmen are interested in the intelligence on the marine waveband, and yet wish to use their radios for general purposes. Of course special sets designed for marine use are available at any yacht chandlers, but their prices are often quite startling. The former sets are often competitive in price with their truly domestic equivalents and are wholly adequate for use by yachtsmen. They will receive:
Radio 2 shipping weather forecasts and gale warnings.
Radio 4 coastal weather forecasts.
BBC local radio stations which broadcast local coastal forecasts.
Post Office and Irish Republic ship-shore stations' weather forecasts.
Continental English language coastal shipping forecasts.
Channel Islands local shipping forecasts, strong winds warnings and gale warnings.

If in addition one possesses a VHF transmitter-receiver, then one can always call a shore station for a weather forecast, even to the extent of speaking to the Meteorological Office, Bracknell, Berks.

Excerpts from Met.O. Leaflet No.3 1974 are as follows:
1. Introduction
The Meteorological Office provides routine weather information for ships operating in the North Sea, the English Channel, the Irish Sea and the eastern North Atlantic. Regular weather bulletins, and gale warnings as necessary, for the coastal sea areas shown are issued by radio-telephony and radio-telegraphy from Post Office coastal radio stations and by radio-telephony from BBC stations.

2. Gale Warnings
Gale warnings are issued when mean winds of at least force 8 or gusts reaching 43 knots are expected. The term 'severe gale' implies mean winds of at least force 9 or gusts reaching 52 knots. The term 'storm' implies a mean wind of at least force 10 or gusts reaching at least 60 knots. The term 'imminent' implies within 6 hours of the time of issue; 'soon' implies between 6 and 12 hours; 'later' implies more than 12 hours. Warnings are issued as follows:
(a) **From Post Office and Irish Coastal Radio Stations**
Gale warnings are broadcast by W/T and R/T from coastal radio stations appropriate to the area within which the gale is expected. These stations and areas are listed below. The date and time of origin are given in each warning, of which the following is an example:
'Gale warning, 8 January, 0150 GMT. Fastnet, Shannon, southerly gale force 8 imminent.'
The R/T transmission is broadcast first at conversation speed and then repeated at dictation speed.
(b) **From the BBC**
See below.

3. Weather Bulletins for Shipping – Post Office and Irish Coastal Stations
The words 'wind', 'force', 'millibar' and 'visibility' are omitted from weather bulletins issued in plain language from Post Office and Irish Coastal Stations. This is to enable the forecast to be given in a clearer and more concise form in the time available. Forecasts cover the period 24 hours from the time of issue.
(a) **Coastal Areas**
Weather forecasts, giving wind speed and direction, weather and visibility, are broadcast on W/T and R/T from coastal radio

stations appropriate to the area to which the forecast refers; these stations and areas are listed below, and the areas are shown on the map. The R/T transmission is broadcast first at conversation speed and then repeated at dictation speed.

4. Weather Bulletins for Shipping – BBC

The words 'wind', 'force', 'millibar' and 'visibility' have been omitted from weather bulletins broadcast by the BBC. This is to enable the forecast to be given in a clearer and more concise form in the time available.

(a) BBC Radio 2

Weather bulletins for shipping are broadcast on BBC Radio 2 on 200 kHz (1500 m) at the times shown below:

Monday–Saturday	Sunday
(Clocktime)	(Clocktime)
0033–0038	0033–0038
0633–0638	0633–0638
1355–1400	1155–1200
1755–1800	1755–1800

Contents of broadcasts

The broadcasts will consist of the following items and will be broadcast in the order shown:

(i) A statement of the gale warnings in force at the time of issue of the forecasts.

(ii) A general synopsis giving the situation in so far as it affects the area within the next 24 hours, with information as to expected changes within that period.

(iii) Forecasts for the next 24 hours for each coastal sea area, giving wind speed and direction, weather and visibility. The areas will be given in a fixed order (see below). When appropriate, contiguous sea areas may be grouped together.

(iv) The latest reports from a selection of the following stations will be broadcast in this order, the number of stations depending on the time available: Sule Skerry, Bell Rock Lighthouse, *Dowsing, Galloper* and *Varne* light-vessels, Royal Sovereign Light-tower, Portland Bill, Scilly/St. Mary's, Valentia, Ronaldsway, Malin Head and Tiree. The elements given will be wind direction (compass points) and speed (Beaufort force), present weather (including 'past hour' weather), visibility and, if available, sea-level pressure and tendency in qualitative terms.

Order of broadcast of areas

Forecasts for coastal sea areas are normally broadcast in the following order:

Viking, Forties, Cromarty, Forth, Tyne, Dogger, Fisher, German Bight, Humber, Thames, Dover, Wight, Portland, Plymouth, Biscay, Finisterre, Sole, Lundy, Fastnet, Irish Sea, Shannon, Rockall, Malin, Hebrides, Bailey, Fair Isle, Faeroes, South-East Iceland.

Gale Warnings

Gale warnings are broadcast on BBC Radio 2 as soon as possible after receipt and are repeated at the following hour, e.g. a warning received at 1520 will be broadcast as soon as possible

and will be repeated at 1600. A summary of gale warnings in operation is issued on Radios 1 and 2 at 0530 Monday–Saturday and as part of the shipping bulletin at 0630 on Radio 2 on Sunday.

(b) BBC Radio 4

Forecasts for inshore waters (up to 12 miles offshore) of England and Wales 'until 1800 tomorrow' are broadcast at the end of the English and Welsh Radio 4 programmes. The forecast of wind, weather and visibility is followed by the 2200 reports of wind direction (compass points) and speed (Beaufort force), present weather, visibility and, if available, sea-level pressure and tendency in qualitative terms from the following stations: Acklington (nr. Newcastle), Gorleston (nr. Yarmouth), Manston (nr. Ramsgate), Portland Bill, Scilly/St. Mary's, Numbles (nr. Swansea), Aberporth (Cardigan Bay) and Ronaldsway (Isle of Man).

At the end of the Northern Ireland Radio 4 programme a similar forecast for Northern Ireland inshore waters is given with the 2100 or 2200 reports from Kilkeel (Co. Down), Killough (Co. Down), Malin Head, Machrihanish (Kintyre), Ronaldsway (Isle of Man), Valley (nr. Holyhead) and Orlock Head (nr. Bangor, Northern Ireland).

The forecast for Scottish inshore waters is given towards the end of the Scottish Radio 4 programme with the 2200 reports from the following stations: Machrihanish (Kintyre), Tiree, Stornoway, Wick, Aberdeen (Dyce), Leuchars and Lerwick.

Details of precise times and frequencies are published in the *Radio Times.*

Author's Note:

Although Radio 4 broadcasts the same programmes to the whole country, slight differences occur, notably in local news and weather programmes. Perhaps typical of local weather broadcasts are those for the south west of England, broadcast from Plymouth. In this area at about 8.30 a.m. 'Coastal Conditions' are broadcast followed by 'Local and national weather forecasts'. 'Coastal conditions' are, in fact, RAC reports of weather at 7.0 a.m. obtained from coastguards at six stations round the coasts of Devon and Cornwall, one on the Isles of Scilly and one at Jersey, Channel Islands.

It will be agreed that, if these reports are related to BBC 2 shipping forecasts for this area, a wider appreciation of weather at sea, existing and to come, is obtained.

(a) Forecasts issued on request

Procedure for ships at sea

Whenever possible ships at sea are advised to obtain the weather information required direct from the Central Forecasting Office, Bracknell, by R/T link. The telephone number is Bracknell 20242, extension 2508.

Alternatively, the request may be addressed to the nearest radio station . . . . giving the ship's name (or call sign), as in the following example: 'To Land's End Radio. Request weather forecast for next 24 hours, Lundy, s.s. *Juliett.*'

No charge is made by the Meteorological Office for the latest available forecast, but a normal R/T link or other transmission charge is levied by the Post Office.

Procedure for requests originated ashore

Requests can be made by telephone to the Meteorological Office (Bracknell 20242, extension 2508) or by prepaid telegram addressed to Metbrack London Telex (Telex 848160) (allowing 20 words for reply, excluding address).

No charge is made for the latest available forecast providing any telegram is prepaid to allow a reply of 20 words, excluding the address.

(b) Forecasts required at a later time or date after receipt of request

If a forecast is required to cover a stated occasion or period in the future, or if the forecast is to be kept under review and subsequent amendments issued, the request should be addressed to The Director-General, Meteorological Office, Met.O.2a, London Road, Bracknell, Berks. RG12 2SZ, giving full details of the service required and the precise conditions necessary for an amendment to be issued. The charge for the service, including transmission costs, will be advised. When confirming acceptance of the charge the address to which the account is to be forwarded should also be notified.

If a series of notifications of the expected occurrence of particular kinds of weather, e.g. gales, or winds from certain directions, within a specified period is required, full details should be given in writing to The Director-General, Meteorological Office, Met.O.2a, London Road, Bracknell, Berks. RG12 2SZ. The charge will be assessed on a monthly, quarterly or yearly basis according to the volume of service required.

Local Weather Forecasts

The Meteorological Office shipping forecasts are the best available when whole sea areas are considered. However, slight differences may occur between weather at one extremity of a sea area and the other. The sea areas used for forecasting are quite large. There can, for example, be a difference in wind velocities on the French and English coasts during any forecast period. Although both sections of coastline are in the same sea area, the Meteorological Office shipping forecast can give no indication of it. It is these cases in which local forecasts prove of value to yachtsmen, although the differences when they occur are of small consequence to larger vessels. Available lists of local radio stations are listed below.

BBC Local Radio Stations

BBC Radio Humberside. 202m. (medium wave)   96.9 VHF
Coastal weather forecasts daily at the following clock times:

0710	1245
0745	1330
0810	1500
0855	1700
1100	1815

BBC Radio Medway. 290m. (medium wave)   96.7 VHF
Coastal weather forecasts at approximately 0840, Monday to Friday during the summer period.

BBC Radio Brighton. 202m. (medium wave)   55.3 wphf
Sailing forecast, Monday to Friday: 0753 and 0859
Forecast for sailing enthusiasts, Saturday: 0755
Sailing forecast, Sunday between 0845 and 0855 in summer.
Sailing forecast, Sunday between 0855 and 0900 in winter.

BBC Radio Solent. 301m. and 188m. (medium wave) 96.1 VHF

Coastal shipping forecasts (Dover, Wight, Portland, Plymouth):

Monday to Friday:	Between 0630 and 0640
	Between 0730 and 0735
	Between 0830 and 0838
Saturday:	0650
	Between 0710 and 0745
	Between 0810 and 0815
Sunday:	Between 0820 and 0830

Weather and weekend sailing forecast:
Friday:	Between 1500 and 1503
	1955 (The important one)

Weather for sailors and anglers:
Saturday:	Between 1100 and 1105

BBC Radio Bristol. 194m. (medium wave)   95.5 VHF
Coastal weather forecasts at 0759 every morning, May to September inclusive.

BBC Radio Merseyside. 202m. (medium wave)   95.8 VHF
Coastal weather forecasts:

Monday to Friday:		Saturday:	Sunday:
0630		0730	0810
0730		0830	1755
0830		1255	
1200		1755	
1758			

Scheveningen (Holland Radio. 1862, 1939 and 2824 kHz. (marine wave)
Netherlands coastal waters (up to 30 miles offshore) weather forecast valid for 24 hours at the following times GMT by R.T.h 0835 and 2035

Ostende (Belgium) Radio. English language broadcasts. (Marine wave)

Area covered:	Belgian coastal waters.
Radio telephony frequencies:	2761 kHz. after preliminary announcements on 2182 kHz. and 2484 kHz.
Times:	0920 and 1820, continental time.
Gale warnings.	Same frequencies.

Transmitted immediately after receipt at the coast station, and at the end of the two silence periods following receipt.

Jersey (Channel Islands) Radio. After initial announcements on 2182 kHz. (marine wave) and Channel 16 VHF, all broadcasts are made on 1657.5 kHz. (marine wave) and Channel 25 VHF.

Area covered:	bounded by 50°N. latitude and 3°W. longitude to seaward, and by the French coasts to the south and east to landwards. Bulletins also include actual weather at Jersey, Guernsey, Alderney, Cherbourg and Dinard.
Weather broadcasts:	0433 GMT
	0833 GMT
	1633 GMT
	2033 GMT
Gale warnings, on receipt and at:	0307 GMT
	0907 GMT
	1507 GMT
	2107 GMT

Strong wind warnings are also forecast for small craft.

Local Forecasts and Present Weather

8. Special Forecasts for Port Areas

Masters of ships and others interested in the movements of shipping in the vicinity of a port and in the loading and discharging of cargo can obtain local weather forecasts by telephone from the forecasting centre nearest to the port. Enquirers should ask for 'Forecast Office'.

Area	FORECASTING CENTRE	TELEPHONE NO.
N.E. Scotland	Kirkwall Airport, Orkney Aberdeen Airport Kinloss, Morayshire	Kirkwall 2421 Dyce 2334 Forres 2161
E. Scotland	Pitreavie, nr. Dunfermline	Inverkeithing 2566
N.E. England	Newcastle Weather Centre	Newcastle upon Tyne 26453
E. England	Bawtry, Yorks.	Doncaster 710474
S.E. England	London Weather Centre	01-836 4311
S. England	Southampton Weather Centre	Southampton 28844
S.W. England	Plymouth	Plymouth 42534
W. England S. Wales	Gloucester	Gloucester 23122
N. Wales	Valley, Anglesey Manchester Weather Centre	Holyhead 2288 061-832 6701
N.W. England	Liverpool Airport Manchester Weather Centre Preston, Lancs.	051-427 4666 061-832 6701 Preston 52628
W. Scotland	Glasgow Weather Centre	041-248 3451
N. Ireland	Belfast (Aldergrove) Airport	Crumlin 52339

9. Reports of Present Weather

(a) Mariners requiring reports of actual weather conditions prevailing at specified places around the coast of the British Isles may obtain such reports by telephone from any of the Meteorological Office stations in the following list.

Name of Station   *Telephone No.*

Mount Batten (Plymouth) . . . . .Plymouth 42534
Thorney Island . . . . Emsworth 2355
Manston . . . . Manston 351, Ext. 220
Shoeburyness . . . . .Shoeburyness 2271, Ext. 474
Lossiemouth . . . . Lossiemouth 2121
Kinloss (Moray Firth) . . . . Forres 2161, Ext. 116

Wick . . . . Wick 2215
Lerwick . . . . Lerwick 239
Kirkwall (Orkneys) . . . . Kirkwall 2421
Stornoway . . . . Stornoway 2256 (Night: 2282)
Benbecula (Hebrides) . . . . Benbecula 351
Tiree . . . . .Scarinish 41
Prestwick (Firth of Clyde) . . . . .Prestwick 78475
Carlisle . . . . Carlisle 23422, Ext. 440
Ronaldsway (Isle of Man) . . . . . .Castletown 3311 (Night: 3313)
Blackpool . . . . .Blackpool 43061 (Night: 43063)
Valley (Anglesey) . . . . Holyhead 2288
Aberporth (Cardigan Bay) . . . . . . .Aberporth 205/208, Ext. 363

(b) The following Coastguard Stations and Lighthouse (L.H.)

which make weather observations for the Meteorological Office may be prepared to respond to inquiries concerning actual weather conditions. Such information only applies to present weather in the immediate locality of each station and does not include forecasts or information concerning other areas.

Name of Station

Scilly/St. Mary's . . . . Scillonia 651
Tol-Pedn-Penwith (Gwennap Head) . . . . Sennen 219
Lizard . . . . Lizard 444
Prawle Point . . . . Chivelstone 259
Brixham (Berry Head) . . . . Brixham 2156
Beer . . . . Seaton 14
Portland Bill . . . . Portland 3100
Needles . . . . Freshwater 2265
Calshot . . . . Fawley 484
St. Catherine's Point L.H. . . . . Niton 284
Shoreham-by-Sea . . . . Shoreham-by-Sea 2226
Newhaven L.H. . . . . Newhaven 131
Eastbourne . . . . Eastbourne 20634
Fairlight (Hastings) . . . . Pett 3171
Dungeness L.H. . . . . Lydd 236
Folkestone . . . . Folkestone 54230
Dover Strait (St. Margaret's) . . . . St. Margaret's Bay 2515
Thames (Walton-on-Naze) . . . . Frinton-on-Sea 5518
Aldeburgh . . . . Aldeburgh 2779
Gorleston . . . . Gt. Yarmouth 63444
Cromer . . . . Cromer 2507
Spurn Point . . . . Spurn Point 283
Flamborough Head . . . . Flamborough 203

Whitby . . . . Whitby 2107
Tynemouth . . . . North Shields 72691
Seahouses . . . . Seahouses 274
St. Abbs Head L.H. . . . . Coldingham 287
Usan (Montrose) . . . . Montrose 1
Fraserburgh Fraserburgh 3374 Tarbatness (Moray Firth)
L.H. . . . . Portmahomack 210
Cape Wrath L.H. . . . . Scourie 267
Rudh Re (Ross and Cromarty) L.H. . . . . Gairloch 2481
Ardnamurchan (Argyll) L.H. . . . . Kilchoan 210
Rhuvaal (Islay) L.H. . . . . Port Askaig 202
Kildonan (Isle of Arran) . . . . Kildonan 211
Corsewall Point L.H. . . . . Kirkcolm 220
Portpatrick . . . . Portpatrick 209
Mull of Galloway L.H. . . . . Drummore 211
St. Bee's Head L.H. . . . . Whitehaven 2635
Point of Ayre L.H. . . . . Kirkandreas 238
Portrush . . . . Portrush 3356
Ballycastle . . . . Ballycastle 226
Portmuck . . . . Islandmagee 227
Bangor (Co. Down) . . . . Groomsport 284
Killough . . . . Ardglass 203
Kilkeel . . . . Kilkeel 62232
Fleetwood . . . . Fleetwood 3780
Formby . . . . Formby 72903
Rhyl . . . . Rhyl 3284
Porthdynllaen (Caernarvon Bay) . . . . Nevin 204
Tenby (Monkston Point) . . . . Saundersfoot 2722
Mumbles . . . . Swansea 66534
Ilfracombe . . . . Ilfracombe 2117
Hartland . . . . Hartland 235

10. Post Office and Irish Radio Stations which broadcast Weather Information

R/T Transmissions

These stations also give weather information on request.

Name of station	Position	Working frequency (kHZ)	Weather forecast and gale warning areas	Times forecast transmitted (GMT)	Times gale warnings transmitted
Wick	58° 26′N 03° 06′W	1827	S.E. Iceland, Faeroes, Hebrides, Fair Isle, Viking, Cromarty	0803 2003	At end of next silence period* after receipt from the Meteorological office and also at the next of the following times: 0303, 0903, 1503, 2103 GMT.
Stonehaven	56° 57′N 02° 13′W	1856	Forth, Cromarty, Forties, Fisher	0833 2033	
Cullercoats	55° 02′N 01° 26′W	2719	Tyne, Dogger, Fisher	0803 2003	
Humber	53° 20′N 00° 17′E	1869	Humber, German Bight	0833 2033	
North Foreland	51° 22′N 01° 25′E	1848	Thames, Dover, Wight	0803 2003	
Niton	50° 35′N 01° 17′W	1834	Portland, Wight	0833 2033	
Land's End	50° 07′N 05° 40′W	1841	Lundy, Sole, Plymouth, Biscay, Finisterre	0803 2003	
Ilfracombe	51° 11′N 04° 07′W	2670	Lundy, Fastnet	0833 2033	
Portpatrick	54° 51′N 05° 07′W	1883	Irish Sea, Malin	0833 2033	
Oban	56° 28′N 05° 23′W	2740	Malin, Hebrides, Bailey, Rockall	0803 2003	
Valentia	51° 56′N 10° 21′W	1827	Shannon, Fastnet	0833 2033	

*R/T silence periods are from 00 to03 and from 30 to 33 minutes past each hour.

Index